Zombies Calling

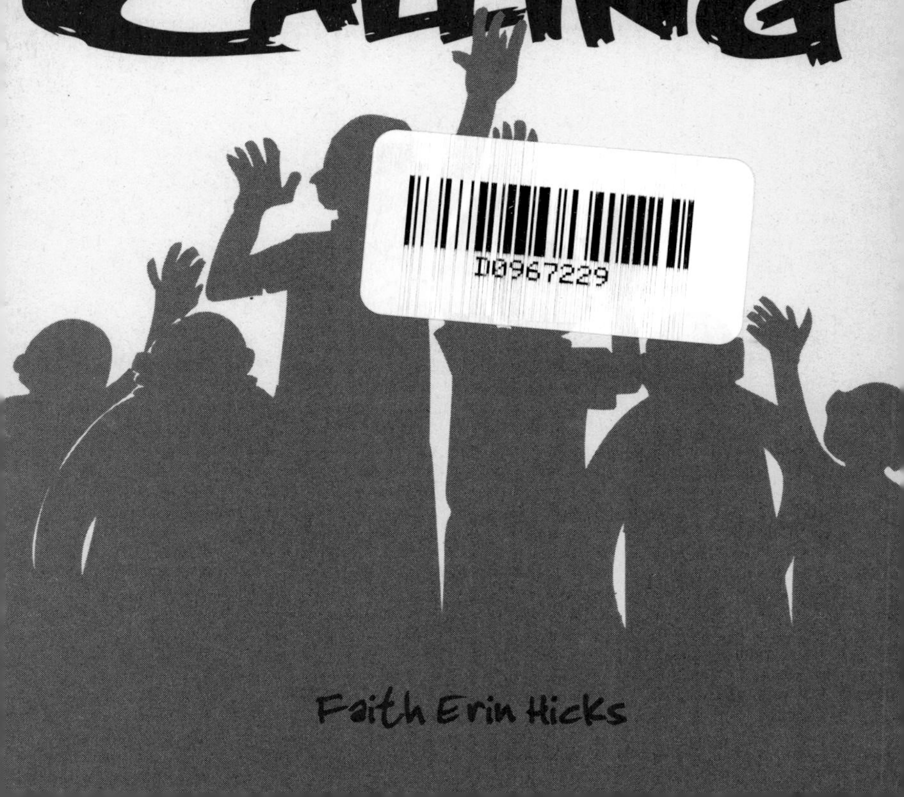

Faith Erin Hicks

Zombies Calling

written and illustrated by Faith Erin Hicks

Zombies Calling logo by Lacey Wood

SLG Publishing

Dan Vado - President & Publisher
Jennifer de Guzman - Editor-in-Chief

P.O. Box 26427
San Jose, CA 95159

First Printing: November 2007
ISBN-13: 978-1-59362-079-0

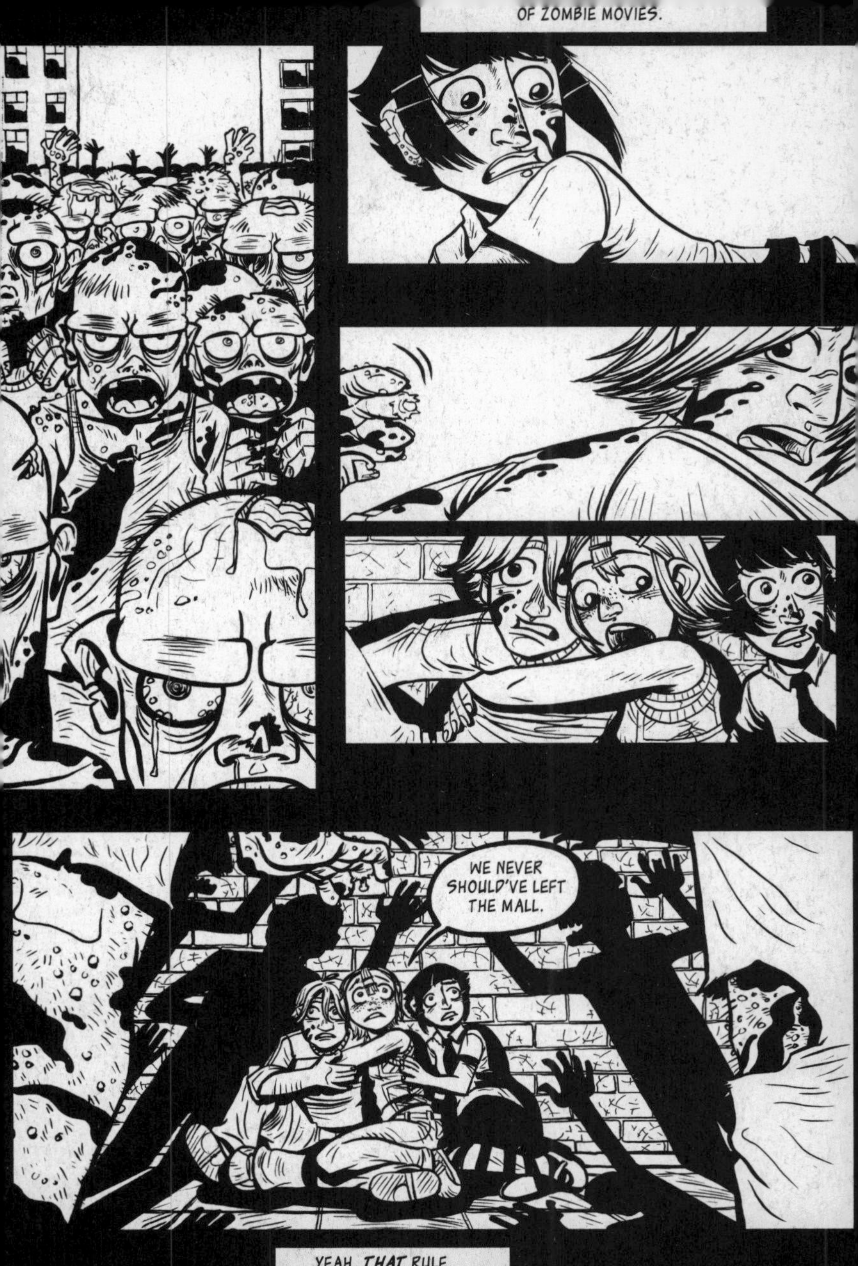
OF ZOMBIE MOVIES.
WE NEVER SHOULD'VE LEFT THE MALL.
YEAH, THAT RULE.

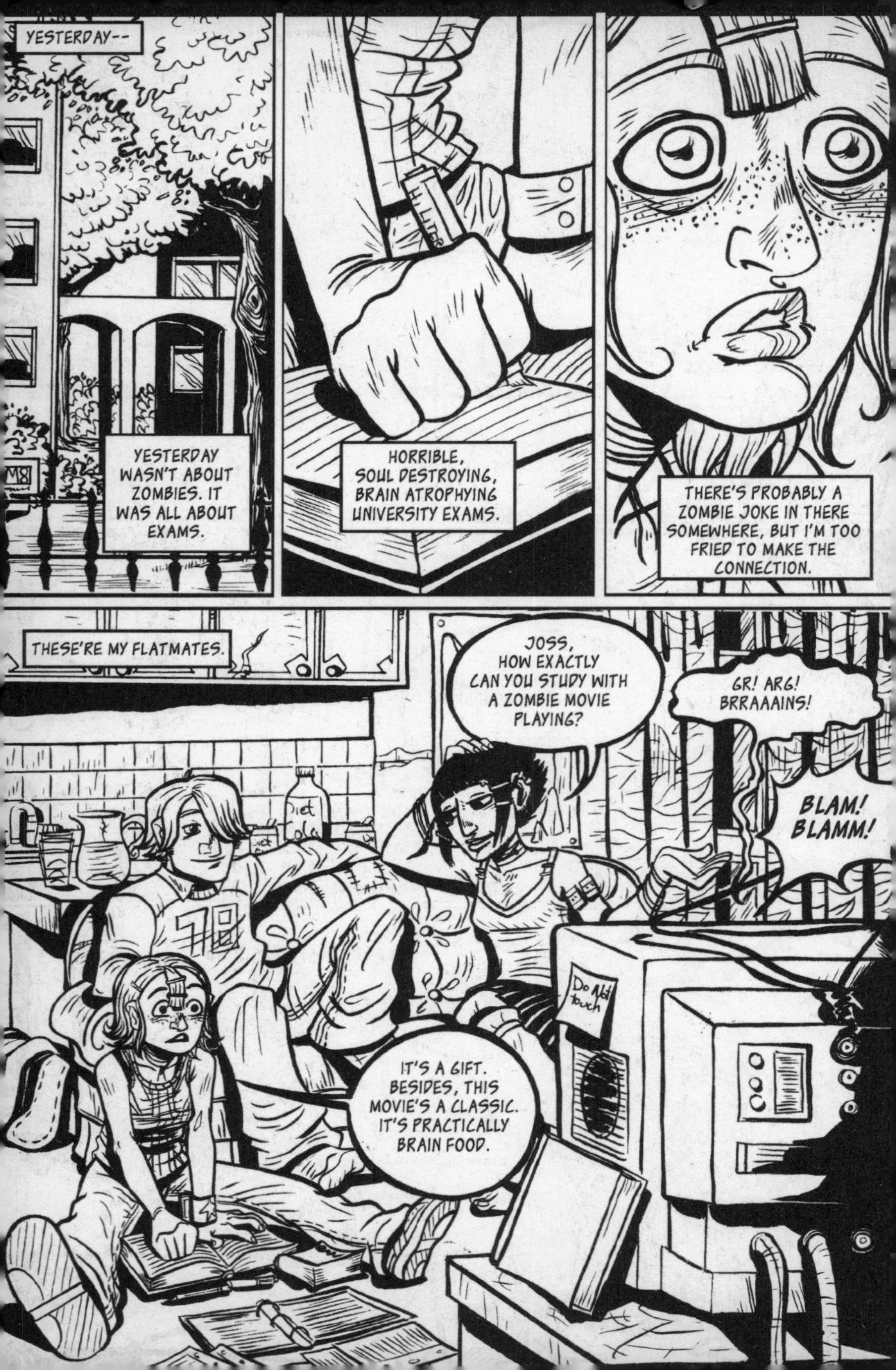
YESTERDAY--
YESTERDAY WASN'T ABOUT ZOMBIES. IT WAS ALL ABOUT EXAMS.
HORRIBLE, SOUL DESTROYING, BRAIN ATROPHYING UNIVERSITY EXAMS.
THERE'S PROBABLY A ZOMBIE JOKE IN THERE SOMEWHERE, BUT I'M TOO FRIED TO MAKE THE CONNECTION.
THESE'RE MY FLATMATES.
JOSS, HOW EXACTLY CAN YOU STUDY WITH A ZOMBIE MOVIE PLAYING?
GR! ARG! BRRAAAINS!
BLAM! BLAMM!
Do Not touch
IT'S A GIFT. BESIDES, THIS MOVIE'S A CLASSIC. IT'S PRACTICALLY BRAIN FOOD.

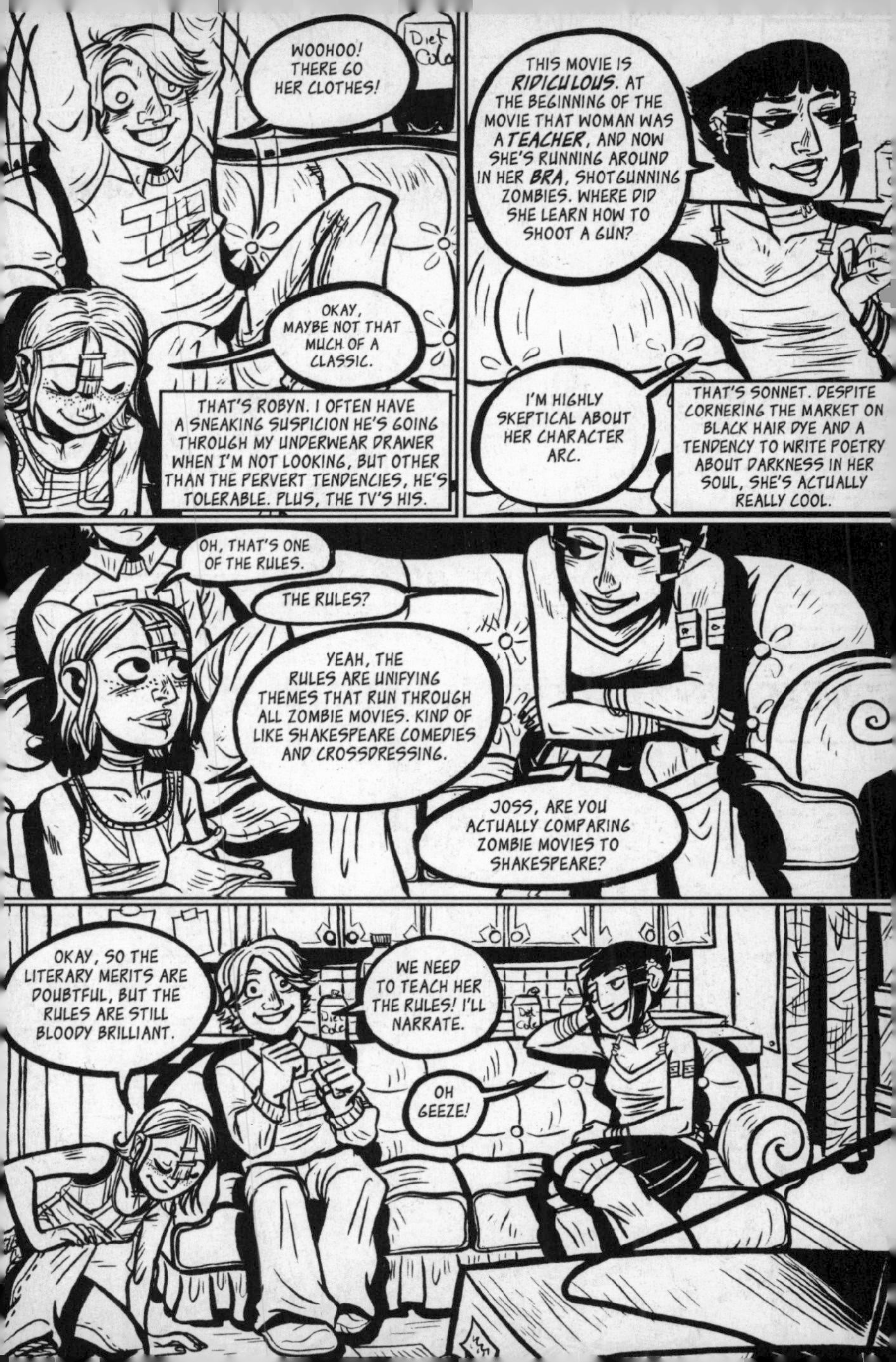
WOOHOO! THERE GO HER CLOTHES!
OKAY, MAYBE NOT THAT MUCH OF A CLASSIC.
THAT'S ROBYN. I OFTEN HAVE A SNEAKING SUSPICION HE'S GOING THROUGH MY UNDERWEAR DRAWER WHEN I'M NOT LOOKING, BUT OTHER THAN THE PERVERT TENDENCIES, HE'S TOLERABLE. PLUS, THE TV'S HIS.
THIS MOVIE IS RIDICULOUS. AT THE BEGINNING OF THE MOVIE THAT WOMAN WAS A TEACHER, AND NOW SHE'S RUNNING AROUND IN HER BRA, SHOTGUNNING ZOMBIES. WHERE DID SHE LEARN HOW TO SHOOT A GUN?
I'M HIGHLY SKEPTICAL ABOUT HER CHARACTER ARC.
THAT'S SONNET. DESPITE CORNERING THE MARKET ON BLACK HAIR DYE AND A TENDENCY TO WRITE POETRY ABOUT DARKNESS IN HER SOUL, SHE'S ACTUALLY REALLY COOL.
OH, THAT'S ONE OF THE RULES.
THE RULES?
YEAH, THE RULES ARE UNIFYING THEMES THAT RUN THROUGH ALL ZOMBIE MOVIES. KIND OF LIKE SHAKESPEARE COMEDIES AND CROSSDRESSING.
JOSS, ARE YOU ACTUALLY COMPARING ZOMBIE MOVIES TO SHAKESPEARE?
OKAY, SO THE LITERARY MERITS ARE DOUBTFUL, BUT THE RULES ARE STILL BLOODY BRILLIANT.
WE NEED TO TEACH HER THE RULES! I'LL NARRATE.
OH GEEZE!

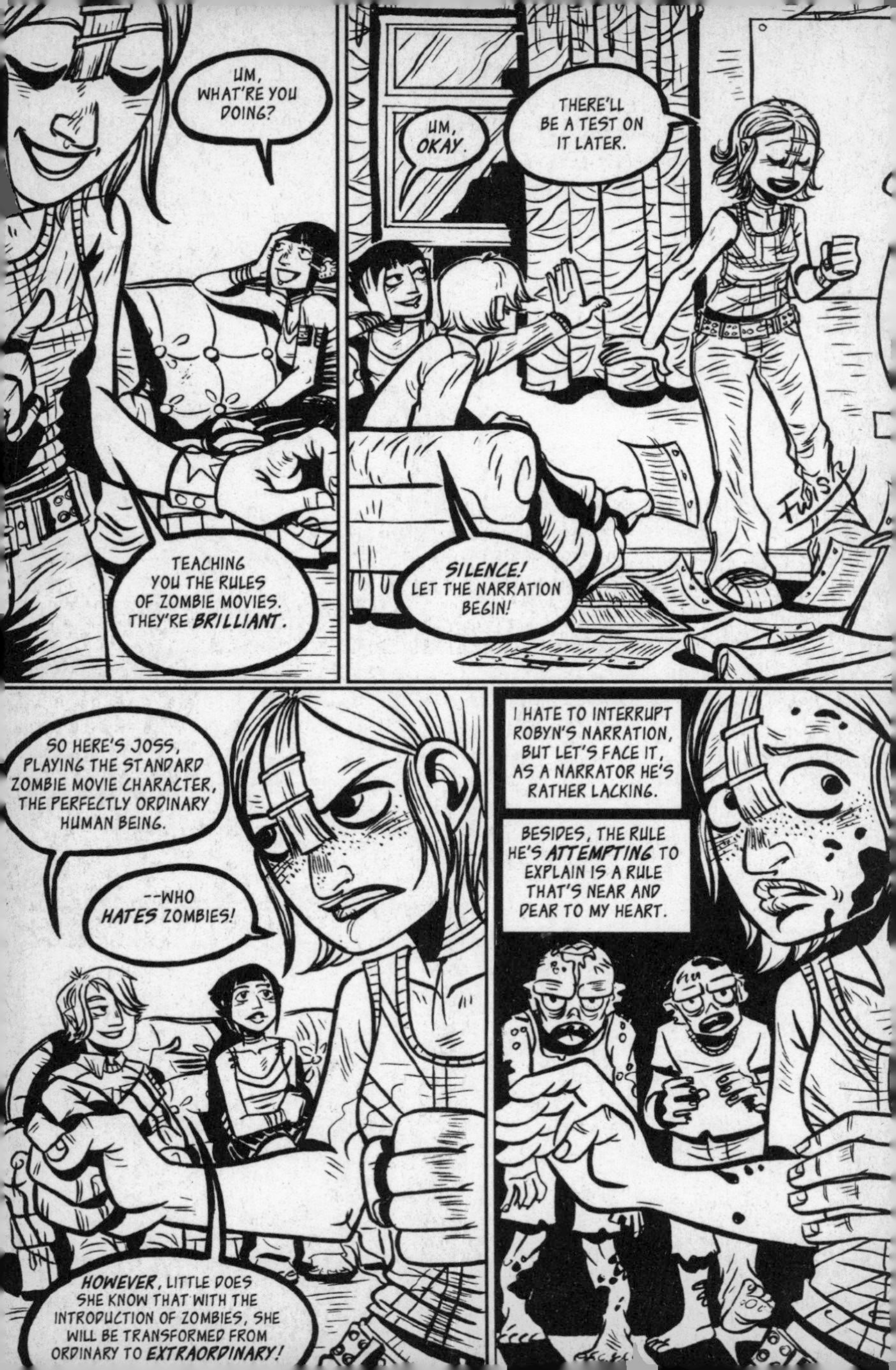
UM, WHAT'RE YOU DOING?
TEACHING YOU THE RULES OF ZOMBIE MOVIES. THEY'RE *BRILLIANT*.
UM, *OKAY*.
THERE'LL BE A TEST ON IT LATER.
SILENCE! LET THE NARRATION BEGIN!
SO HERE'S JOSS, PLAYING THE STANDARD ZOMBIE MOVIE CHARACTER, THE PERFECTLY ORDINARY HUMAN BEING.
--WHO *HATES* ZOMBIES!
HOWEVER, LITTLE DOES SHE KNOW THAT WITH THE INTRODUCTION OF ZOMBIES, SHE WILL BE TRANSFORMED FROM ORDINARY TO *EXTRAORDINARY!*
I HATE TO INTERRUPT ROBYN'S NARRATION, BUT LET'S FACE IT, AS A NARRATOR HE'S RATHER LACKING.
BESIDES, THE RULE HE'S *ATTEMPTING* TO EXPLAIN IS A RULE THAT'S NEAR AND DEAR TO MY HEART.

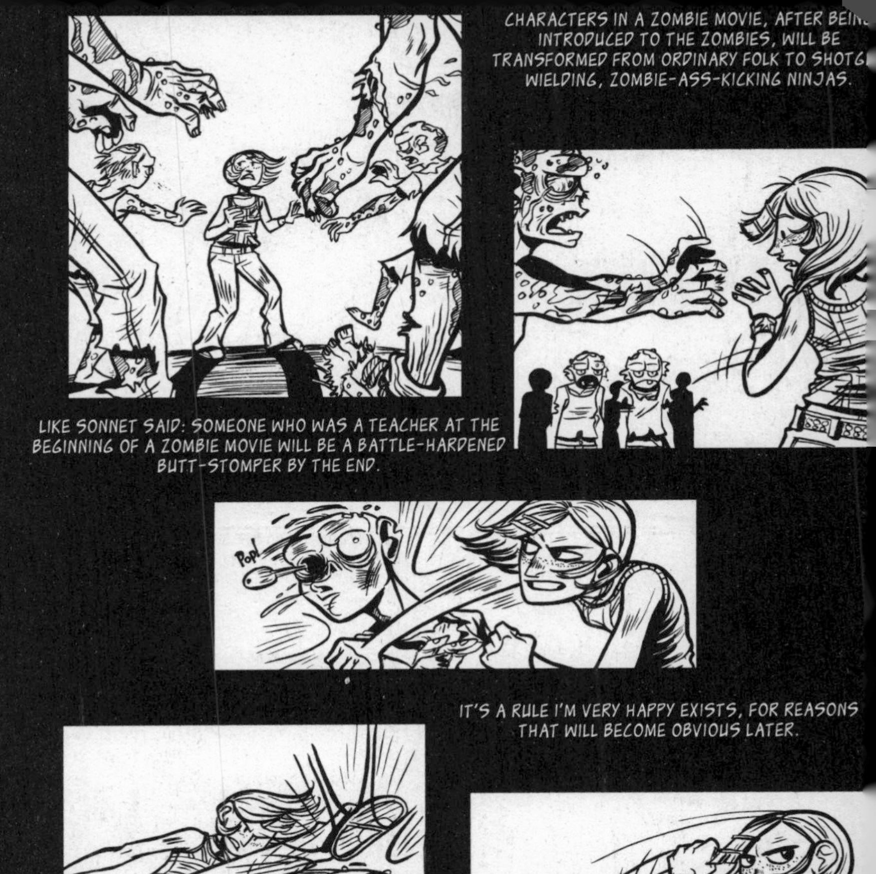
CHARACTERS IN A ZOMBIE MOVIE, AFTER BEIN
INTRODUCED TO THE ZOMBIES, WILL BE
TRANSFORMED FROM ORDINARY FOLK TO SHOTG
WIELDING, ZOMBIE-ASS-KICKING NINJAS.
LIKE SONNET SAID: SOMEONE WHO WAS A TEACHER AT THE BEGINNING OF A ZOMBIE MOVIE WILL BE A BATTLE-HARDENED BUTT-STOMPER BY THE END.
POP!
IT'S A RULE I'M VERY HAPPY EXISTS, FOR REASONS THAT WILL BECOME OBVIOUS LATER.

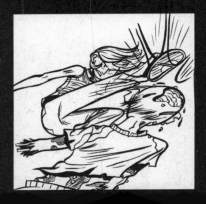

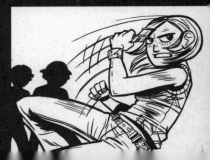

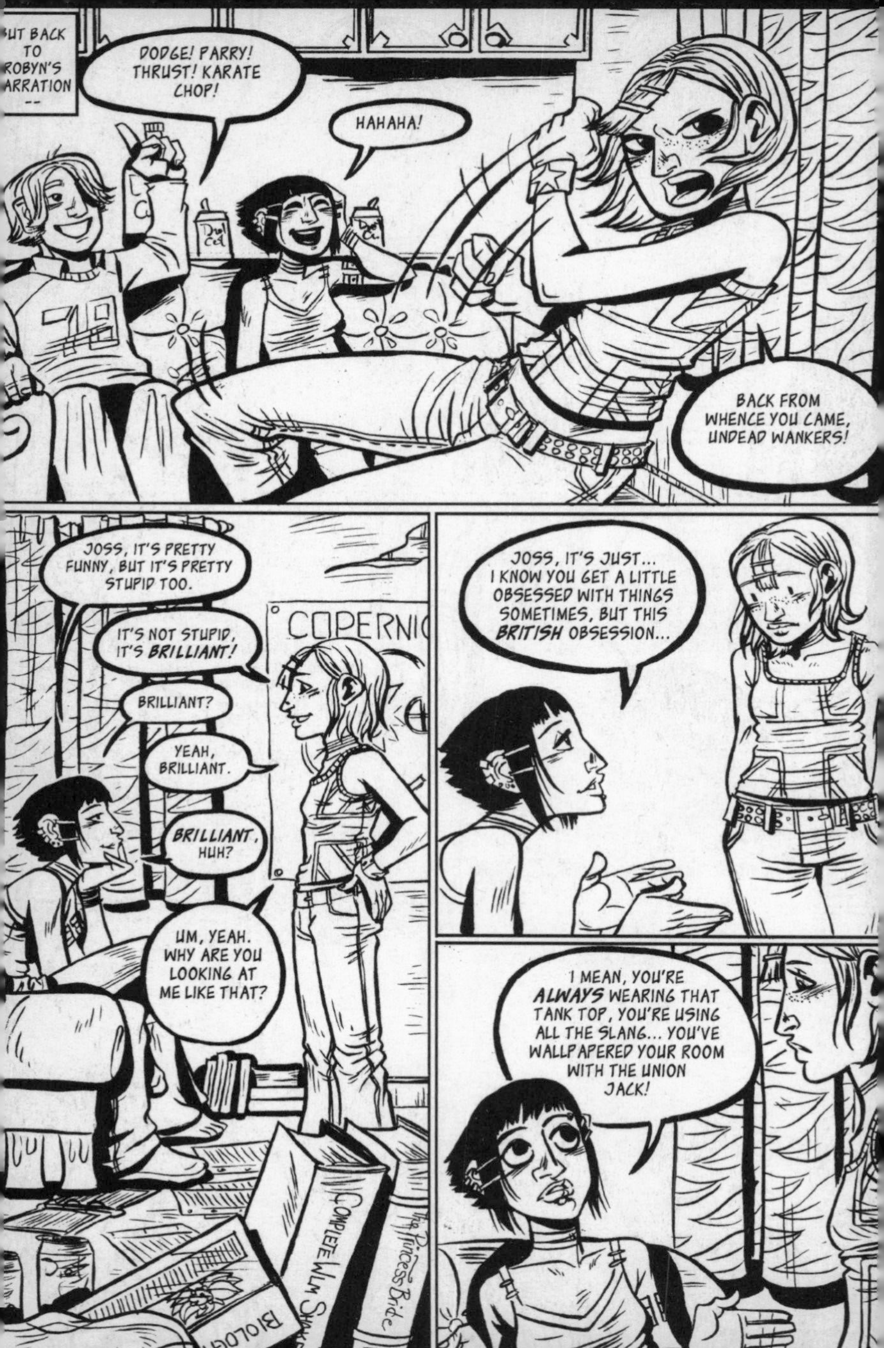

UT BACK TO ROBYN'S ARRATION --
DODGE! PARRY! THRUST! KARATE CHOP!
HAHAHA!
BACK FROM WHENCE YOU CAME, UNDEAD WANKERS!
JOSS, IT'S PRETTY FUNNY, BUT IT'S PRETTY STUPID TOO.
IT'S NOT STUPID, IT'S BRILLIANT!
BRILLIANT?
YEAH, BRILLIANT.
BRILLIANT, HUH?
UM, YEAH. WHY ARE YOU LOOKING AT ME LIKE THAT?
COPERNIC
COMPLETE WLM SHAKE
The Princess Bride
BIOLOGY
JOSS, IT'S JUST... I KNOW YOU GET A LITTLE OBSESSED WITH THINGS SOMETIMES, BUT THIS BRITISH OBSESSION...
I MEAN, YOU'RE ALWAYS WEARING THAT TANK TOP, YOU'RE USING ALL THE SLANG... YOU'VE WALLPAPERED YOUR ROOM WITH THE UNION JACK!

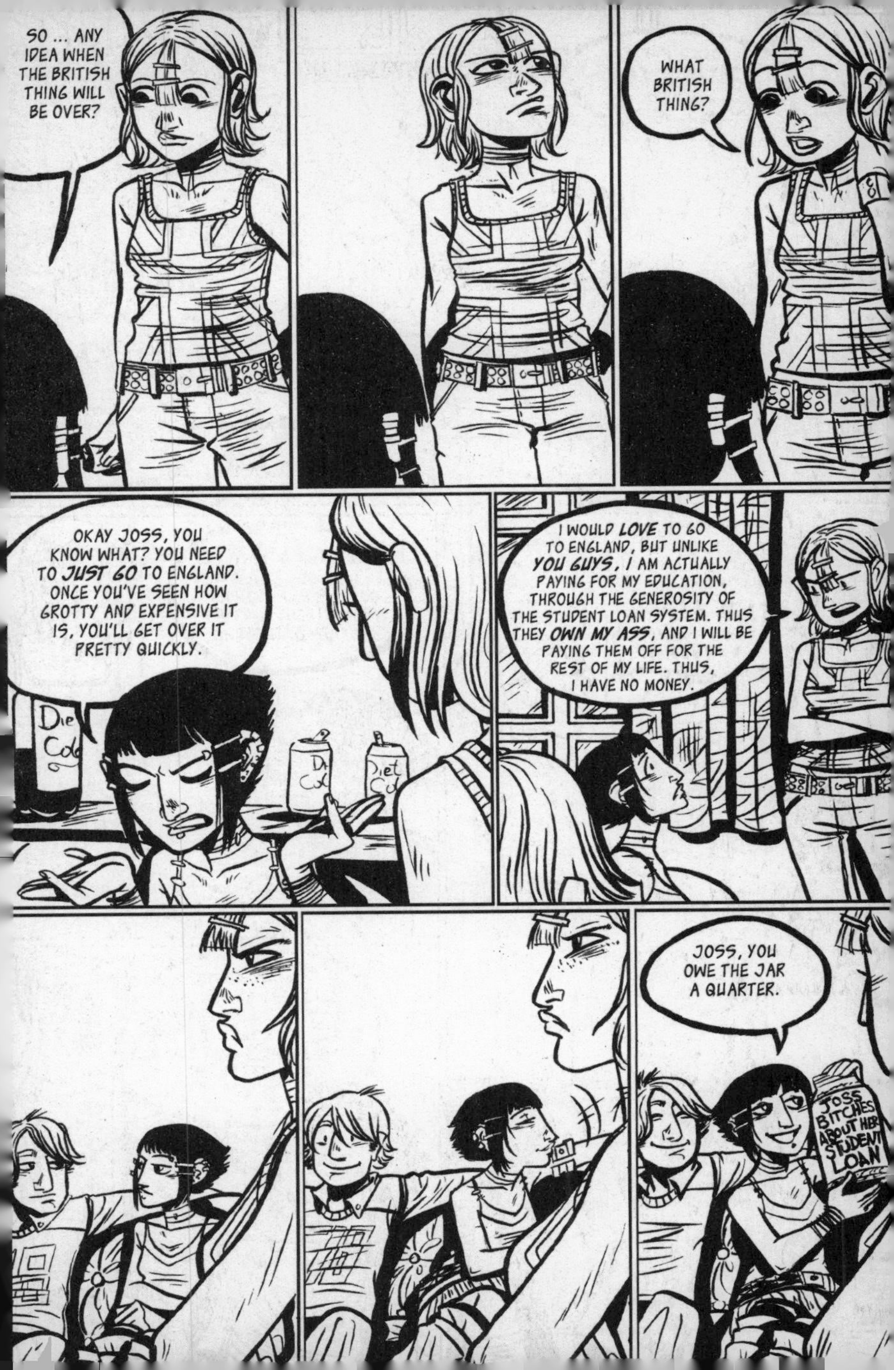
SO ... ANY IDEA WHEN THE BRITISH THING WILL BE OVER?
WHAT BRITISH THING?
OKAY JOSS, YOU KNOW WHAT? YOU NEED TO JUST GO TO ENGLAND. ONCE YOU'VE SEEN HOW GROTTY AND EXPENSIVE IT IS, YOU'LL GET OVER IT PRETTY QUICKLY.
I WOULD LOVE TO GO TO ENGLAND, BUT UNLIKE YOU GUYS, I AM ACTUALLY PAYING FOR MY EDUCATION, THROUGH THE GENEROSITY OF THE STUDENT LOAN SYSTEM. THUS THEY OWN MY ASS, AND I WILL BE PAYING THEM OFF FOR THE REST OF MY LIFE. THUS, I HAVE NO MONEY.
JOSS, YOU OWE THE JAR A QUARTER.
JOSS BITCHES ABOUT HER STUDENT LOAN

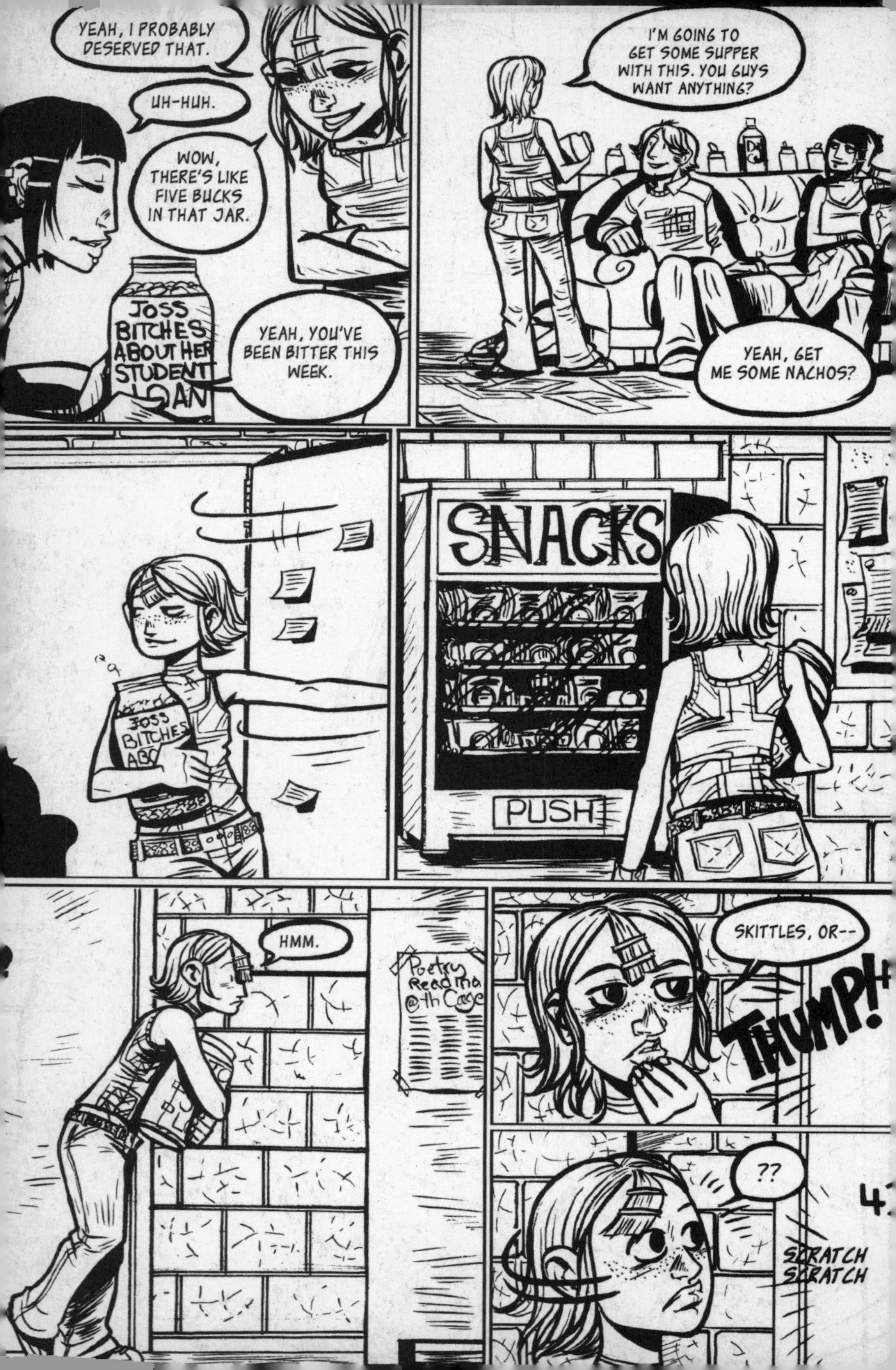
YEAH, I PROBABLY DESERVED THAT.
UH-HUH.
WOW, THERE'S LIKE FIVE BUCKS IN THAT JAR.
JOSS BITCHES ABOUT HER STUDENT LOAN
YEAH, YOU'VE BEEN BITTER THIS WEEK.
I'M GOING TO GET SOME SUPPER WITH THIS. YOU GUYS WANT ANYTHING?
YEAH, GET ME SOME NACHOS?
JOSS BITCHES ABO
SNACKS
PUSH
HMM.
Poetry Reading @th Cage
SKITTLES, OR--
THUMP!
??
SCRATCH SCRATCH

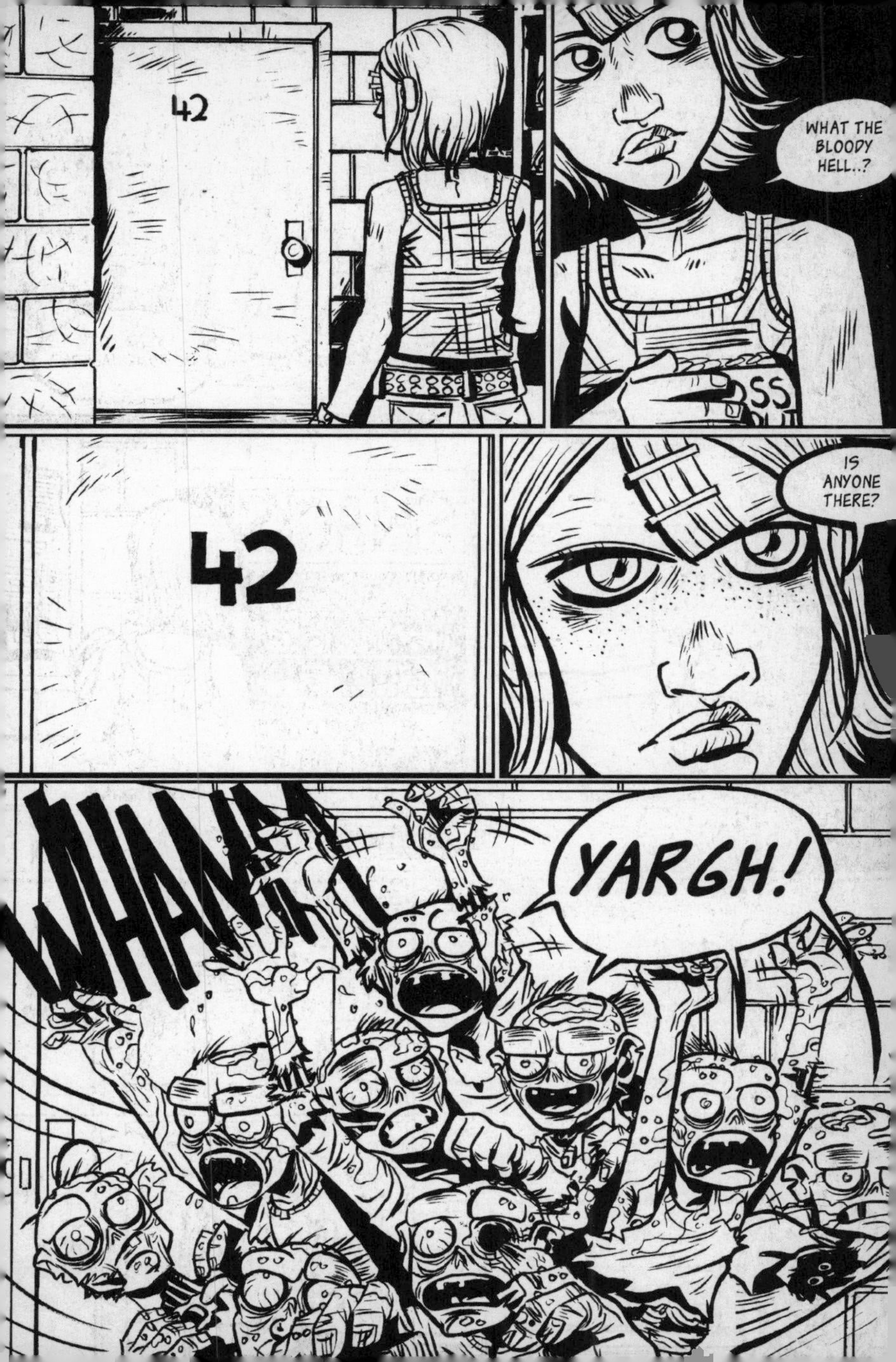
42
WHAT THE BLOODY HELL..?
42
IS ANYONE THERE?
WHAM!
YARGH!

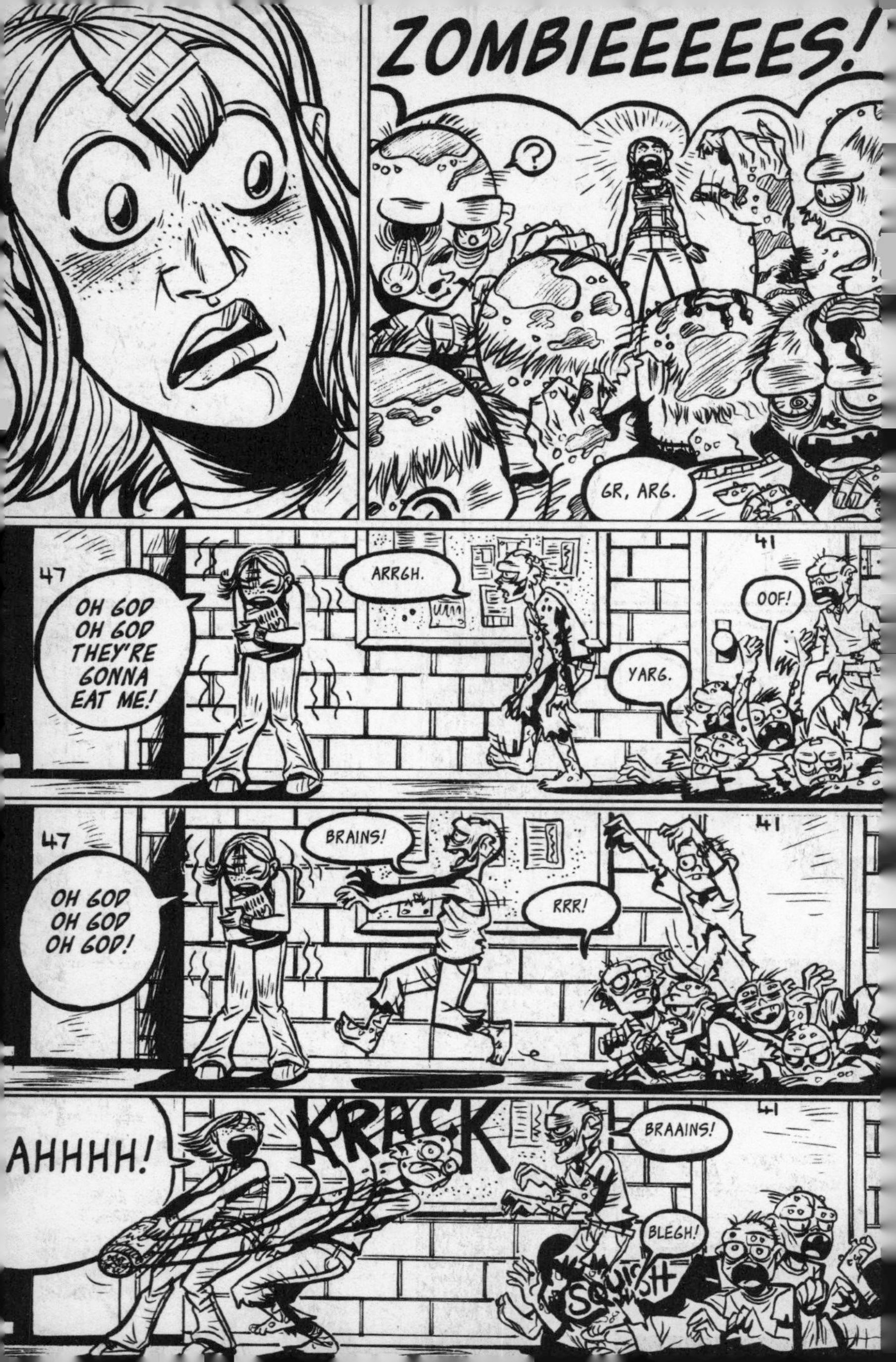
ZOMBIEEEEEES!
?
GR, ARG.
47
OH GOD OH GOD THEY'RE GONNA EAT ME!
ARRGH.
41
OOF!
YARG.
47
OH GOD OH GOD OH GOD!
BRAINS!
41
RRR!
AHHHH!
KRACK
41
BRAAINS!
BLEGH!
SQUISH

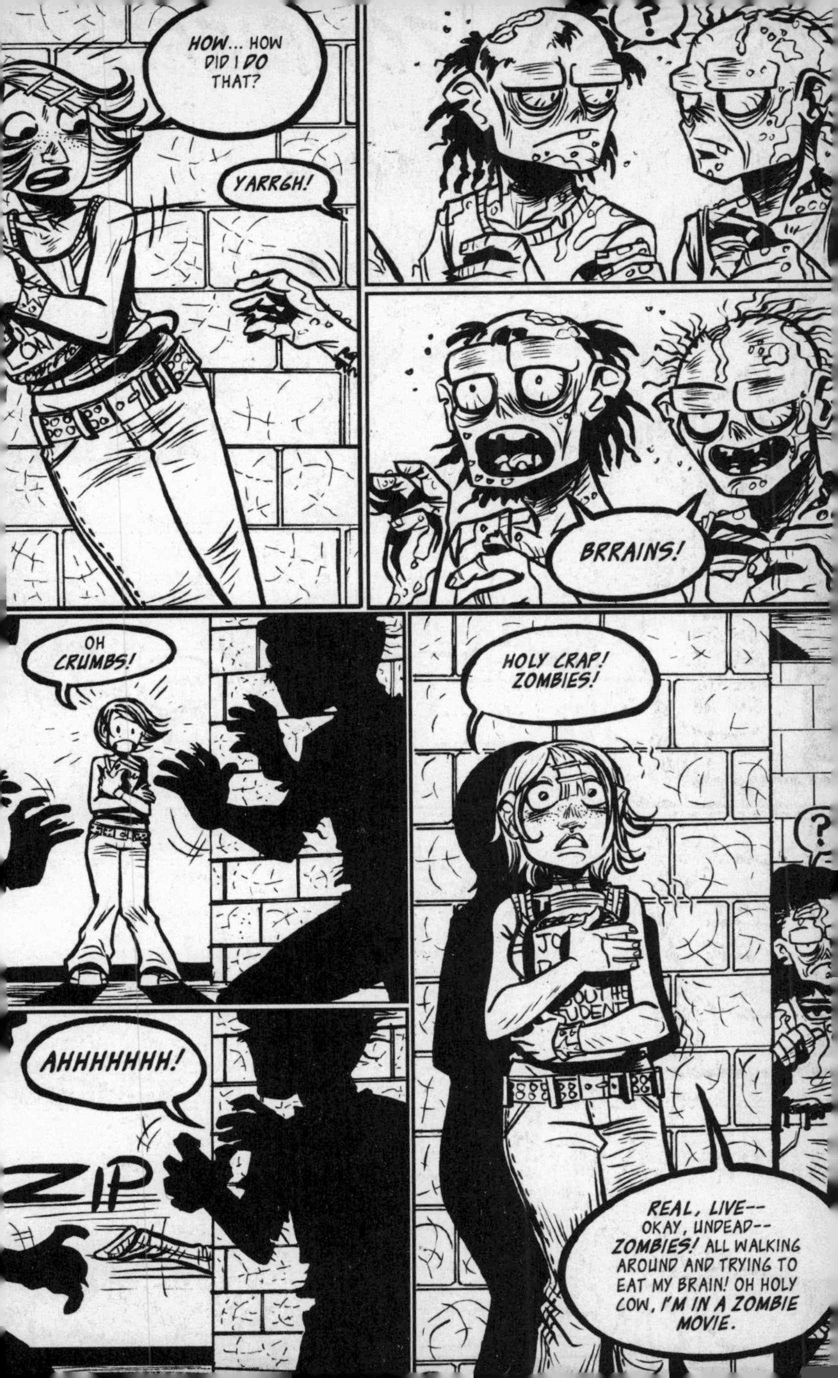
HOW... HOW DID I DO THAT?
YARRGH!
?
BRRAINS!
OH CRUMBS!
AHHHHHHH!
ZIP
HOLY CRAP! ZOMBIES!
?
REAL, LIVE-- OKAY, UNDEAD-- ZOMBIES! ALL WALKING AROUND AND TRYING TO EAT MY BRAIN! OH HOLY COW, I'M IN A ZOMBIE MOVIE.

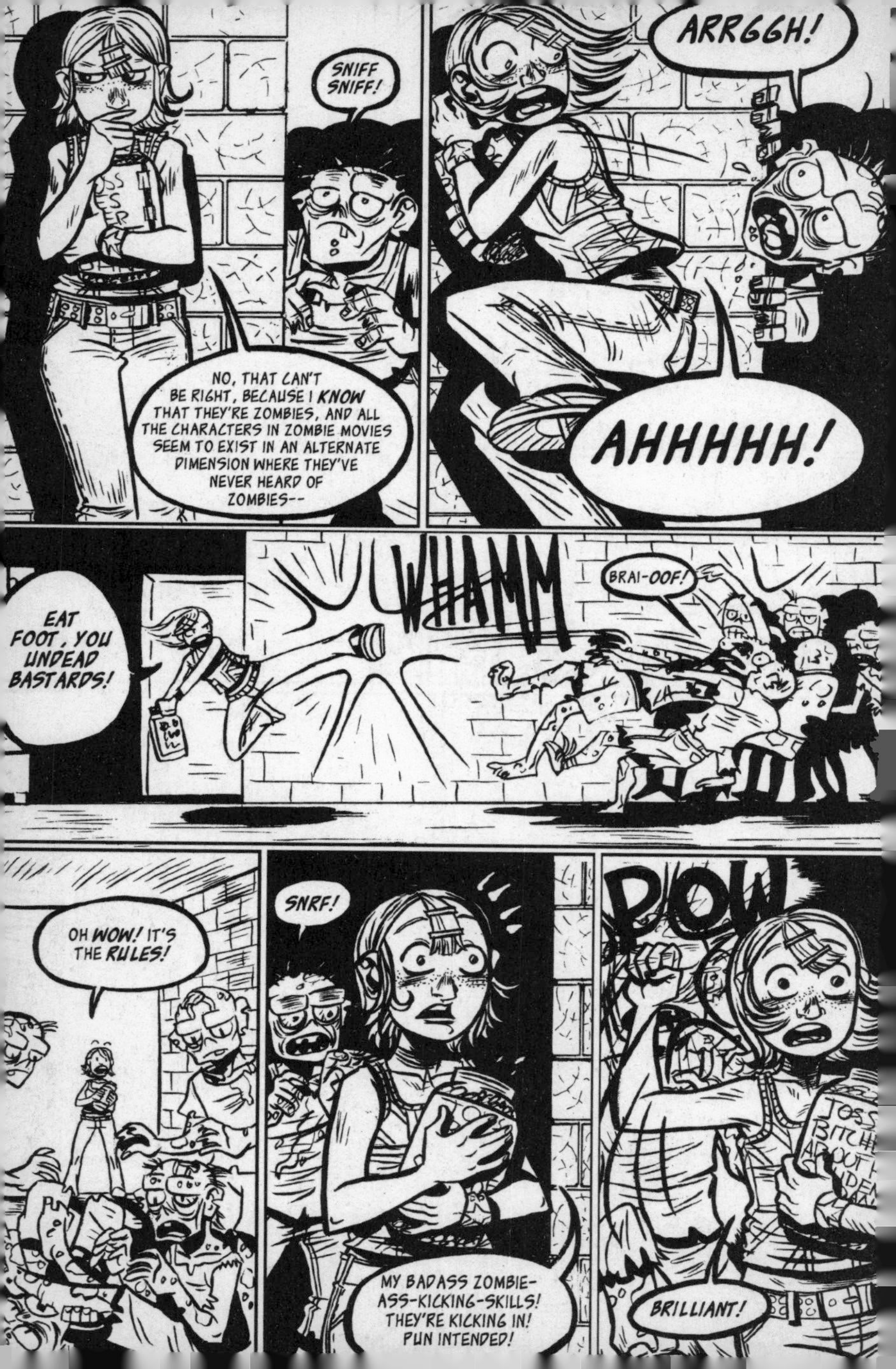
SNIFF SNIFF!
NO, THAT CAN'T BE RIGHT, BECAUSE I KNOW THAT THEY'RE ZOMBIES, AND ALL THE CHARACTERS IN ZOMBIE MOVIES SEEM TO EXIST IN AN ALTERNATE DIMENSION WHERE THEY'VE NEVER HEARD OF ZOMBIES--
ARRGGH!
AHHHHH!
EAT FOOT, YOU UNDEAD BASTARDS!
WHAMM
BRAI-OOF!
OH WOW! IT'S THE RULES!
SNRF!
MY BADASS ZOMBIE-ASS-KICKING-SKILLS! THEY'RE KICKING IN! PUN INTENDED!
POW
BRILLIANT!

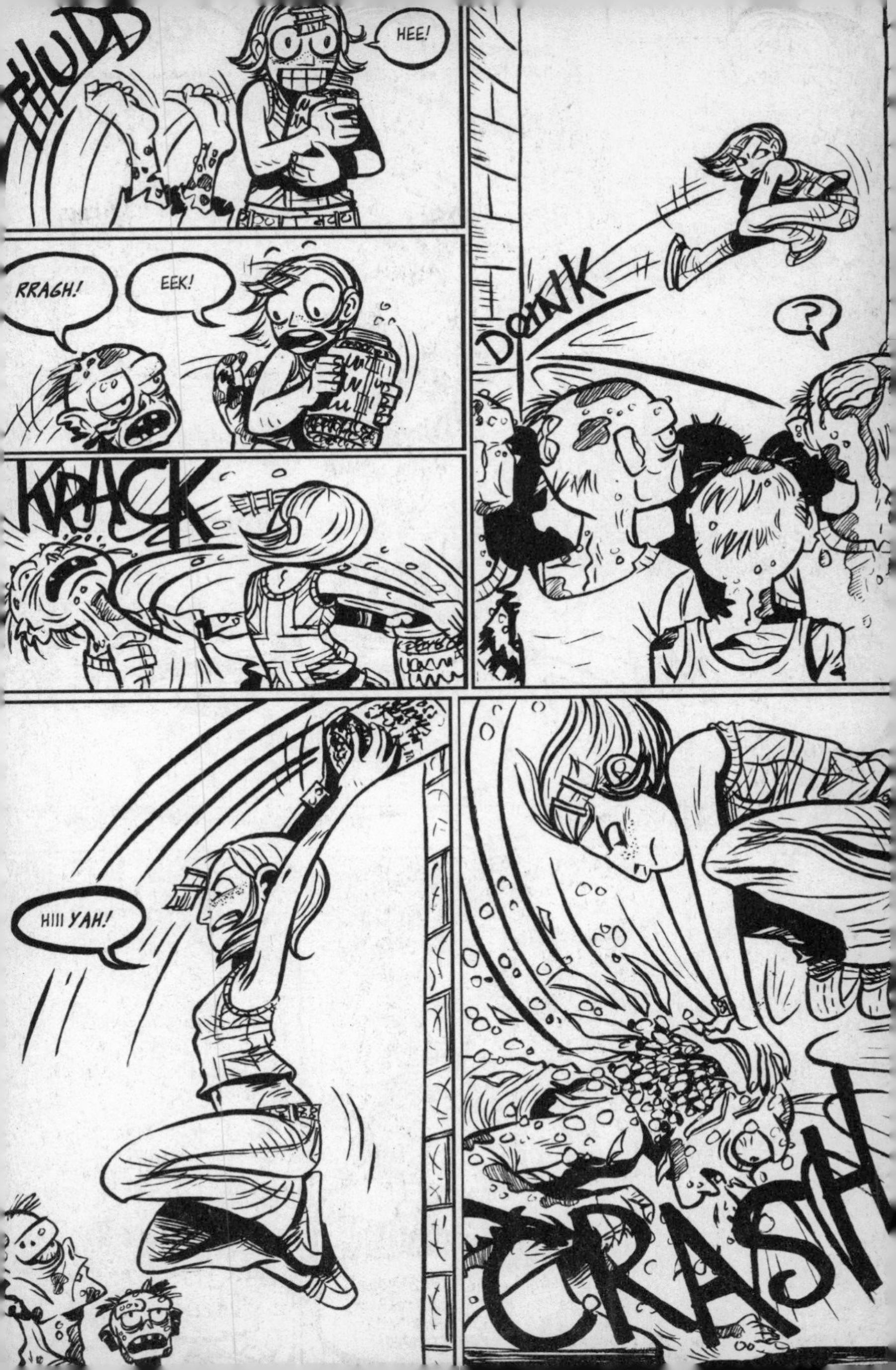

THUDD
HEE!
RRAGH!
EEK!
KRACK
DONK
?
HIII YAH!
CRASH

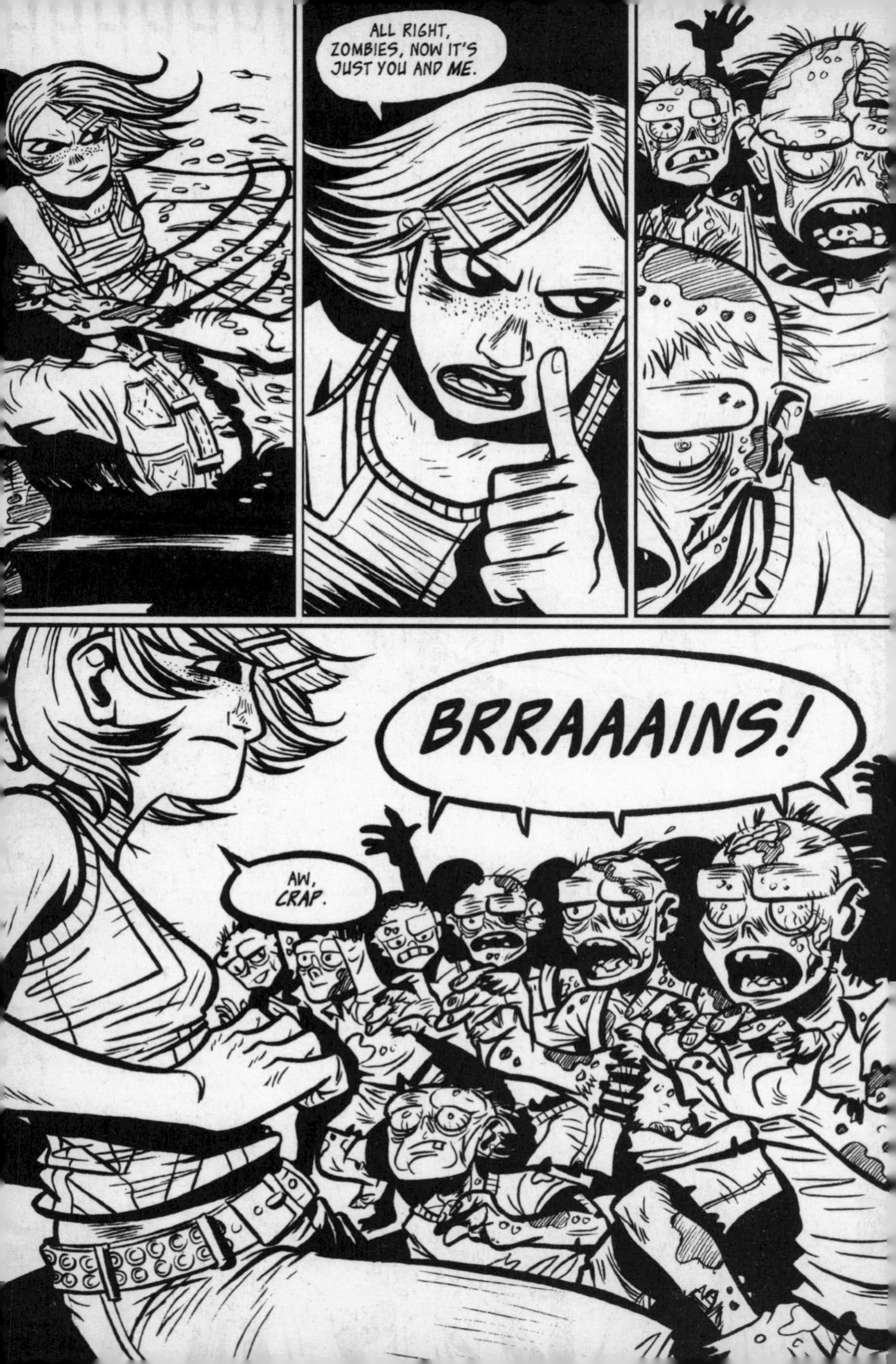
ALL RIGHT, ZOMBIES, NOW IT'S JUST YOU AND ME.
BRRAAAINS!
AW, CRAP.

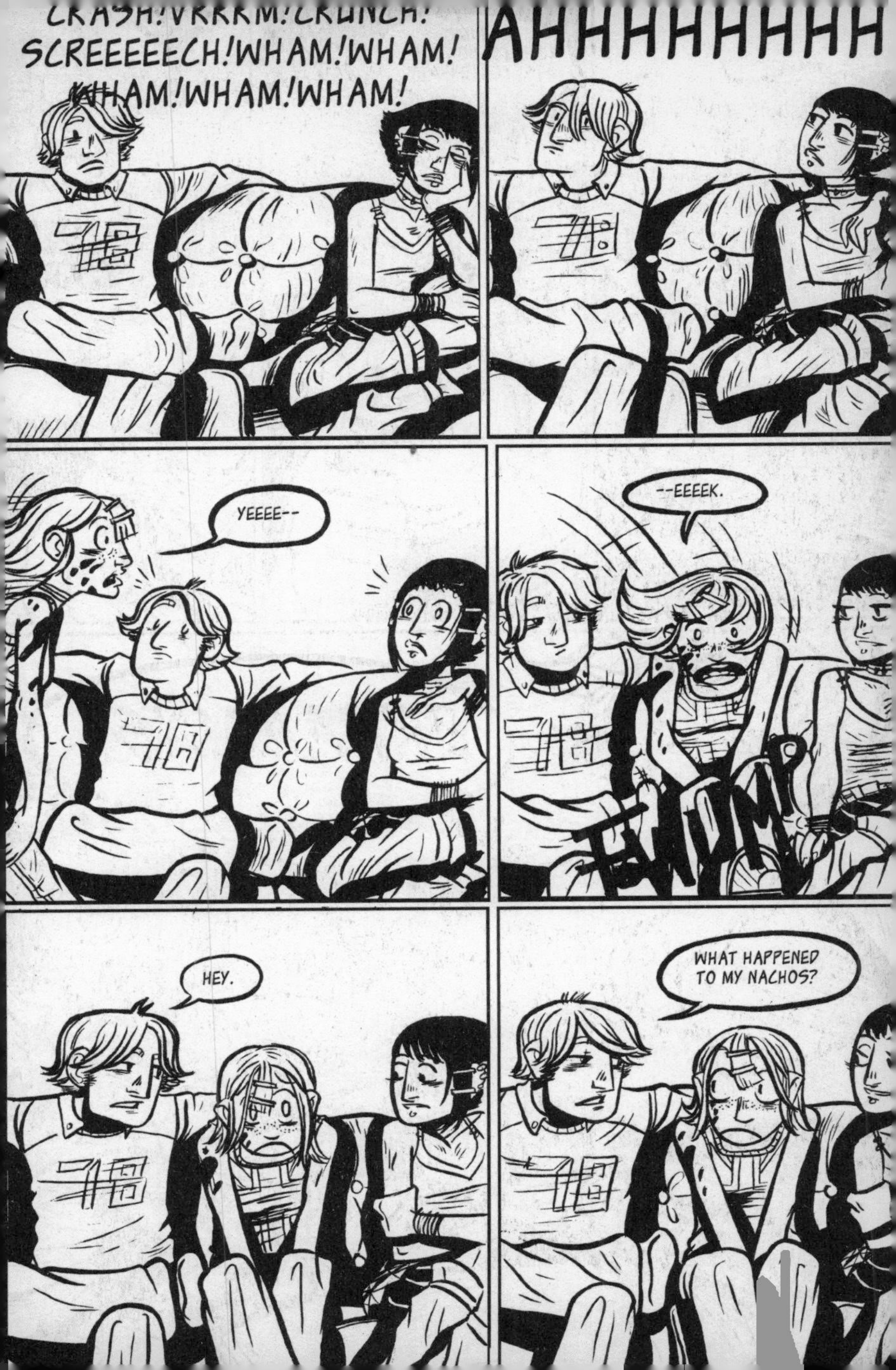
CRASH!VRRRM!CRUNCH!
SCREEEEECH!WHAM!WHAM!
WHAM!WHAM!WHAM!
AHHHHHHHH
YEEEE--
--EEEEK.
THOMP
HEY.
WHAT HAPPENED TO MY NACHOS?

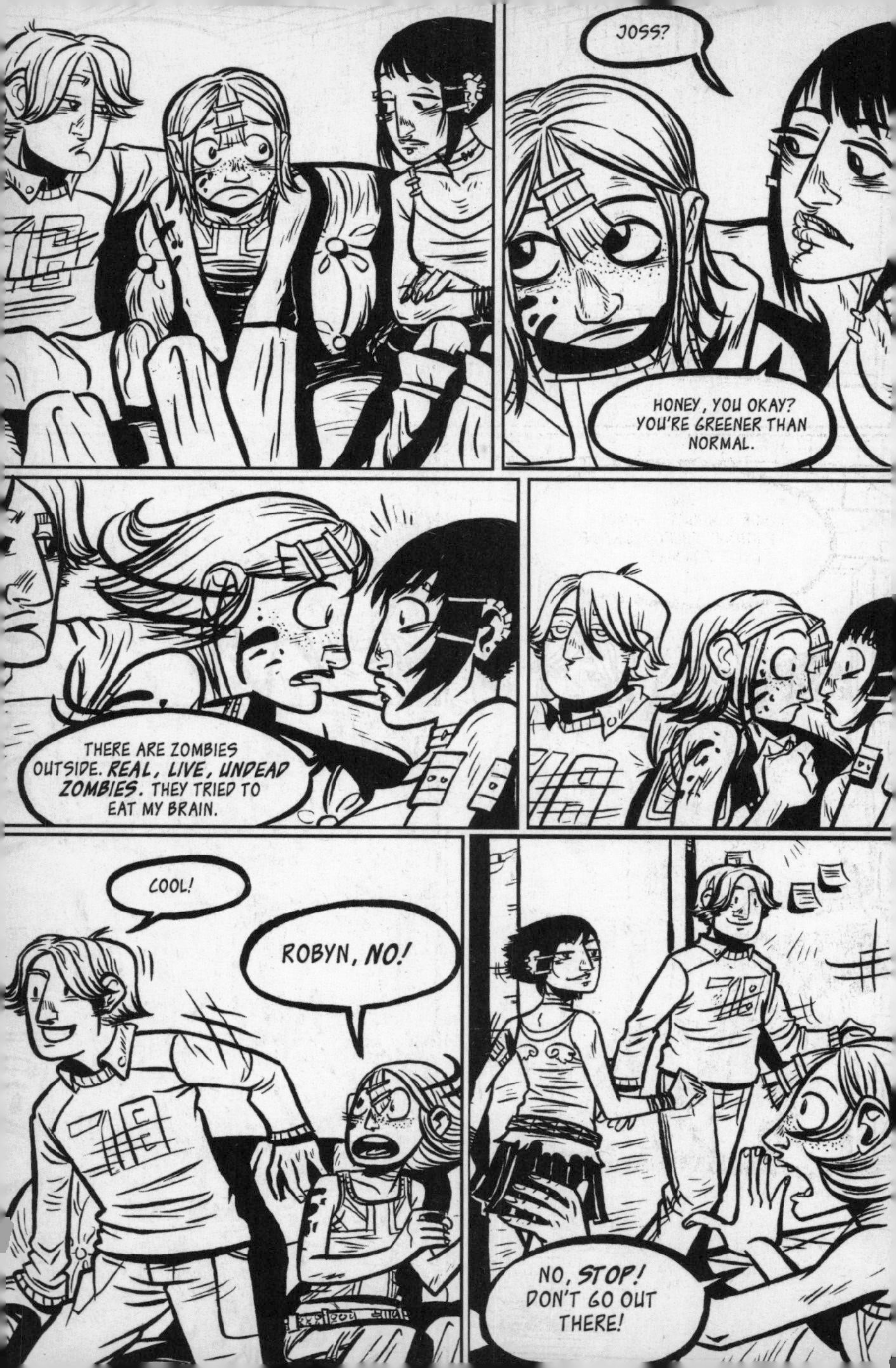
JOSS?
HONEY, YOU OKAY? YOU'RE GREENER THAN NORMAL.
THERE ARE ZOMBIES OUTSIDE. *REAL, LIVE, UNDEAD ZOMBIES*. THEY TRIED TO EAT MY BRAIN.
COOL!
ROBYN, *NO!*
NO, *STOP!* DON'T GO OUT THERE!

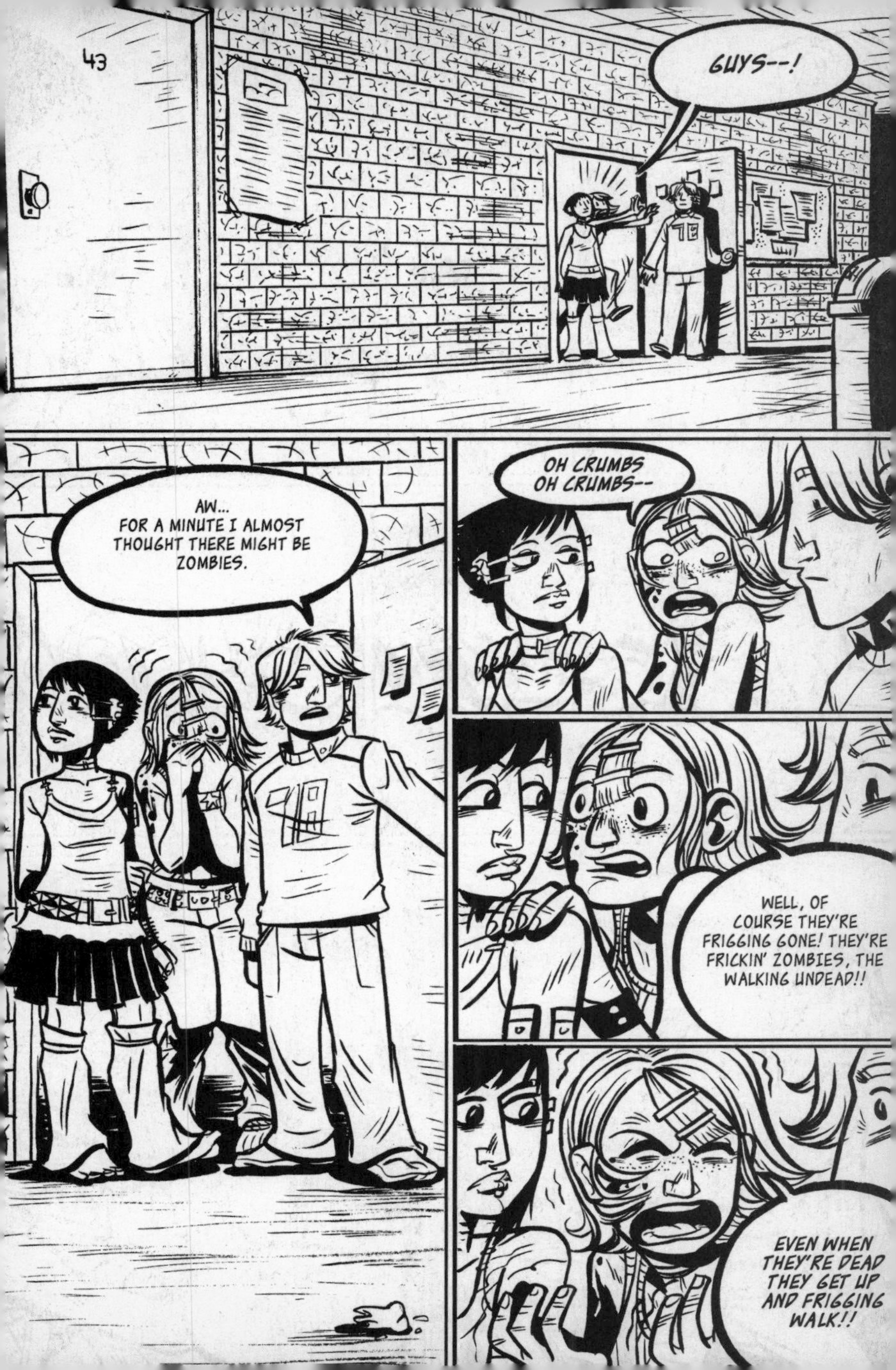
GUYS--!
AW...
FOR A MINUTE I ALMOST
THOUGHT THERE MIGHT BE
ZOMBIES.
OH CRUMBS
OH CRUMBS--
WELL, OF COURSE THEY'RE FRIGGING GONE! THEY'RE FRICKIN' ZOMBIES, THE WALKING UNDEAD!!
EVEN WHEN THEY'RE DEAD THEY GET UP AND FRIGGING WALK!!

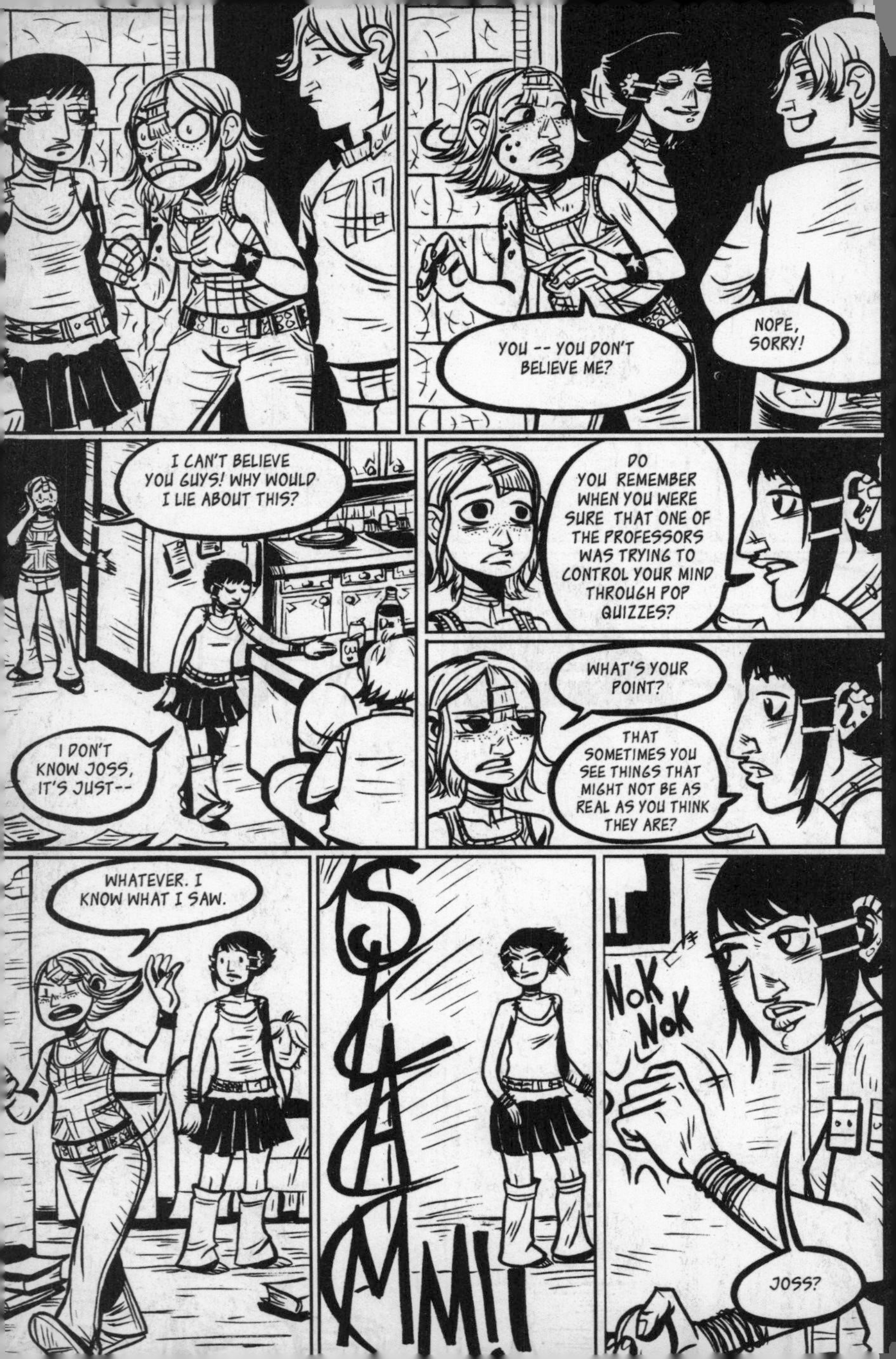
YOU -- YOU DON'T BELIEVE ME?
NOPE, SORRY!
I CAN'T BELIEVE YOU GUYS! WHY WOULD I LIE ABOUT THIS?
I DON'T KNOW JOSS, IT'S JUST--
DO YOU REMEMBER WHEN YOU WERE SURE THAT ONE OF THE PROFESSORS WAS TRYING TO CONTROL YOUR MIND THROUGH POP QUIZZES?
WHAT'S YOUR POINT?
THAT SOMETIMES YOU SEE THINGS THAT MIGHT NOT BE AS REAL AS YOU THINK THEY ARE?
WHATEVER. I KNOW WHAT I SAW.
SLAMM!
NOK NOK
JOSS?

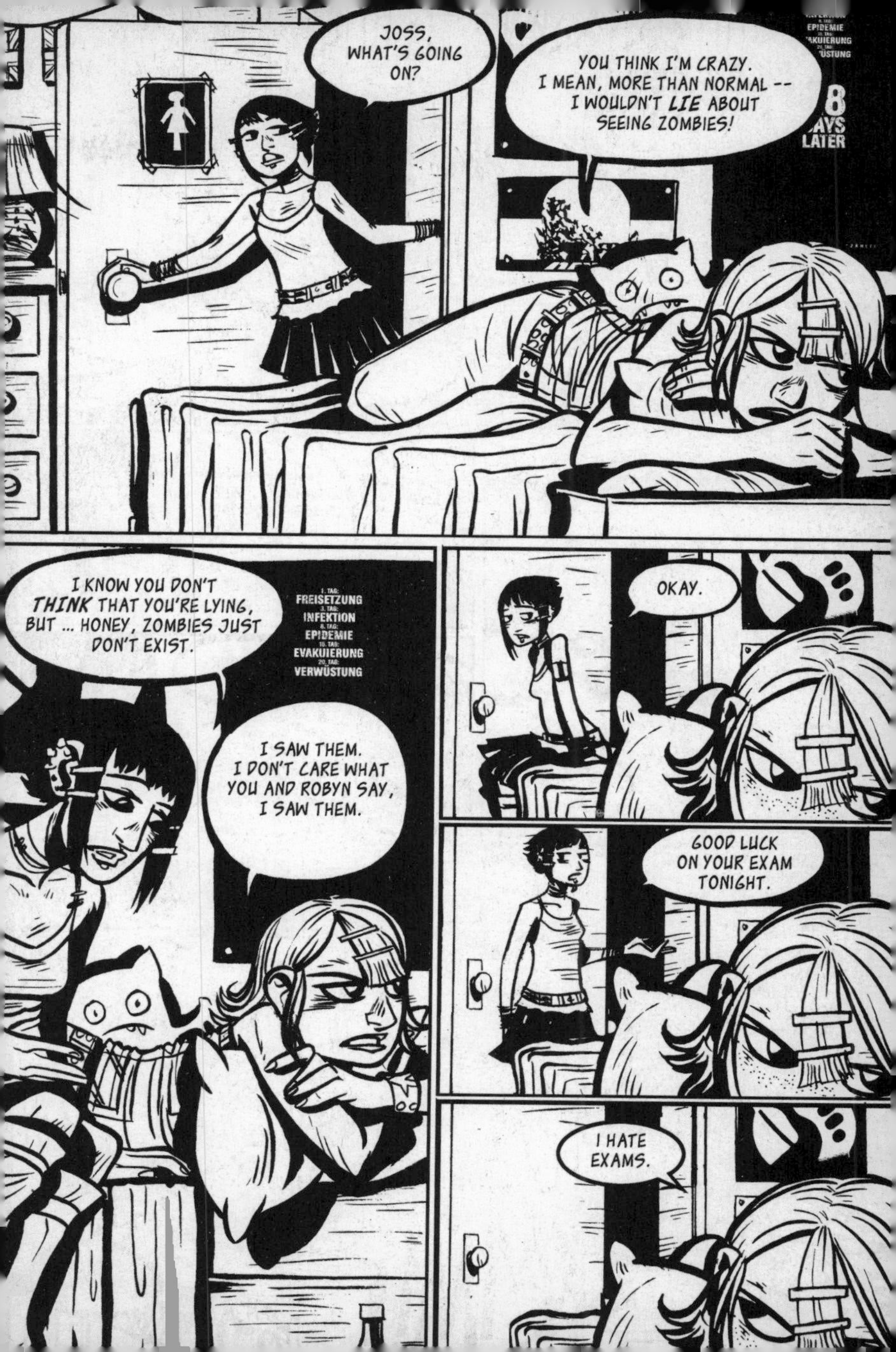
JOSS, WHAT'S GOING ON?
YOU THINK I'M CRAZY. I MEAN, MORE THAN NORMAL -- I WOULDN'T *LIE* ABOUT SEEING ZOMBIES!
EPIDEMIE
I KNOW YOU DON'T *THINK* THAT YOU'RE LYING, BUT ... HONEY, ZOMBIES JUST DON'T EXIST.
FREISETZUNG
INFEKTION
EPIDEMIE
EVAKUIERUNG
VERWÜSTUNG
I SAW THEM. I DON'T CARE WHAT YOU AND ROBYN SAY, I SAW THEM.
OKAY.
GOOD LUCK ON YOUR EXAM TONIGHT.
I HATE EXAMS.

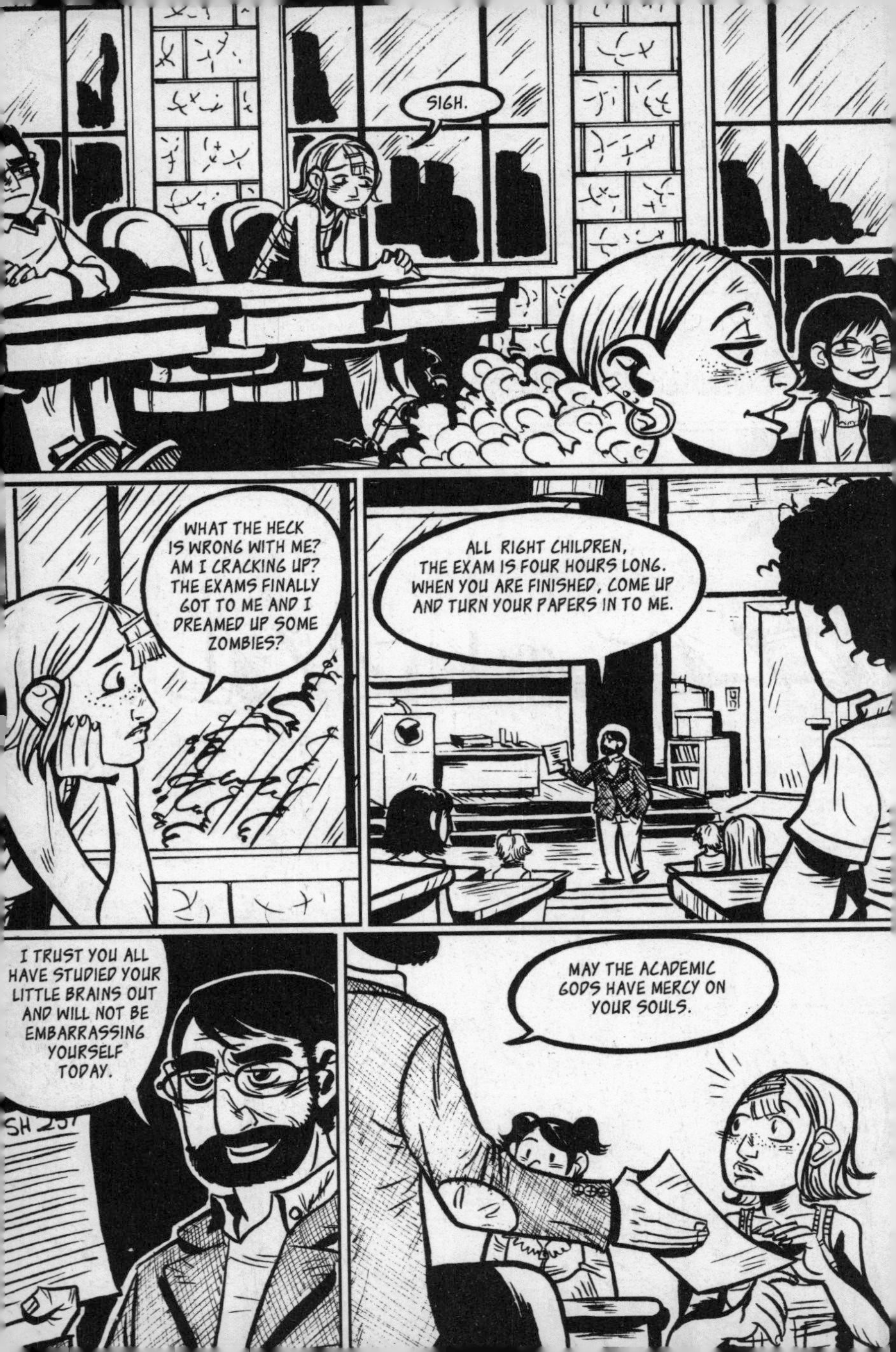
SIGH.
WHAT THE HECK IS WRONG WITH ME? AM I CRACKING UP? THE EXAMS FINALLY GOT TO ME AND I DREAMED UP SOME ZOMBIES?
ALL RIGHT CHILDREN, THE EXAM IS FOUR HOURS LONG. WHEN YOU ARE FINISHED, COME UP AND TURN YOUR PAPERS IN TO ME.
I TRUST YOU ALL HAVE STUDIED YOUR LITTLE BRAINS OUT AND WILL NOT BE EMBARRASSING YOURSELF TODAY.
MAY THE ACADEMIC GODS HAVE MERCY ON YOUR SOULS.

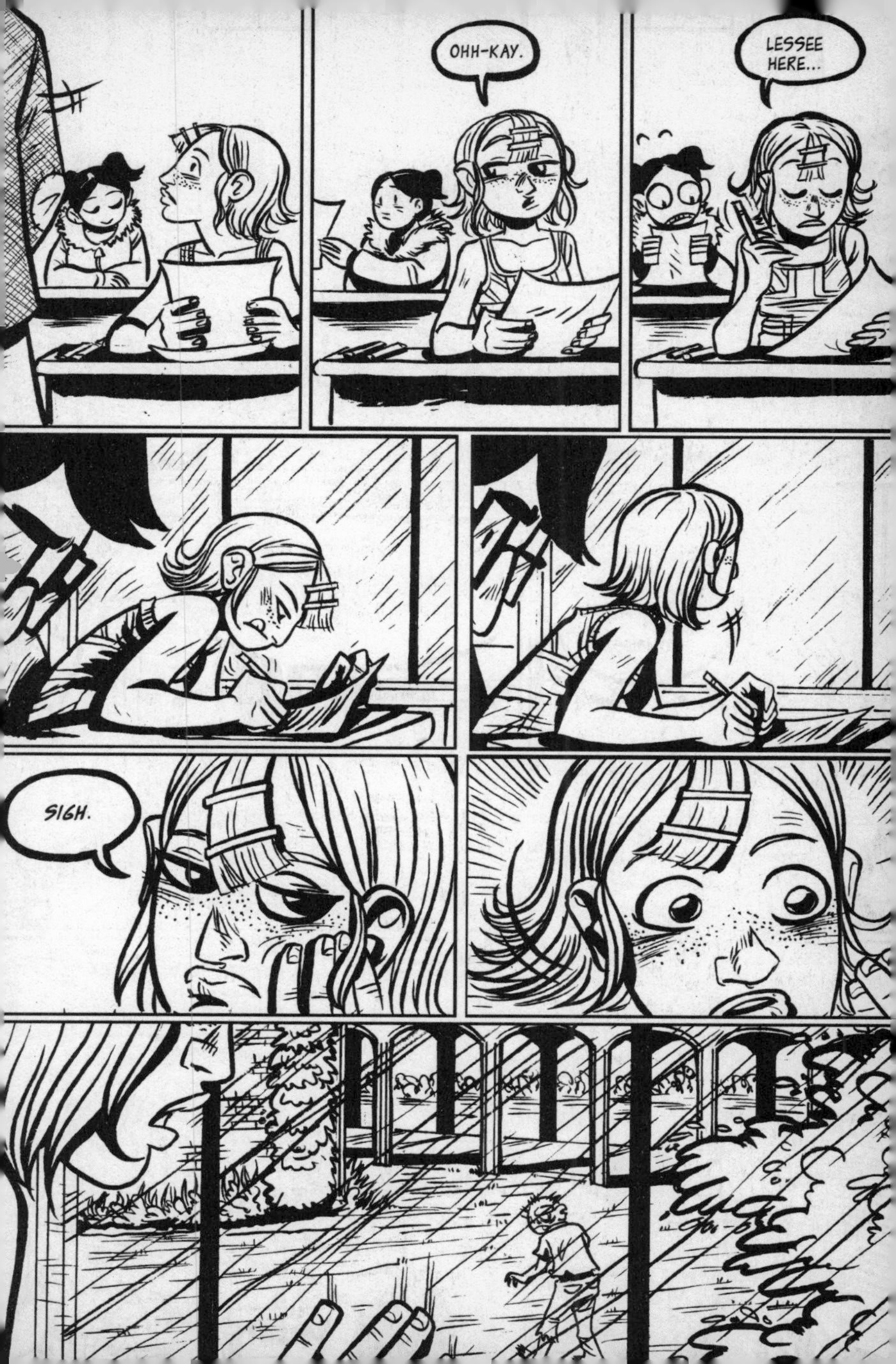
OHH-KAY.
LESSEE HERE...
SIGH.

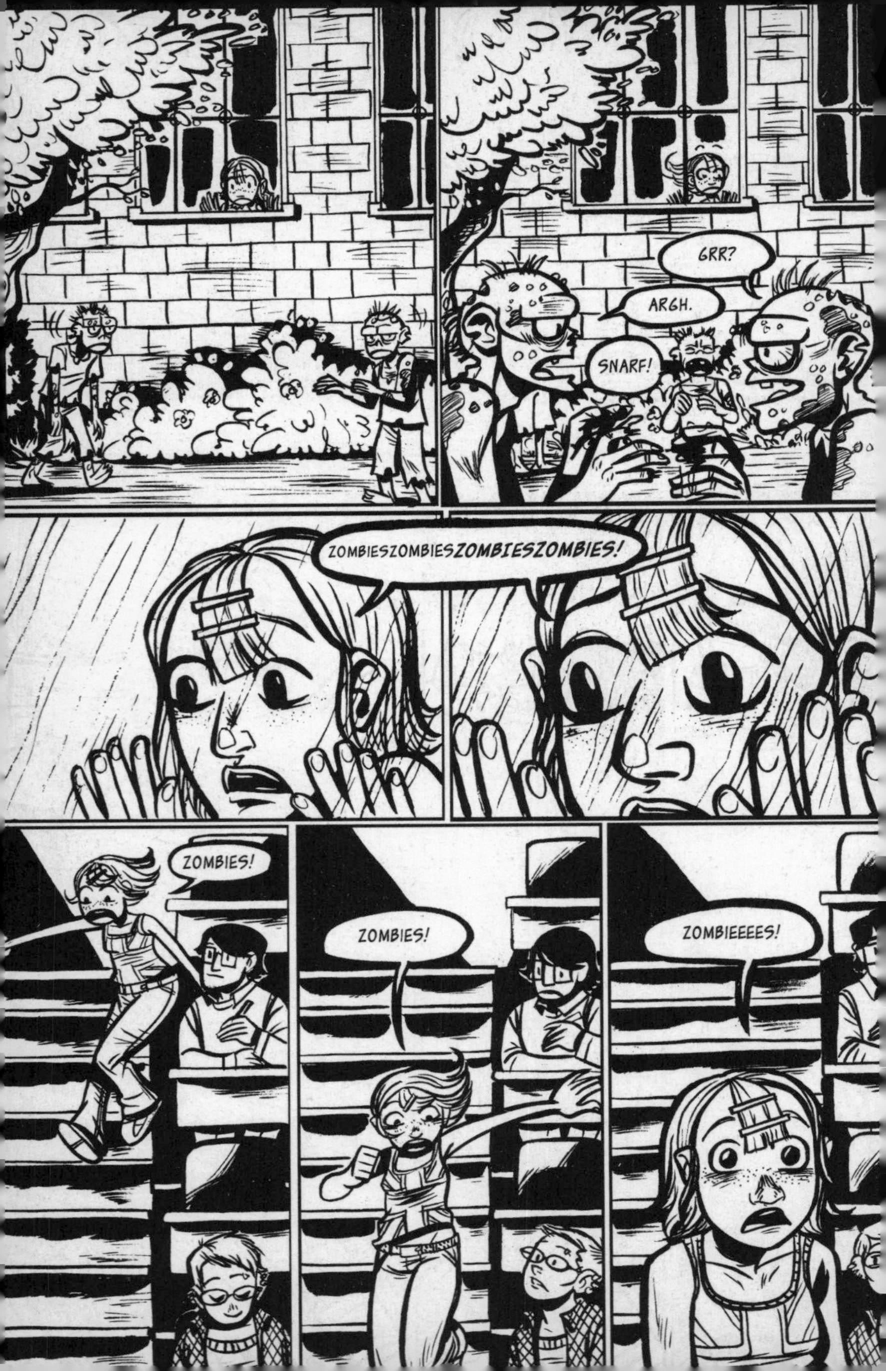
GRR?
ARGH.
SNARF!
ZOMBIESZOMBIESZOMBIESZOMBIES!
ZOMBIES!
ZOMBIES!
ZOMBIEEEES!

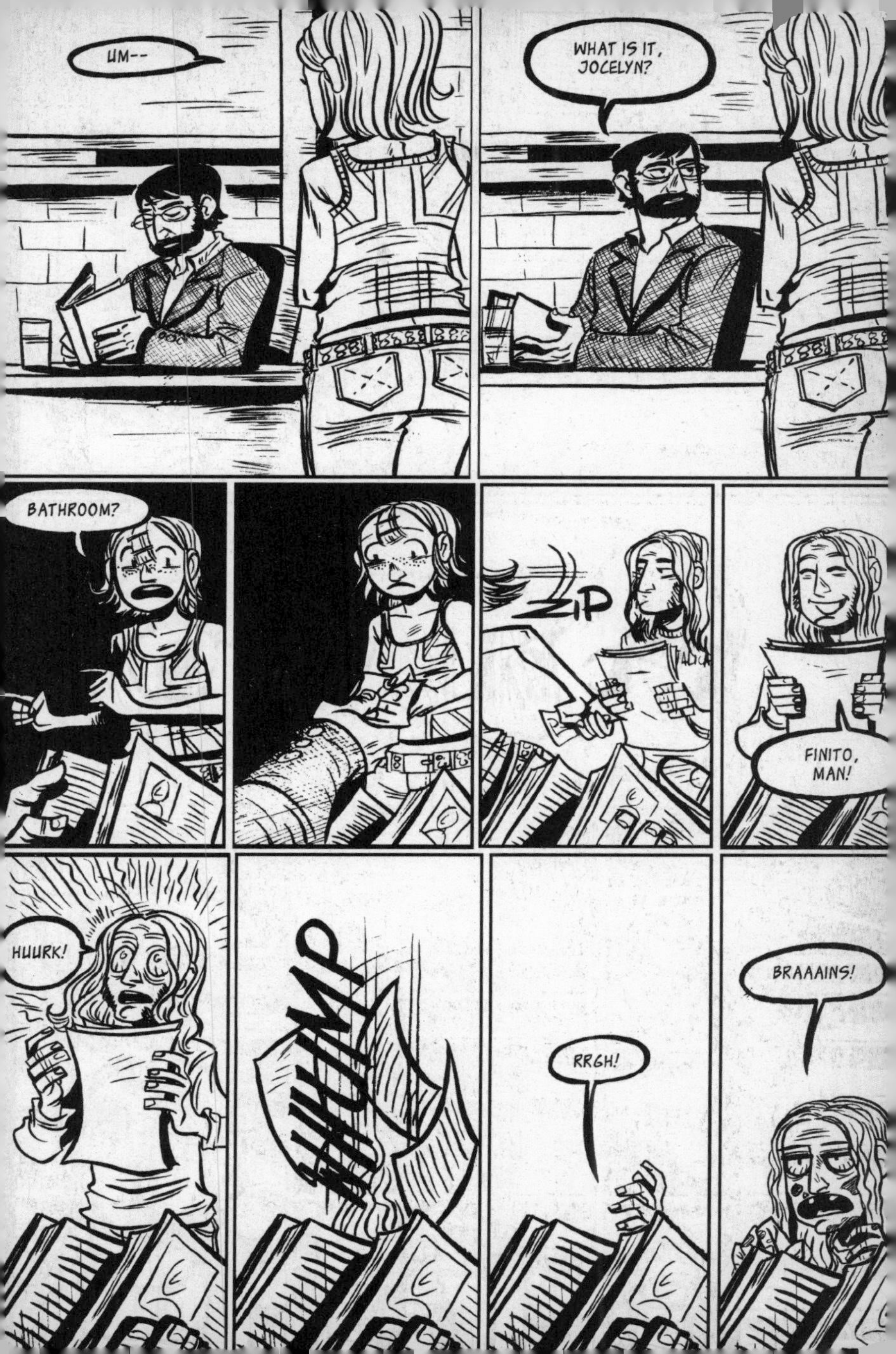
UM--
WHAT IS IT, JOCELYN?
BATHROOM?
ZIP
FINITO, MAN!
HUURK!
THUMP
RRGH!
BRAAAINS!

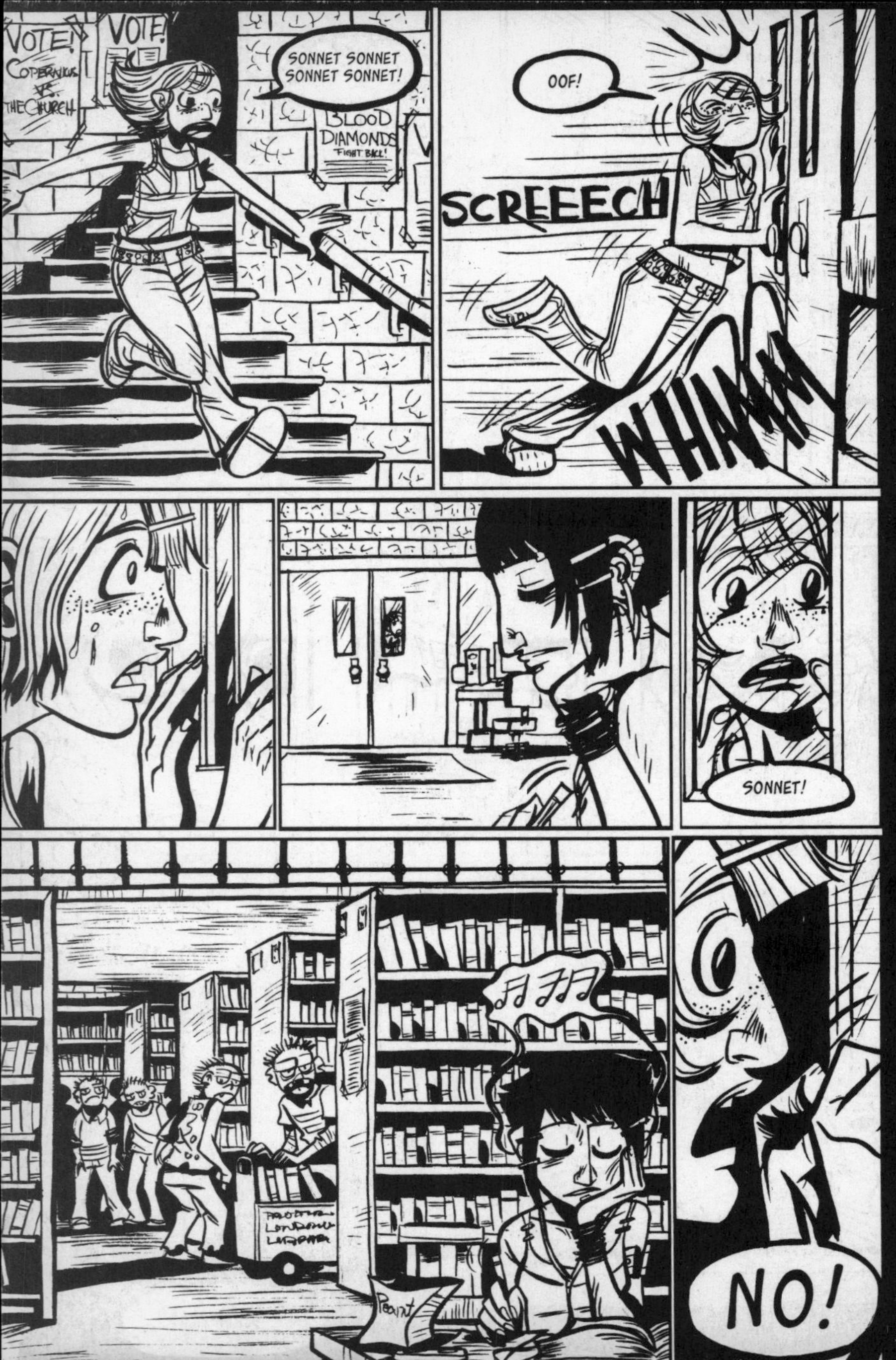
VOTE!
VOTE!
COPERNICUS VS. THE CHURCH
SONNET SONNET SONNET SONNET!
BLOOD DIAMONDS FIGHT BACK!
OOF!
SCREEECH
WHAMM
SONNET!
NO!

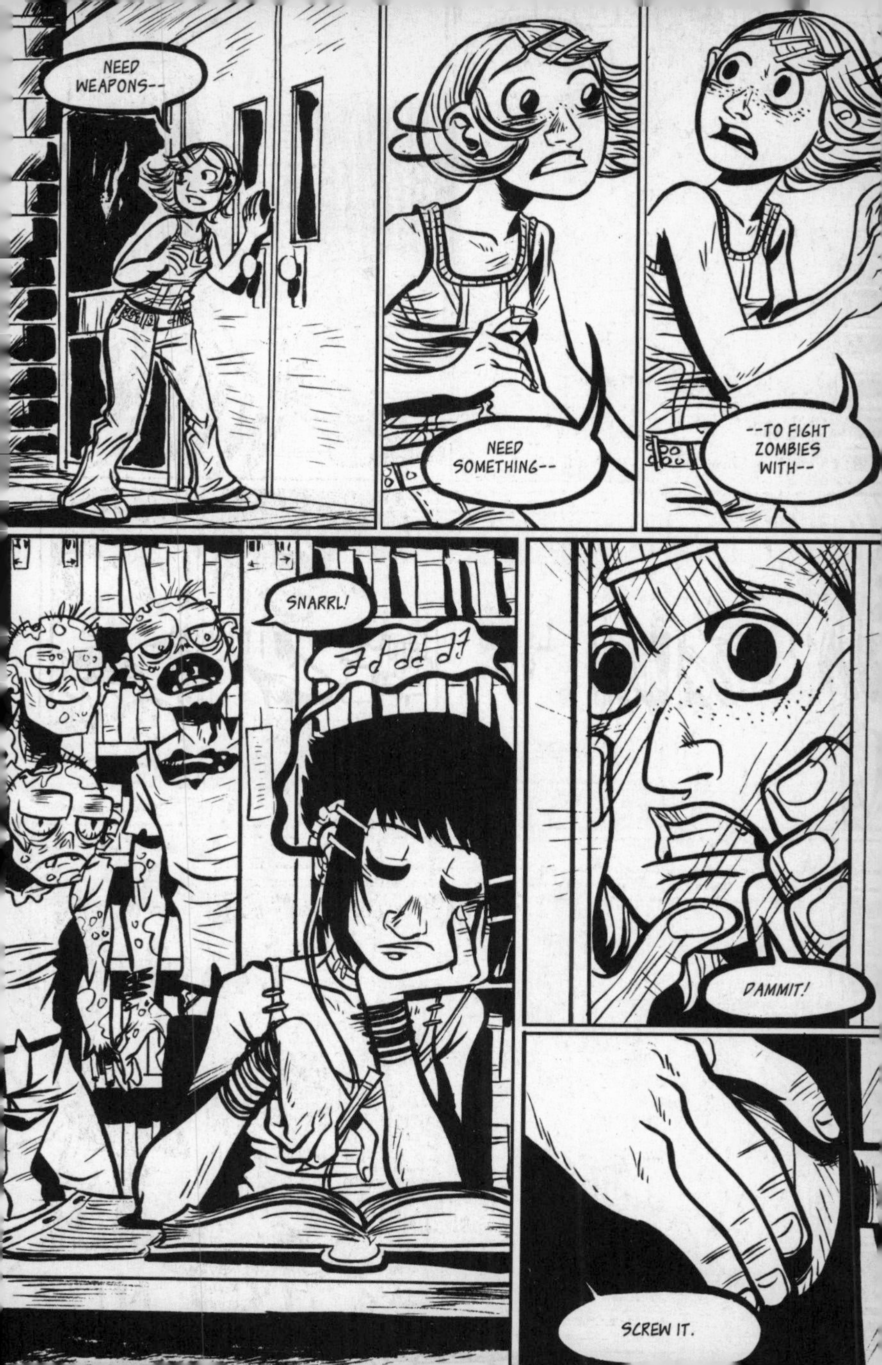
NEED WEAPONS--
NEED SOMETHING--
--TO FIGHT ZOMBIES WITH--
SNARRL!
DAMMIT!
SCREW IT.

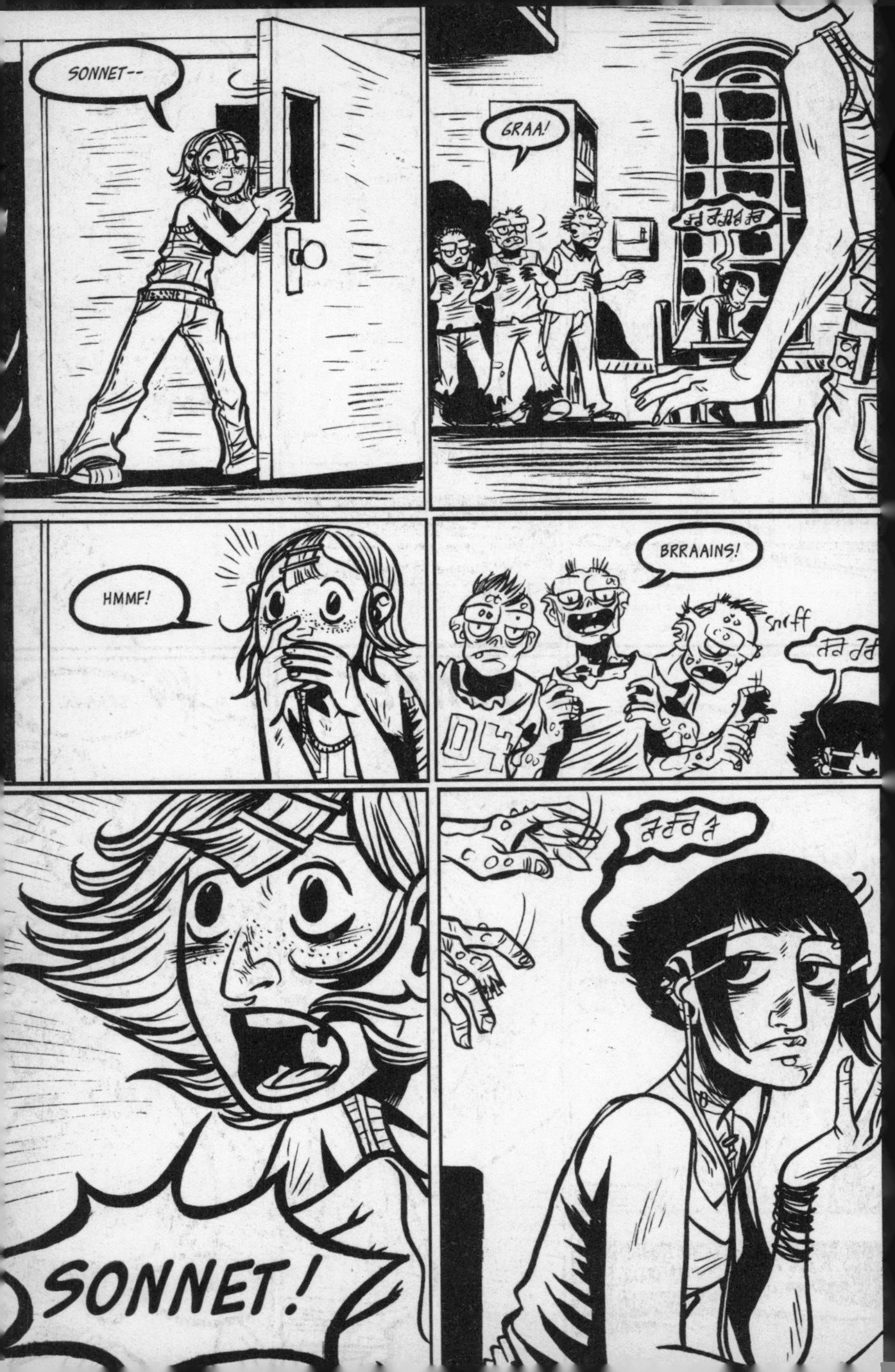
SONNET--
GRAA!
HMMF!
BRRAAINS!
Sniff
SONNET!

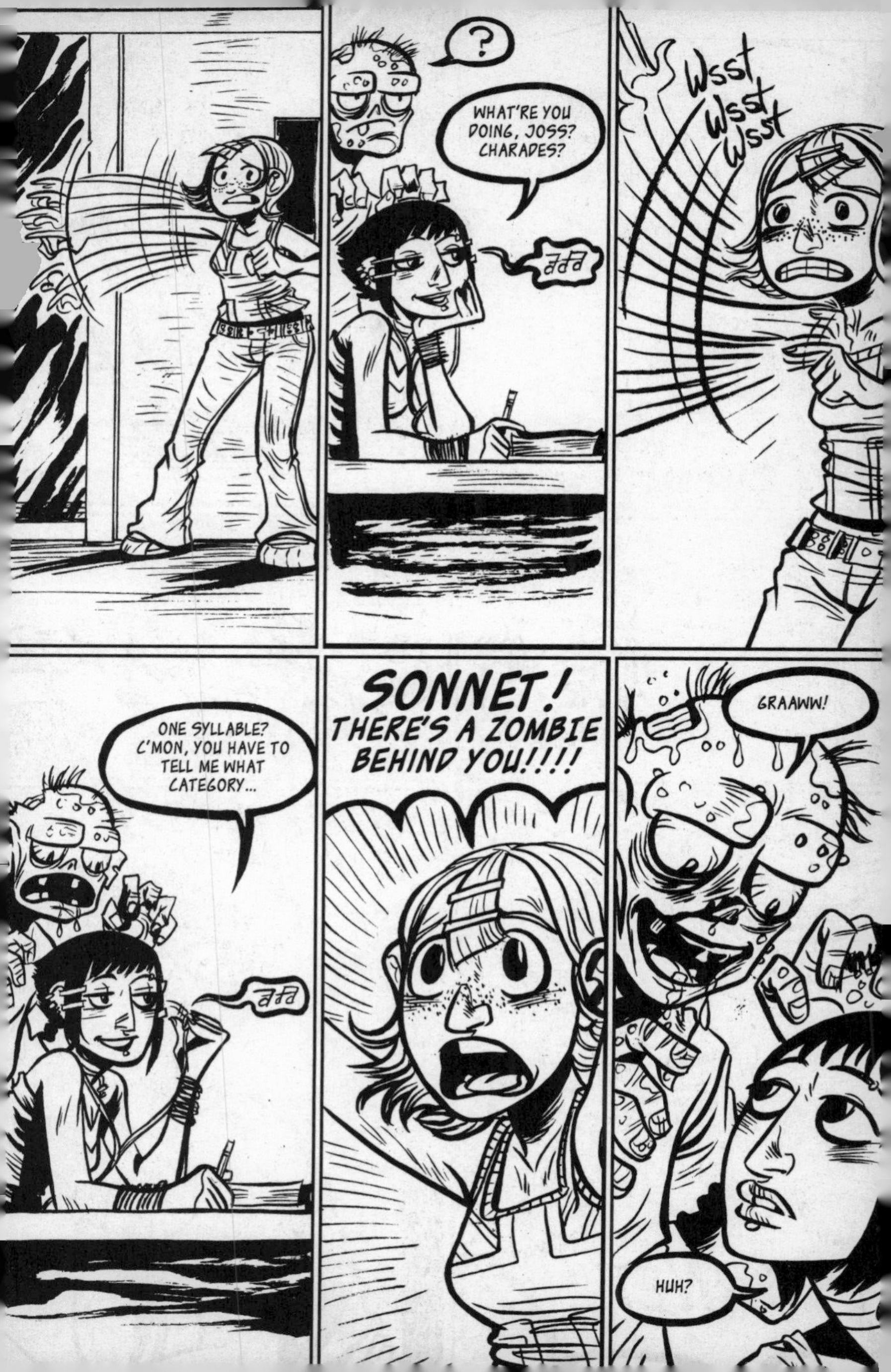
?
WHAT'RE YOU DOING, JOSS? CHARADES?
Wsst Wsst Wsst
ONE SYLLABLE? C'MON, YOU HAVE TO TELL ME WHAT CATEGORY...
SONNET! THERE'S A ZOMBIE BEHIND YOU!!!!
GRAAWW!
HUH?

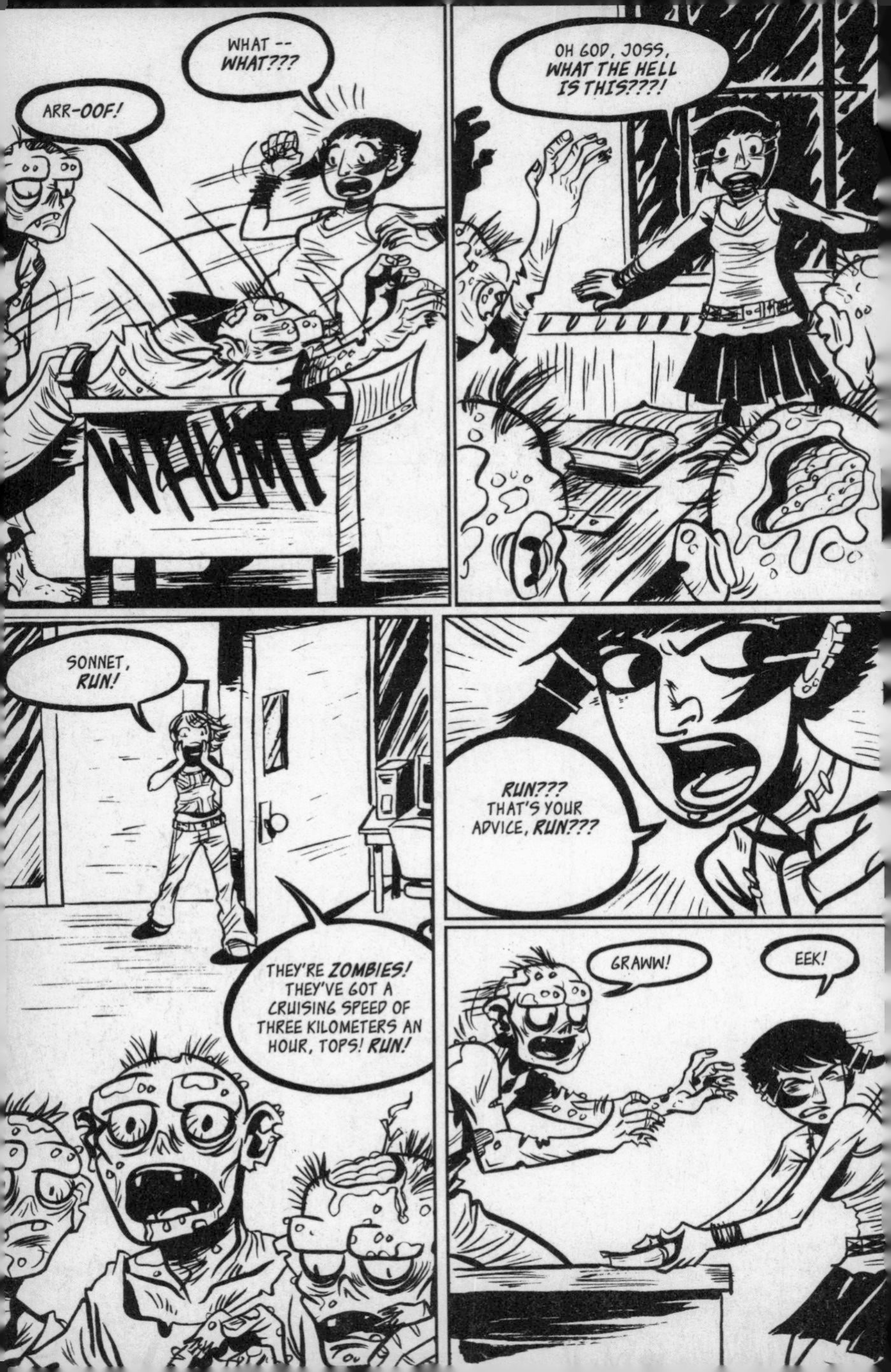
WHAT -- WHAT???
ARR-OOF!
WHUMP
OH GOD, JOSS, WHAT THE HELL IS THIS???!
SONNET, RUN!
RUN??? THAT'S YOUR ADVICE, RUN???
THEY'RE ZOMBIES! THEY'VE GOT A CRUISING SPEED OF THREE KILOMETERS AN HOUR, TOPS! RUN!
GRAWW!
EEK!

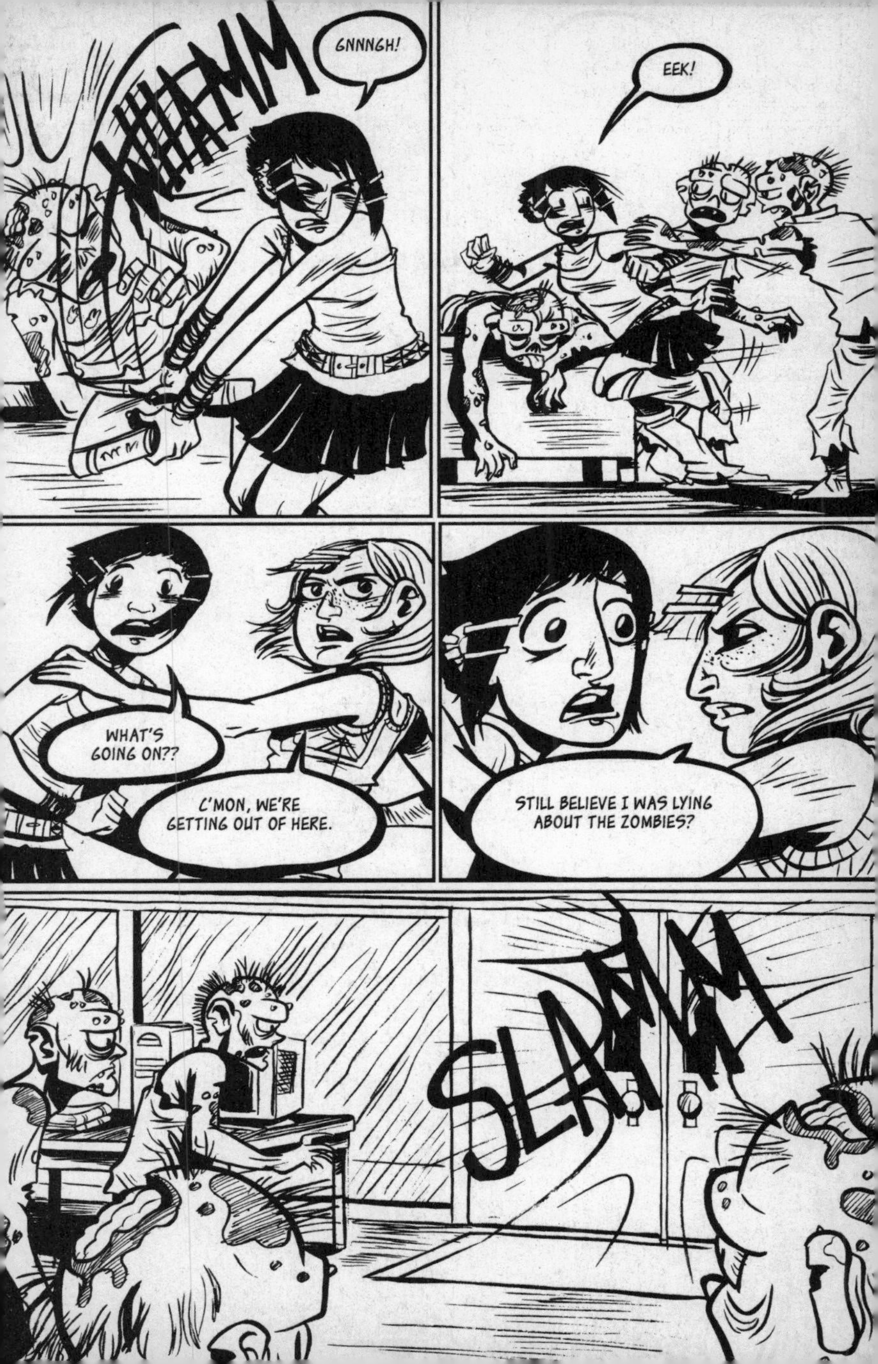
WHAMM
GNNNGH!
EEK!
WHAT'S GOING ON??
C'MON, WE'RE GETTING OUT OF HERE.
STILL BELIEVE I WAS LYING ABOUT THE ZOMBIES?
SLAMM

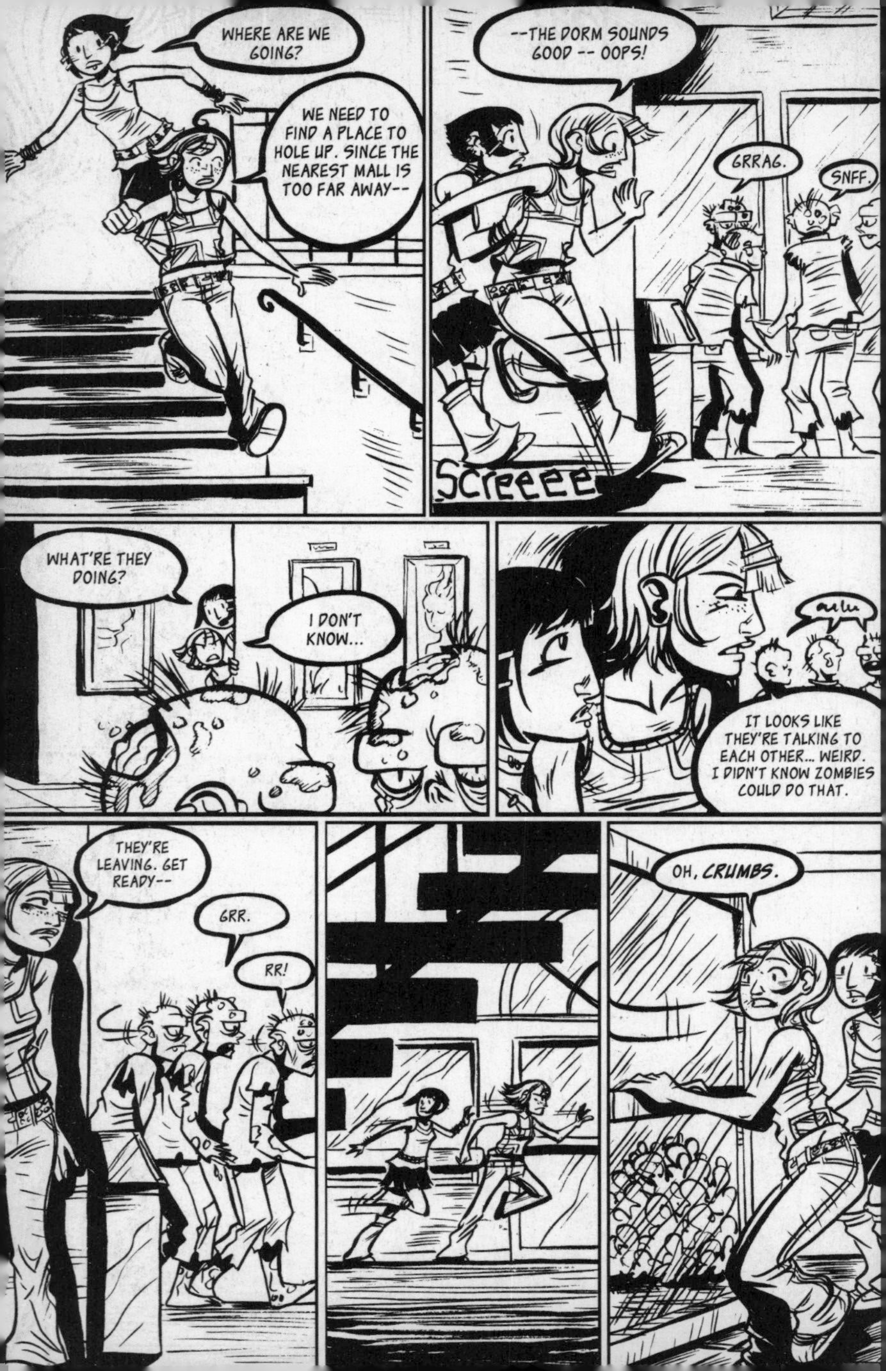
WHERE ARE WE GOING?
WE NEED TO FIND A PLACE TO HOLE UP. SINCE THE NEAREST MALL IS TOO FAR AWAY--
--THE DORM SOUNDS GOOD -- OOPS!
GRRAG.
SNFF.
SCREEEE
WHAT'RE THEY DOING?
I DON'T KNOW...
IT LOOKS LIKE THEY'RE TALKING TO EACH OTHER... WEIRD. I DIDN'T KNOW ZOMBIES COULD DO THAT.
THEY'RE LEAVING. GET READY--
GRR.
RR!
OH, CRUMBS.

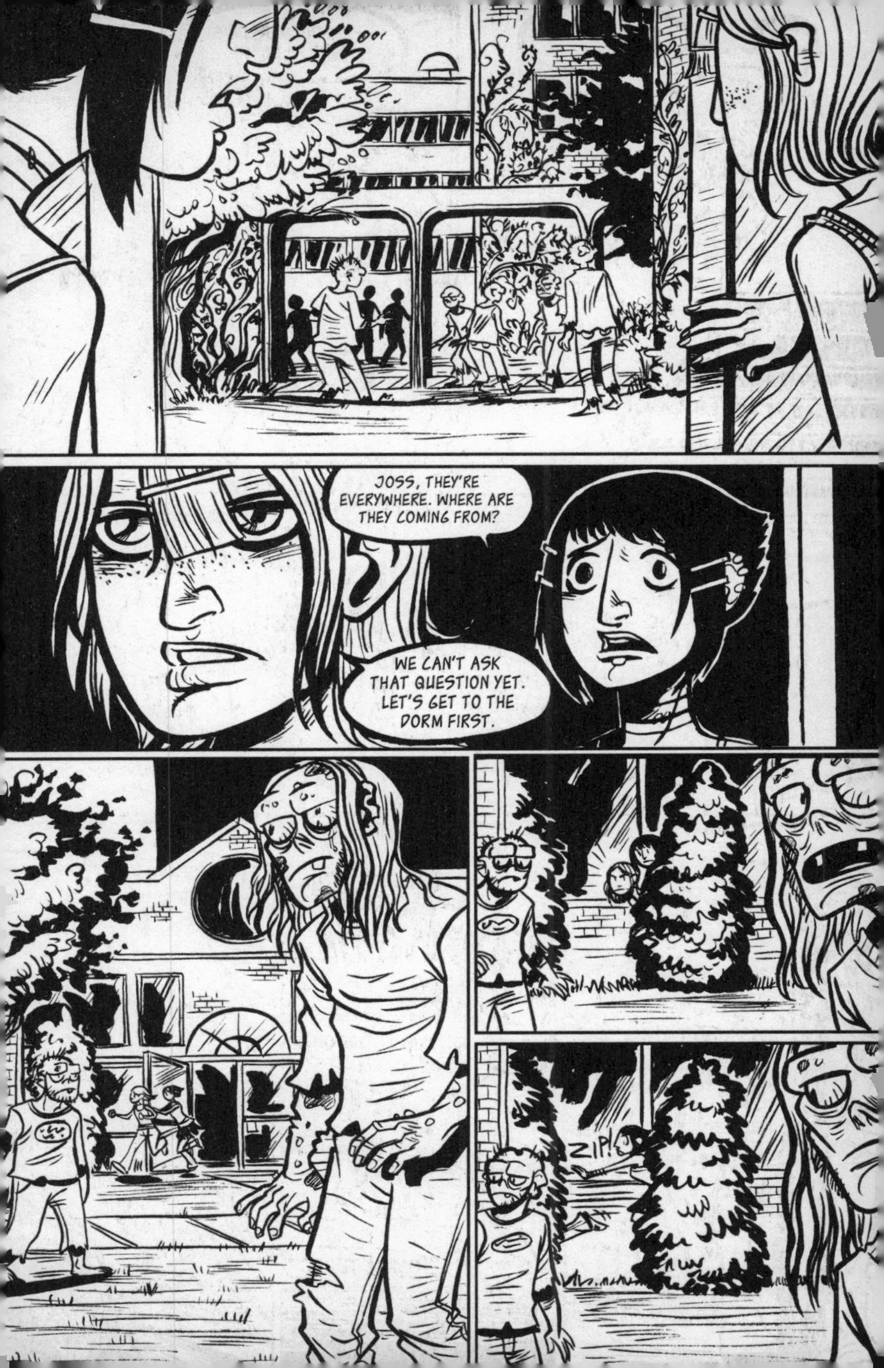
JOSS, THEY'RE EVERYWHERE. WHERE ARE THEY COMING FROM?
WE CAN'T ASK THAT QUESTION YET. LET'S GET TO THE DORM FIRST.
ZIP!

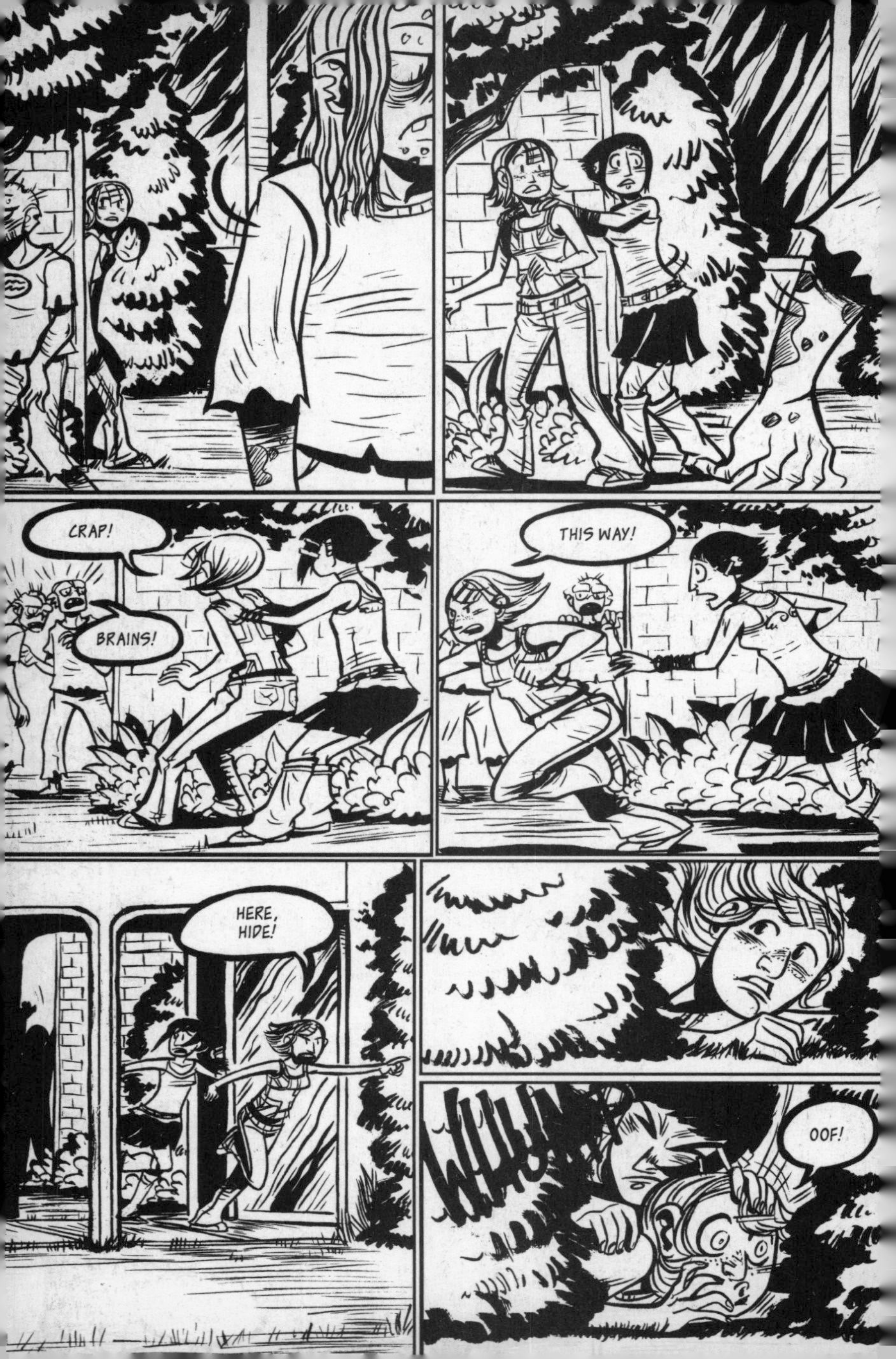
CRAP!
BRAINS!
THIS WAY!
HERE, HIDE!
OOF!

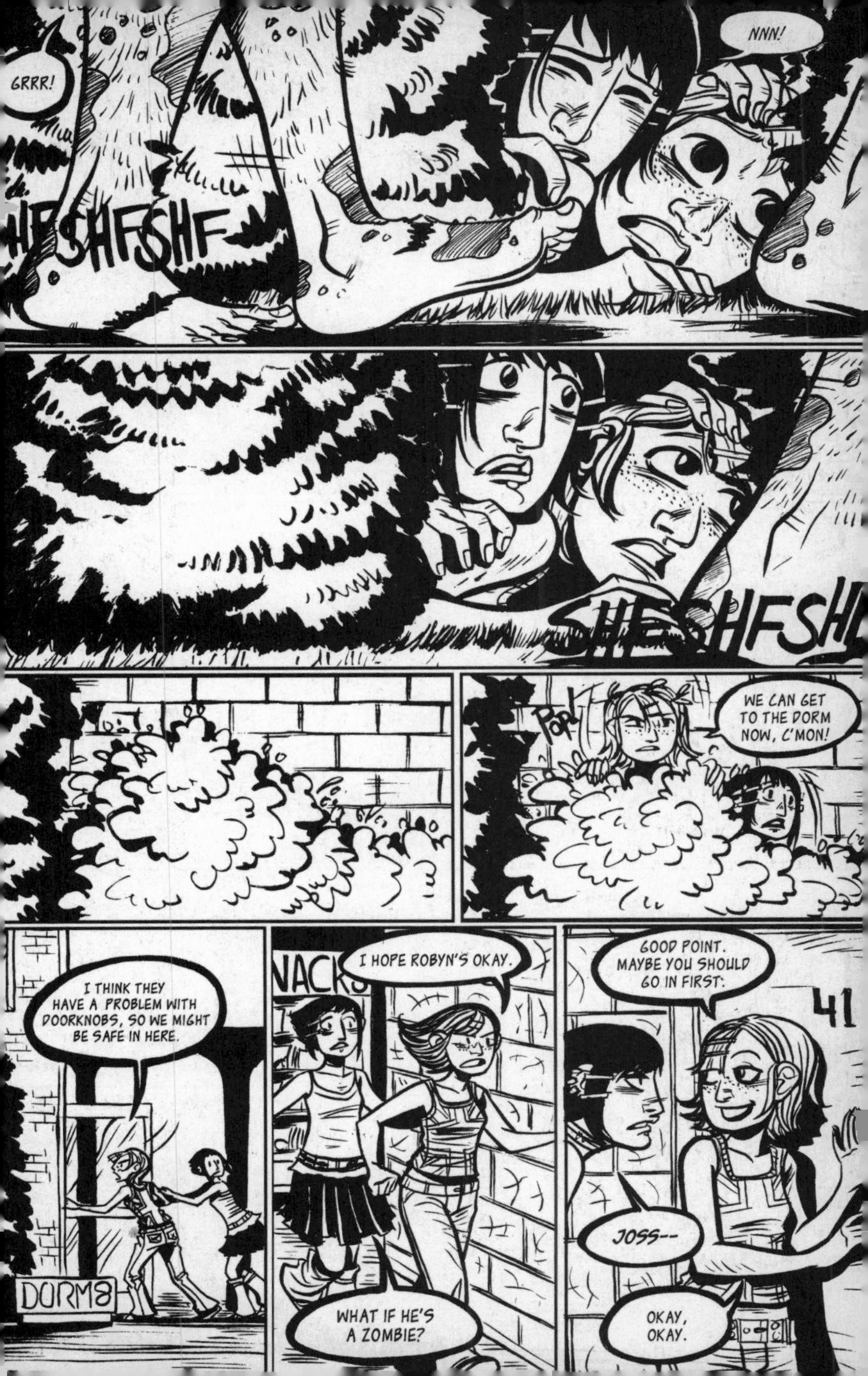
GRRR!
NNN!
SHFSHFSHF
SHFSHFSHF
POP!
WE CAN GET TO THE DORM NOW, C'MON!
I THINK THEY HAVE A PROBLEM WITH DOORKNOBS, SO WE MIGHT BE SAFE IN HERE.
DORM8
I HOPE ROBYN'S OKAY.
WHAT IF HE'S A ZOMBIE?
GOOD POINT. MAYBE YOU SHOULD GO IN FIRST.
JOSS--
OKAY, OKAY.

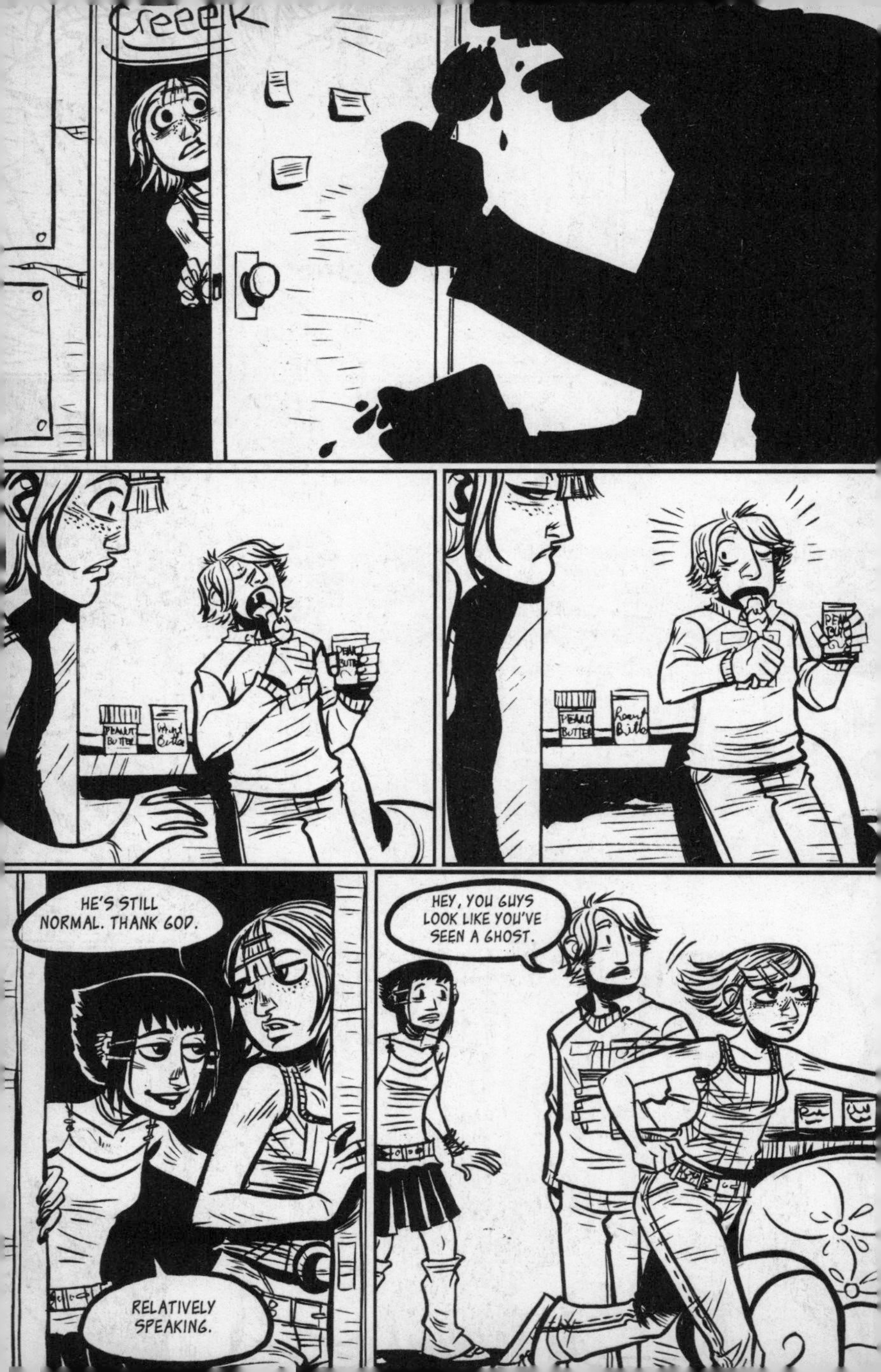
CREEEK
HE'S STILL NORMAL. THANK GOD.
RELATIVELY SPEAKING.
HEY, YOU GUYS LOOK LIKE YOU'VE SEEN A GHOST.

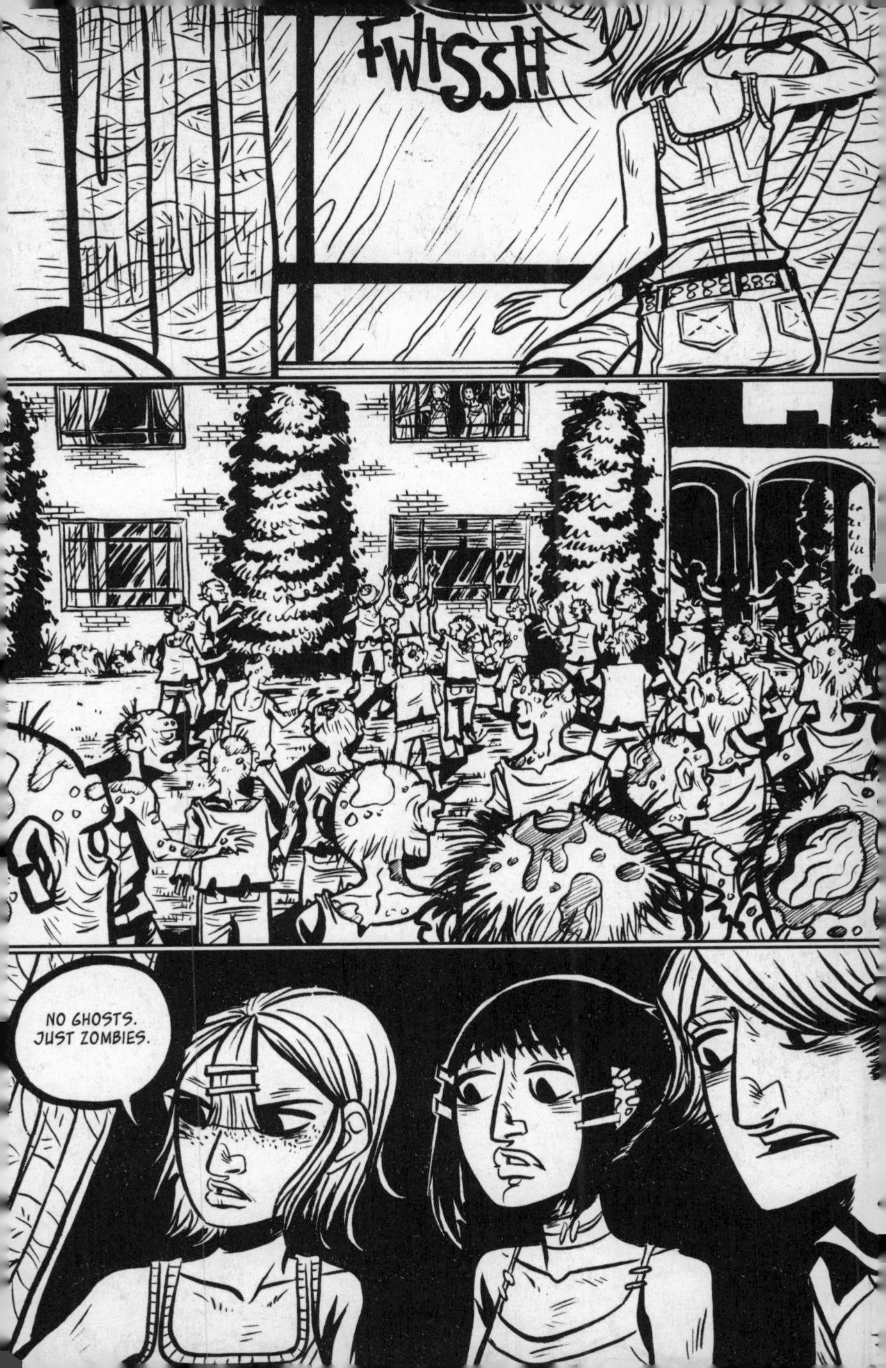
FWISSH
NO GHOSTS. JUST ZOMBIES.

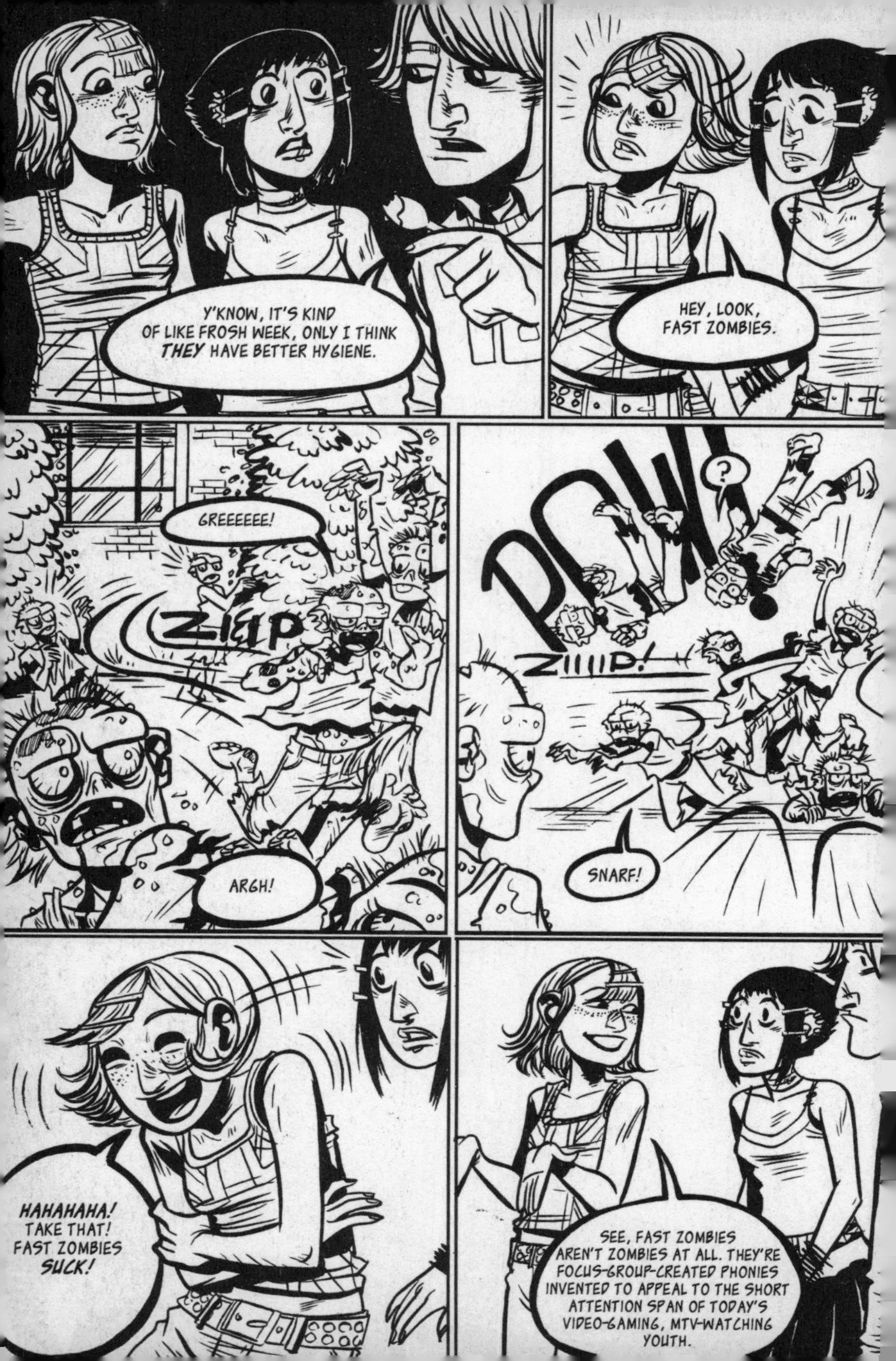
Y'KNOW, IT'S KIND OF LIKE FROSH WEEK, ONLY I THINK *THEY* HAVE BETTER HYGIENE.
HEY, LOOK, FAST ZOMBIES.
GREEEEEE!
ZIIP
ARGH!
POW!
?
ZIIIIP!
SNARF!
HAHAHAHA! TAKE THAT! FAST ZOMBIES *SUCK!*
SEE, FAST ZOMBIES AREN'T ZOMBIES AT ALL. THEY'RE FOCUS-GROUP-CREATED PHONIES INVENTED TO APPEAL TO THE SHORT ATTENTION SPAN OF TODAY'S VIDEO-GAMING, MTV-WATCHING YOUTH.

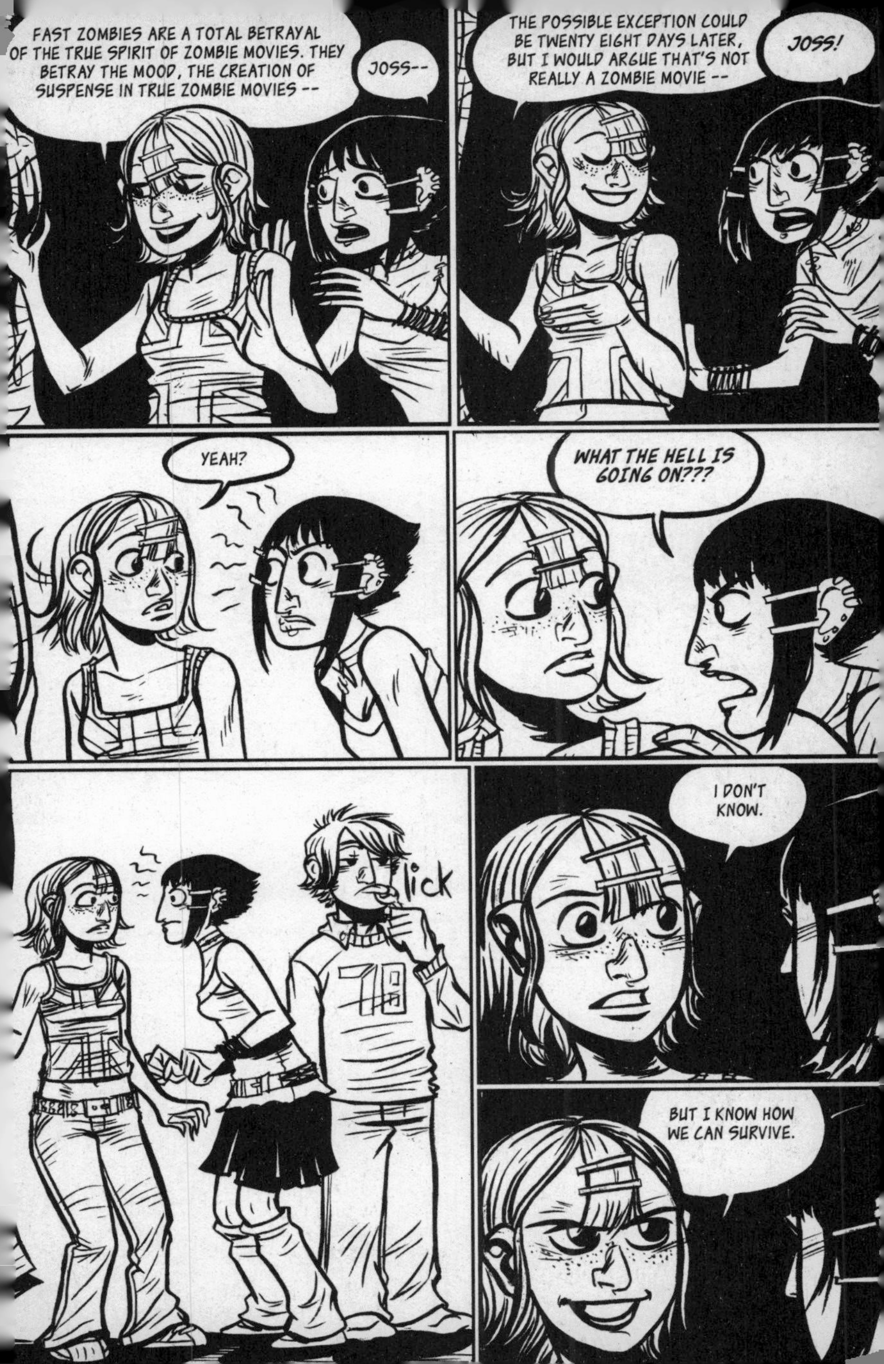
FAST ZOMBIES ARE A TOTAL BETRAYAL OF THE TRUE SPIRIT OF ZOMBIE MOVIES. THEY BETRAY THE MOOD, THE CREATION OF SUSPENSE IN TRUE ZOMBIE MOVIES --
JOSS--
THE POSSIBLE EXCEPTION COULD BE TWENTY EIGHT DAYS LATER, BUT I WOULD ARGUE THAT'S NOT REALLY A ZOMBIE MOVIE --
JOSS!
YEAH?
WHAT THE HELL IS GOING ON???
lick
I DON'T KNOW.
BUT I KNOW HOW WE CAN SURVIVE.

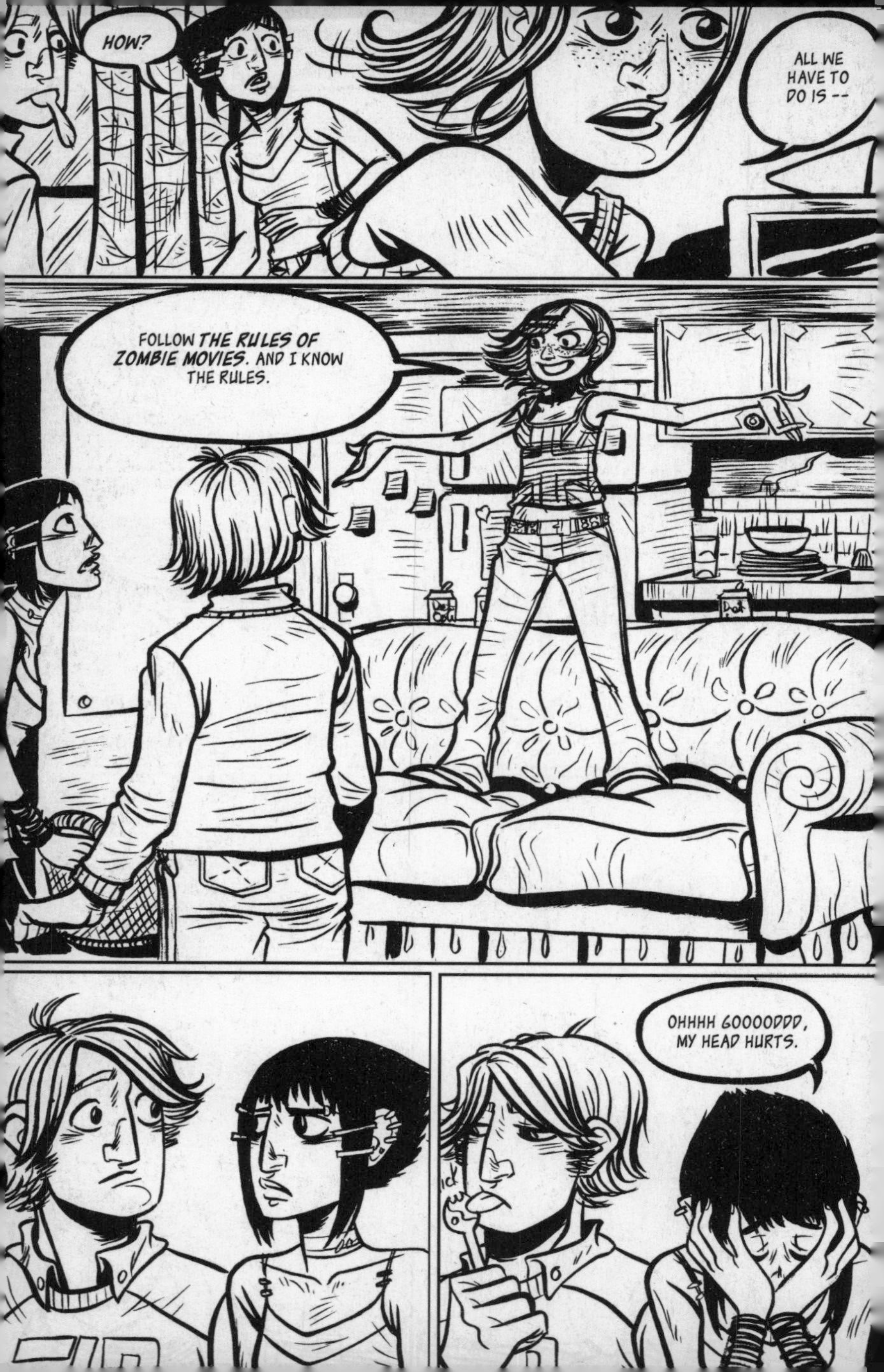
HOW?
ALL WE HAVE TO DO IS --
FOLLOW *THE RULES OF ZOMBIE MOVIES*. AND I KNOW THE RULES.
ICK
OHHHH GOOOODDD, MY HEAD HURTS.

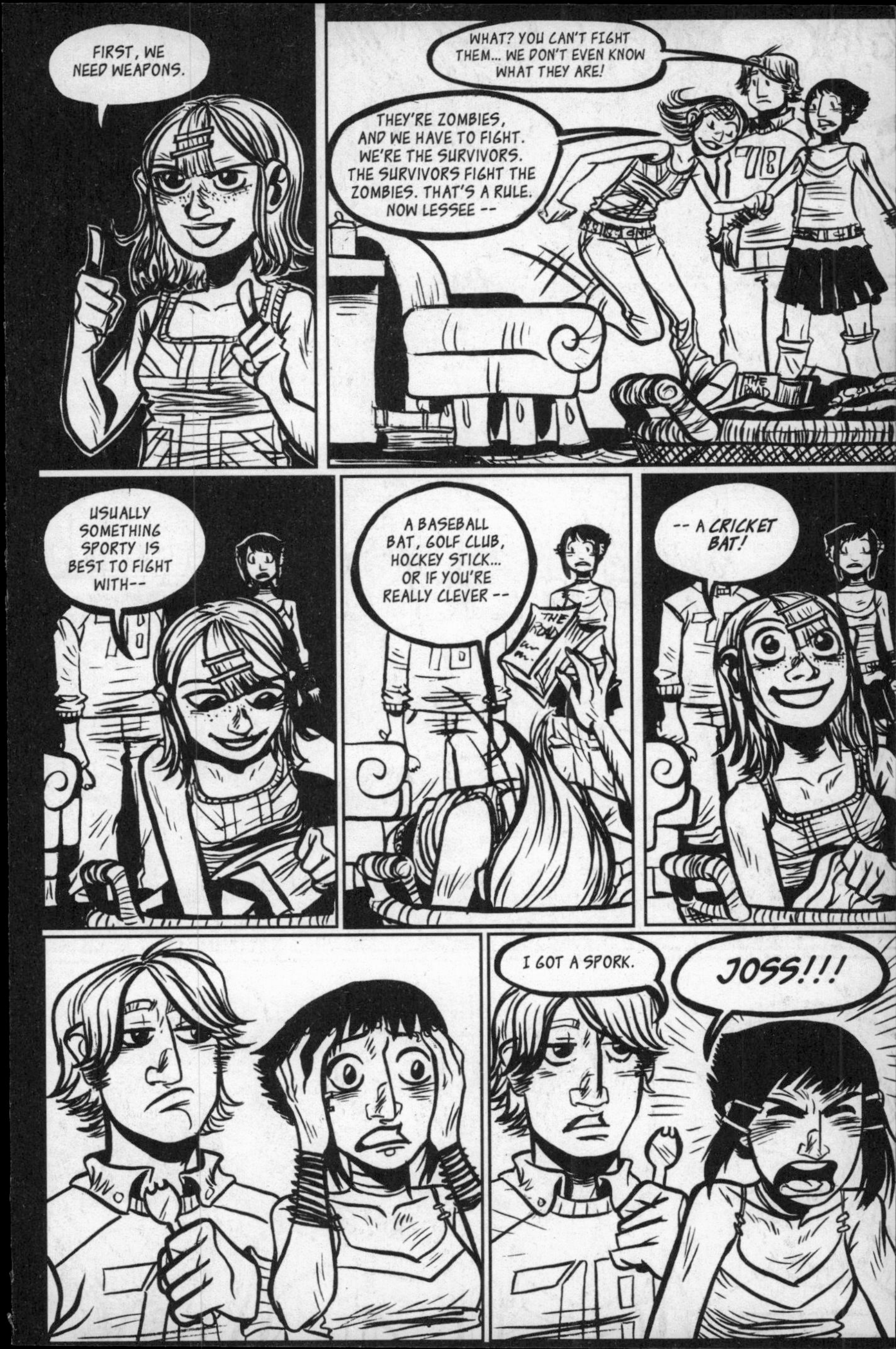
FIRST, WE NEED WEAPONS.
WHAT? YOU CAN'T FIGHT THEM... WE DON'T EVEN KNOW WHAT THEY ARE!
THEY'RE ZOMBIES, AND WE HAVE TO FIGHT. WE'RE THE SURVIVORS. THE SURVIVORS FIGHT THE ZOMBIES. THAT'S A RULE. NOW LESSEE --
THE ROAD
USUALLY SOMETHING SPORTY IS BEST TO FIGHT WITH--
A BASEBALL BAT, GOLF CLUB, HOCKEY STICK... OR IF YOU'RE REALLY CLEVER --
THE ROAD
-- A CRICKET BAT!
I GOT A SPORK.
JOSS!!!

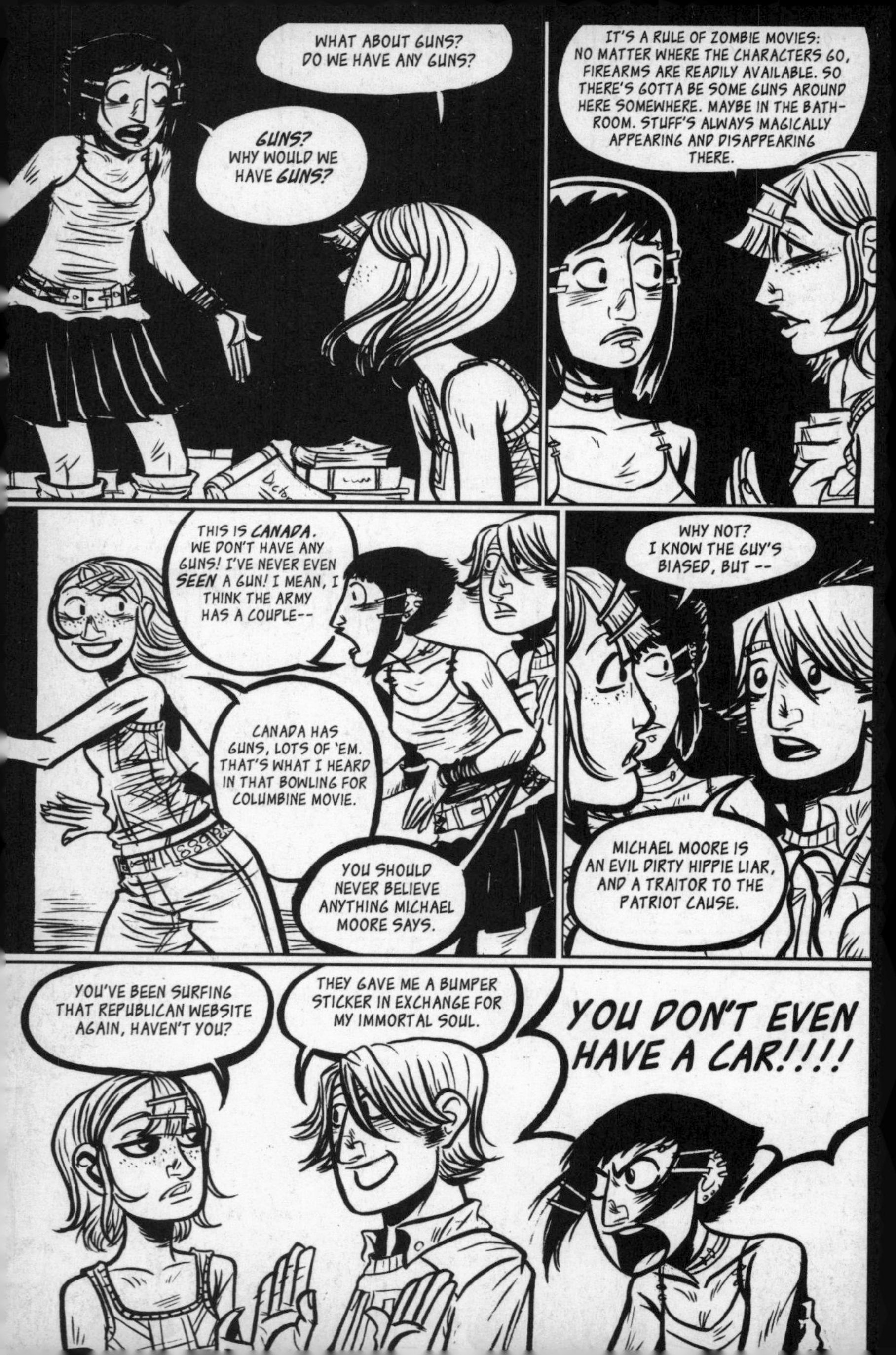
WHAT ABOUT GUNS? DO WE HAVE ANY GUNS?
GUNS? WHY WOULD WE HAVE GUNS?
IT'S A RULE OF ZOMBIE MOVIES: NO MATTER WHERE THE CHARACTERS GO, FIREARMS ARE READILY AVAILABLE. SO THERE'S GOTTA BE SOME GUNS AROUND HERE SOMEWHERE. MAYBE IN THE BATHROOM. STUFF'S ALWAYS MAGICALLY APPEARING AND DISAPPEARING THERE.
THIS IS CANADA. WE DON'T HAVE ANY GUNS! I'VE NEVER EVEN SEEN A GUN! I MEAN, I THINK THE ARMY HAS A COUPLE--
CANADA HAS GUNS, LOTS OF 'EM. THAT'S WHAT I HEARD IN THAT BOWLING FOR COLUMBINE MOVIE.
YOU SHOULD NEVER BELIEVE ANYTHING MICHAEL MOORE SAYS.
WHY NOT? I KNOW THE GUY'S BIASED, BUT --
MICHAEL MOORE IS AN EVIL DIRTY HIPPIE LIAR, AND A TRAITOR TO THE PATRIOT CAUSE.
YOU'VE BEEN SURFING THAT REPUBLICAN WEBSITE AGAIN, HAVEN'T YOU?
THEY GAVE ME A BUMPER STICKER IN EXCHANGE FOR MY IMMORTAL SOUL.
YOU DON'T EVEN HAVE A CAR!!!!

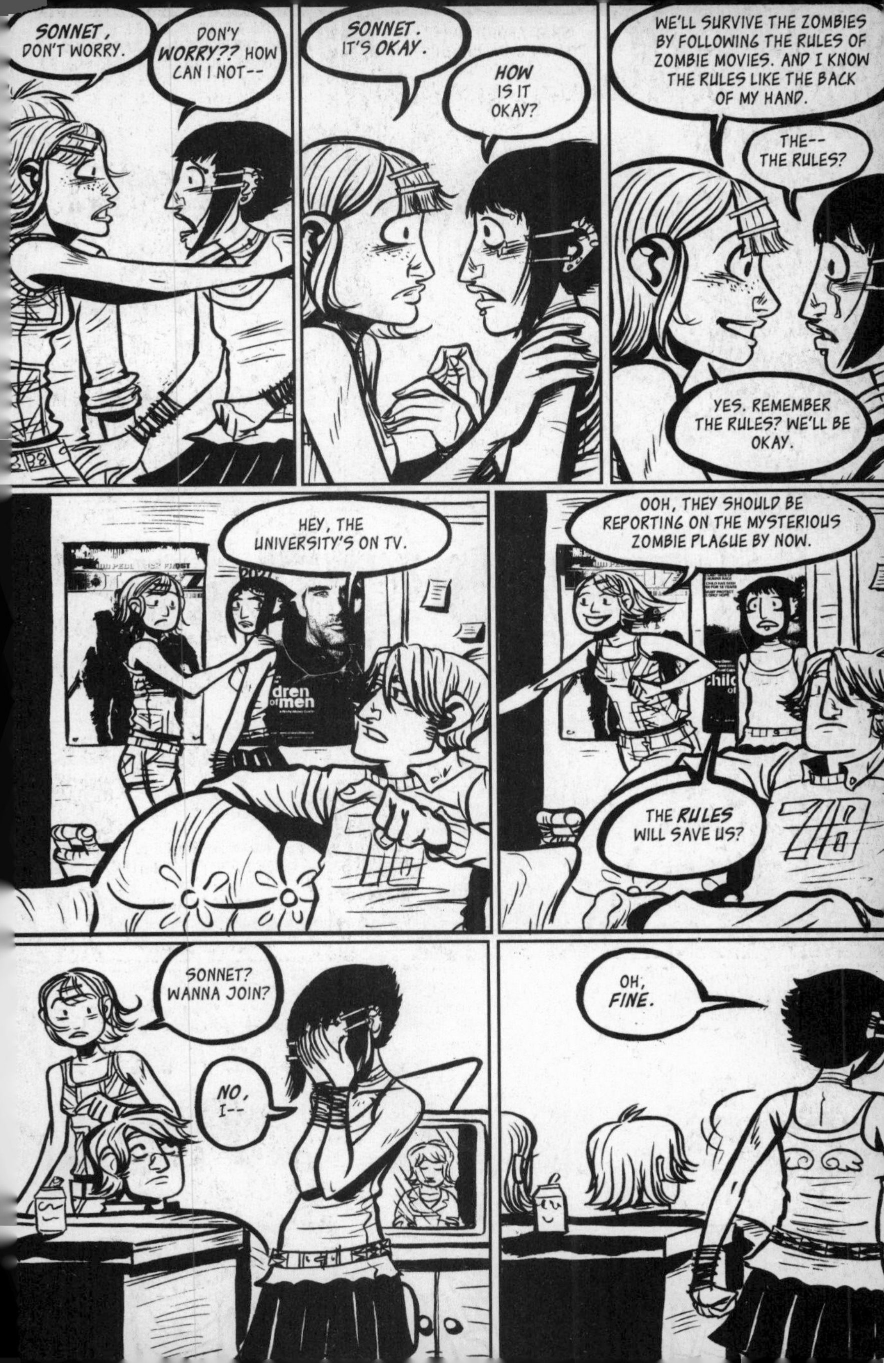
SONNET, DON'T WORRY.
DON'Y WORRY?? HOW CAN I NOT--
SONNET. IT'S OKAY.
HOW IS IT OKAY?
WE'LL SURVIVE THE ZOMBIES BY FOLLOWING THE RULES OF ZOMBIE MOVIES. AND I KNOW THE RULES LIKE THE BACK OF MY HAND.
THE-- THE RULES?
YES. REMEMBER THE RULES? WE'LL BE OKAY.
HEY, THE UNIVERSITY'S ON TV.
OOH, THEY SHOULD BE REPORTING ON THE MYSTERIOUS ZOMBIE PLAGUE BY NOW.
THE RULES WILL SAVE US?
SONNET? WANNA JOIN?
NO, I--
OH, FINE.

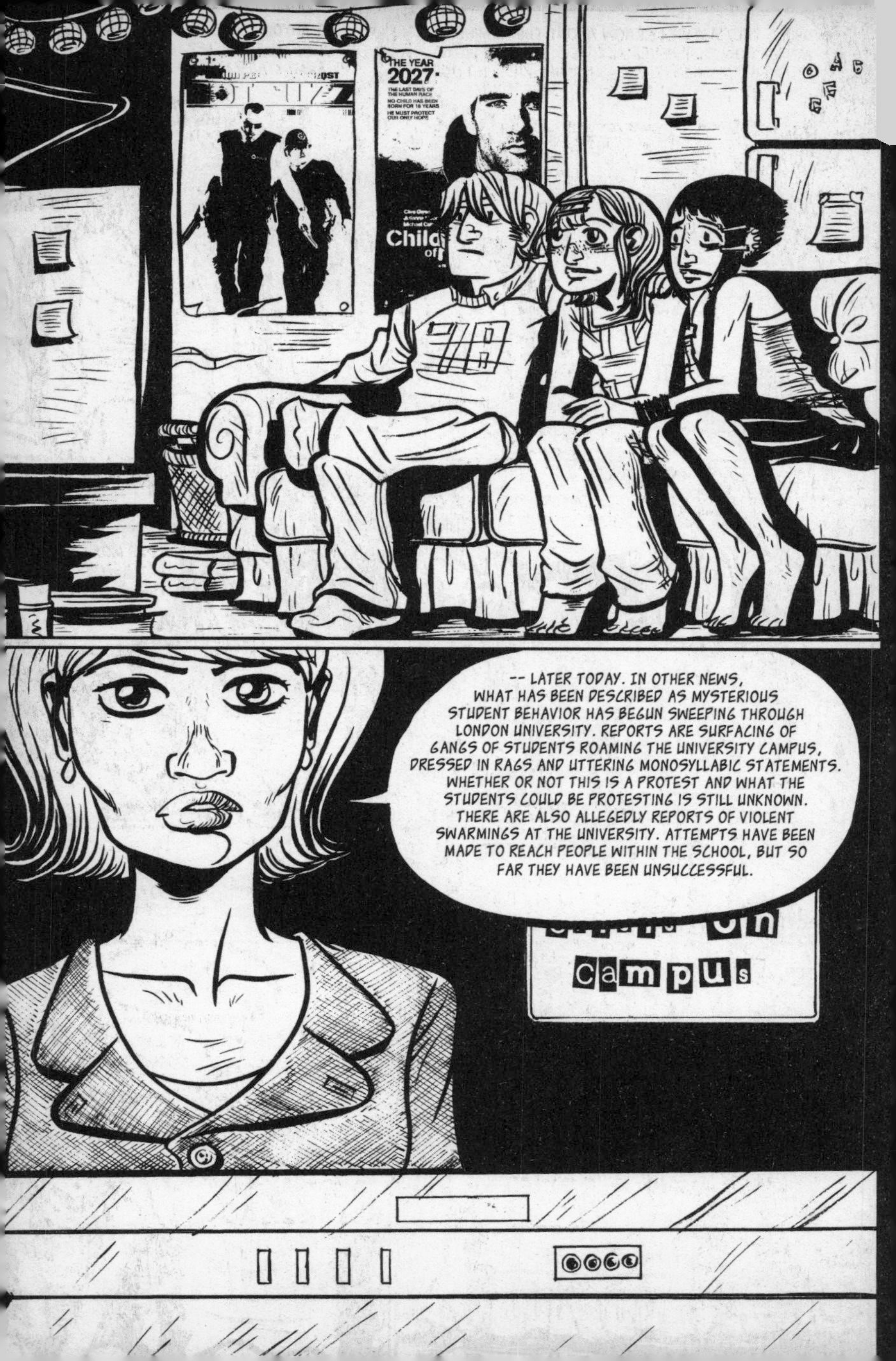
THE YEAR 2027
THE LAST DAYS OF THE HUMAN RACE
NO CHILD HAS BEEN BORN FOR 18 YEARS
HE MUST PROTECT OUR ONLY HOPE
-- LATER TODAY. IN OTHER NEWS, WHAT HAS BEEN DESCRIBED AS MYSTERIOUS STUDENT BEHAVIOR HAS BEGUN SWEEPING THROUGH LONDON UNIVERSITY. REPORTS ARE SURFACING OF GANGS OF STUDENTS ROAMING THE UNIVERSITY CAMPUS, DRESSED IN RAGS AND UTTERING MONOSYLLABIC STATEMENTS. WHETHER OR NOT THIS IS A PROTEST AND WHAT THE STUDENTS COULD BE PROTESTING IS STILL UNKNOWN. THERE ARE ALSO ALLEGEDLY REPORTS OF VIOLENT SWARMINGS AT THE UNIVERSITY. ATTEMPTS HAVE BEEN MADE TO REACH PEOPLE WITHIN THE SCHOOL, BUT SO FAR THEY HAVE BEEN UNSUCCESSFUL.
campus

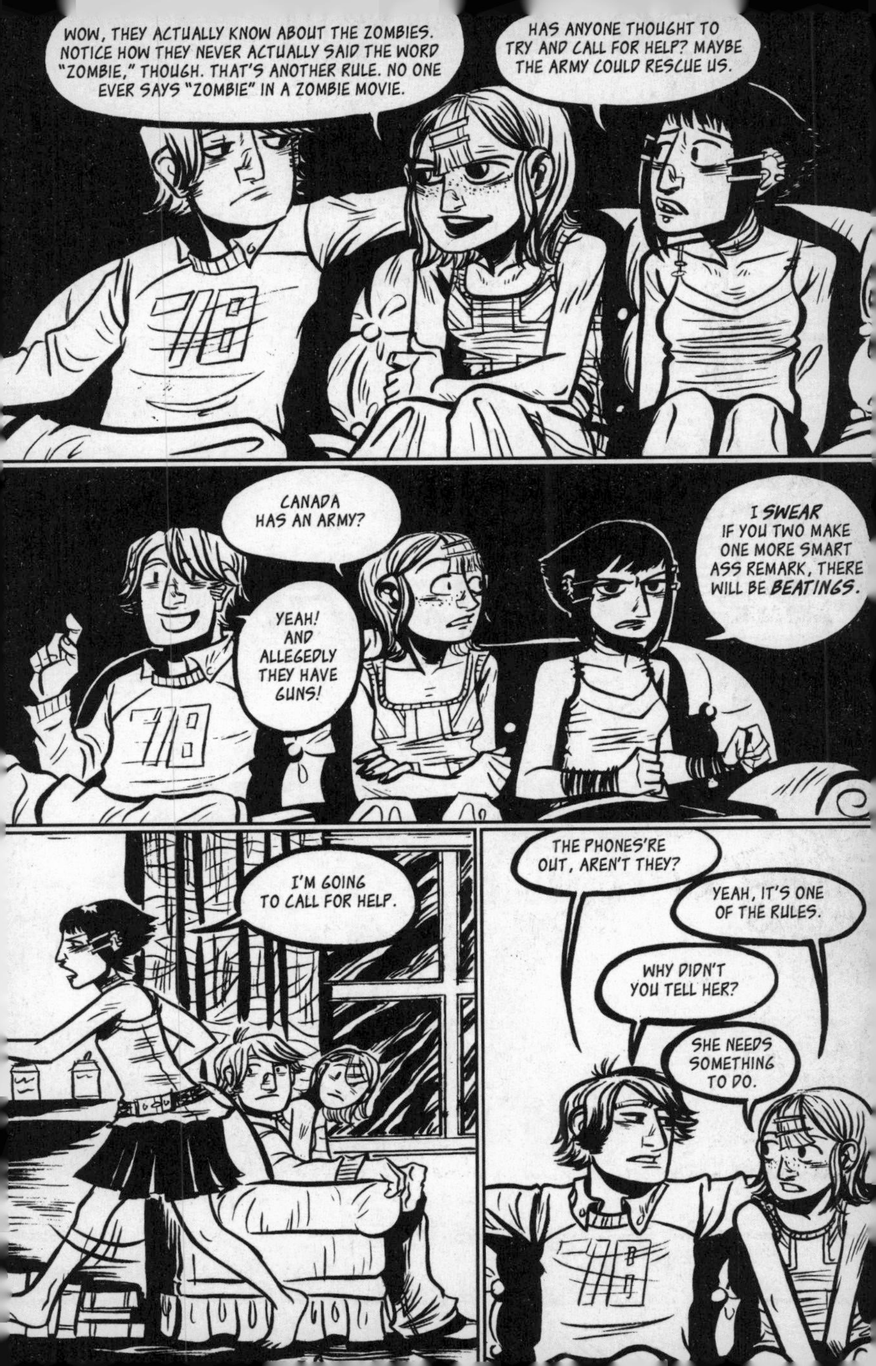
WOW, THEY ACTUALLY KNOW ABOUT THE ZOMBIES. NOTICE HOW THEY NEVER ACTUALLY SAID THE WORD "ZOMBIE," THOUGH. THAT'S ANOTHER RULE. NO ONE EVER SAYS "ZOMBIE" IN A ZOMBIE MOVIE.
HAS ANYONE THOUGHT TO TRY AND CALL FOR HELP? MAYBE THE ARMY COULD RESCUE US.
CANADA HAS AN ARMY?
YEAH! AND ALLEGEDLY THEY HAVE GUNS!
I *SWEAR* IF YOU TWO MAKE ONE MORE SMART ASS REMARK, THERE WILL BE *BEATINGS*.
I'M GOING TO CALL FOR HELP.
THE PHONES'RE OUT, AREN'T THEY?
YEAH, IT'S ONE OF THE RULES.
WHY DIDN'T YOU TELL HER?
SHE NEEDS SOMETHING TO DO.

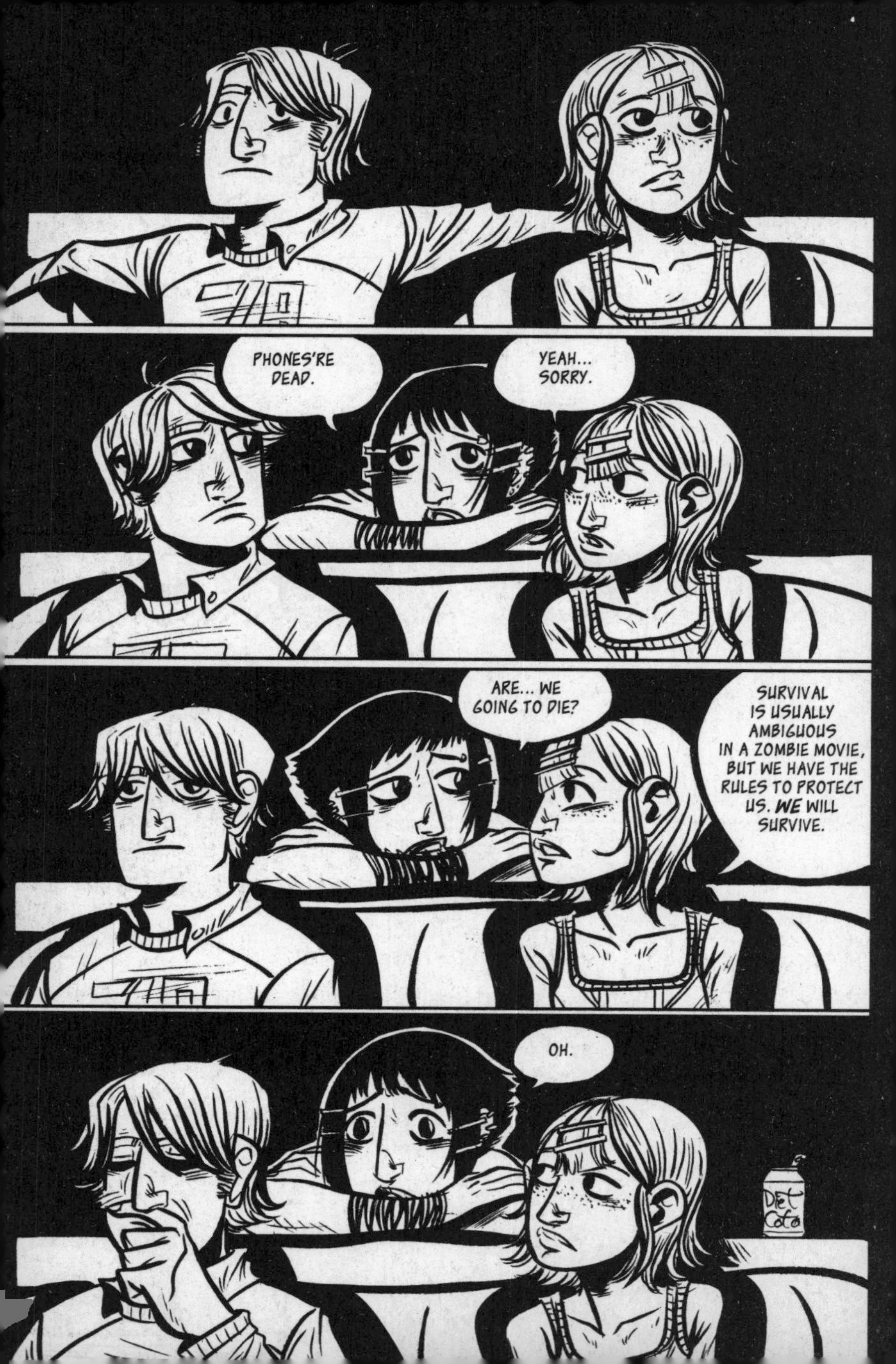
PHONES'RE DEAD.
YEAH... SORRY.
ARE... WE GOING TO DIE?
SURVIVAL IS USUALLY AMBIGUOUS IN A ZOMBIE MOVIE, BUT WE HAVE THE RULES TO PROTECT US. WE WILL SURVIVE.
OH.
DIET COKE

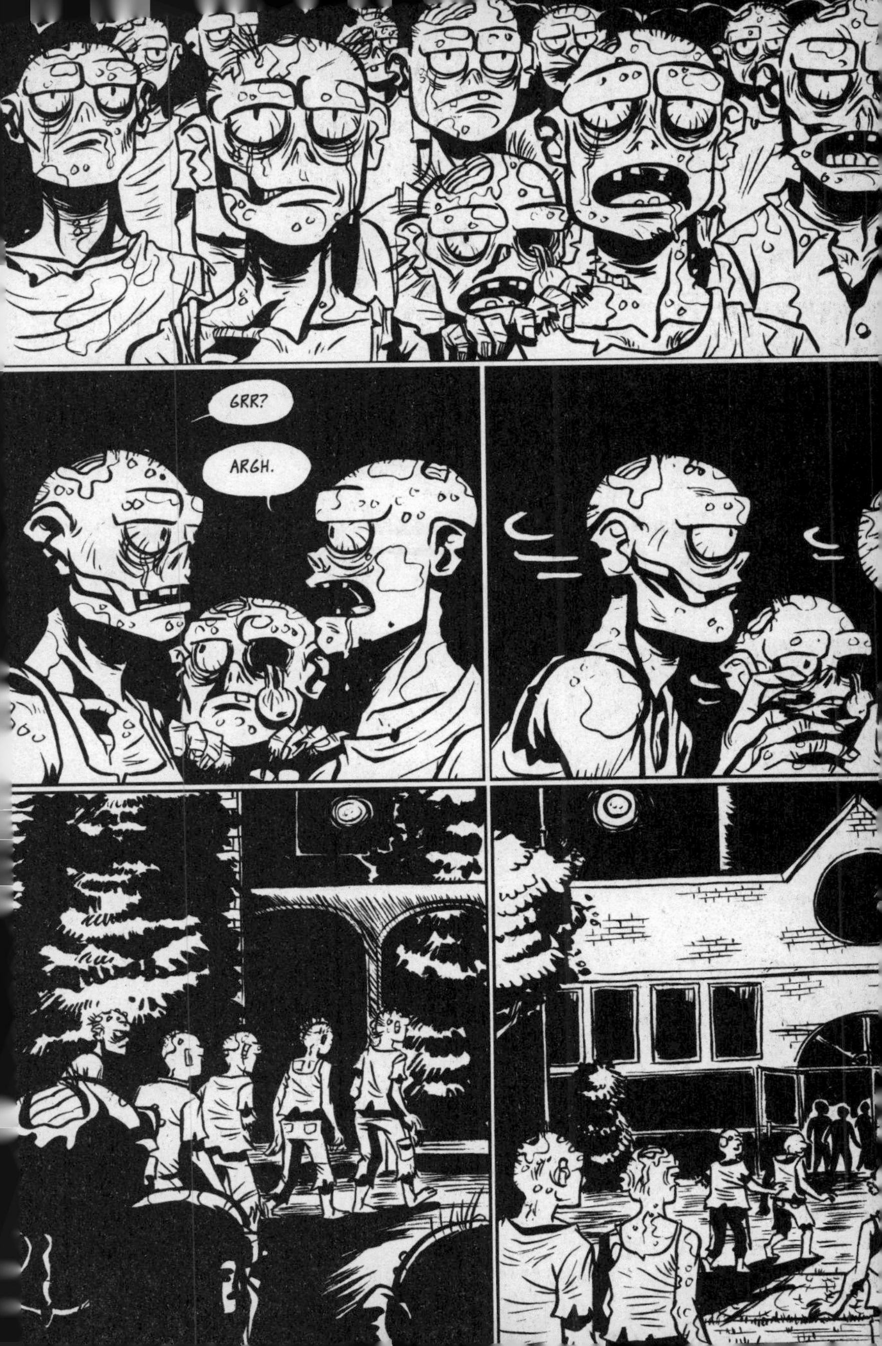
GRR?
ARGH.

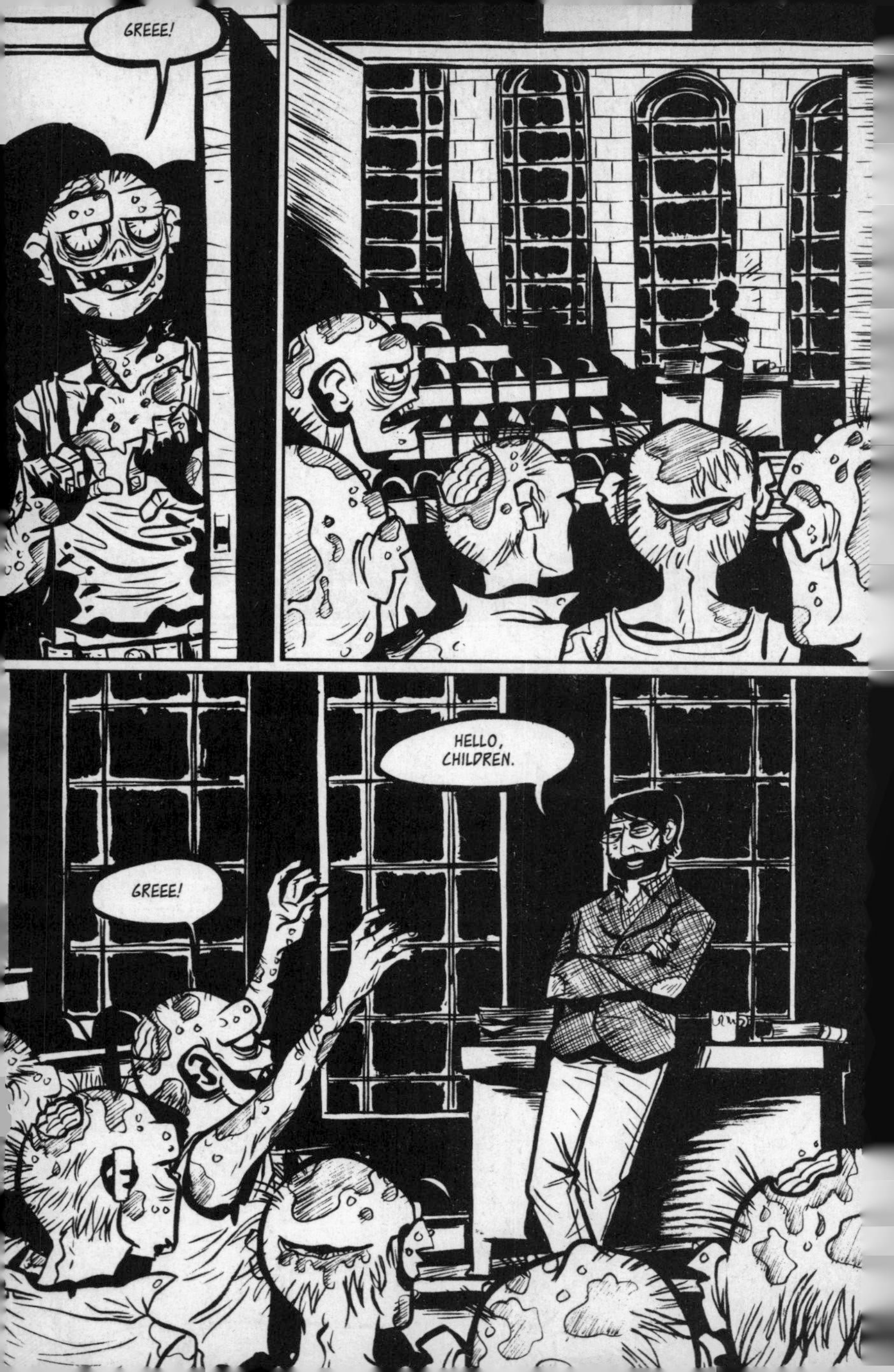
GREEE!
HELLO, CHILDREN.
GREEE!

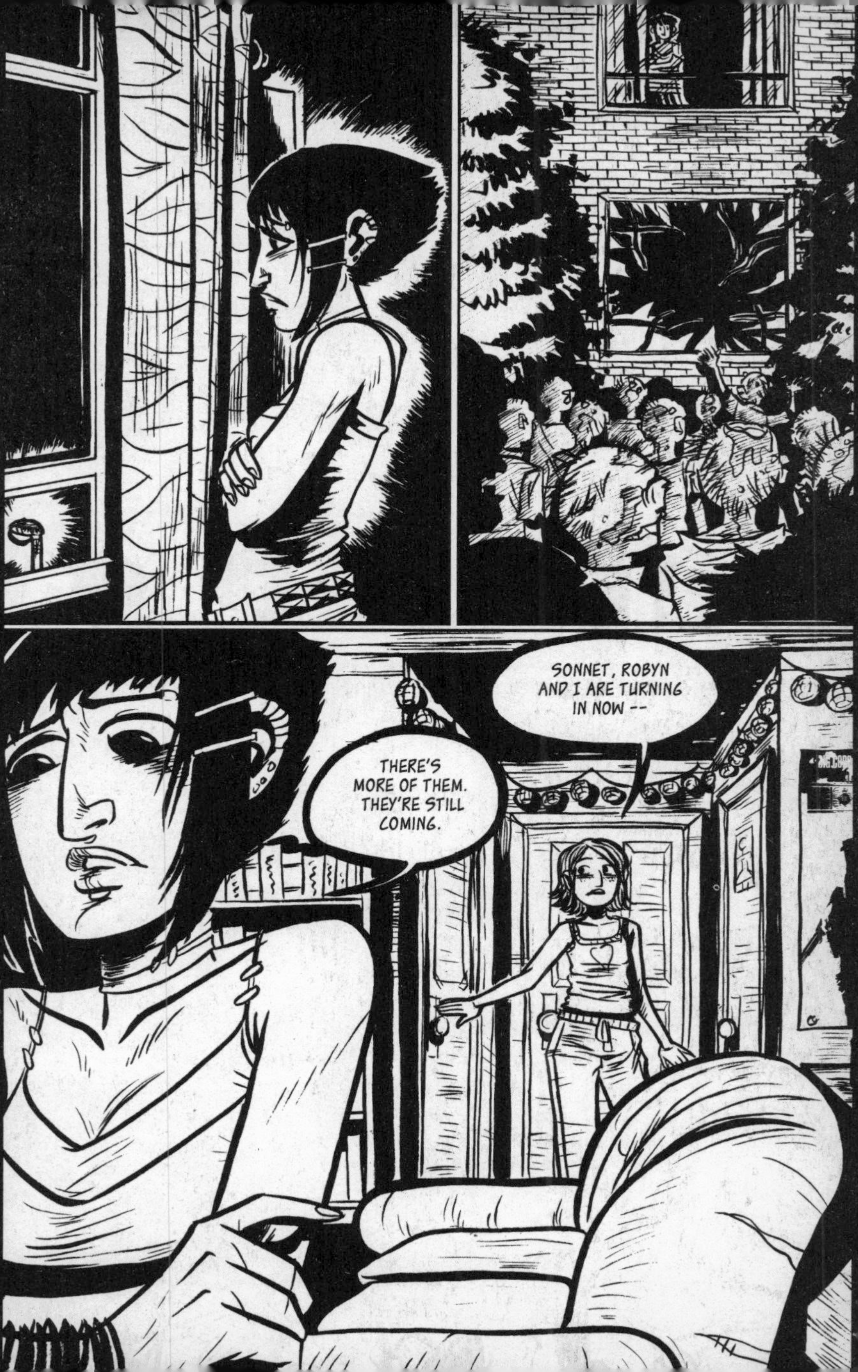
SONNET, ROBYN AND I ARE TURNING IN NOW --
THERE'S MORE OF THEM. THEY'RE STILL COMING.

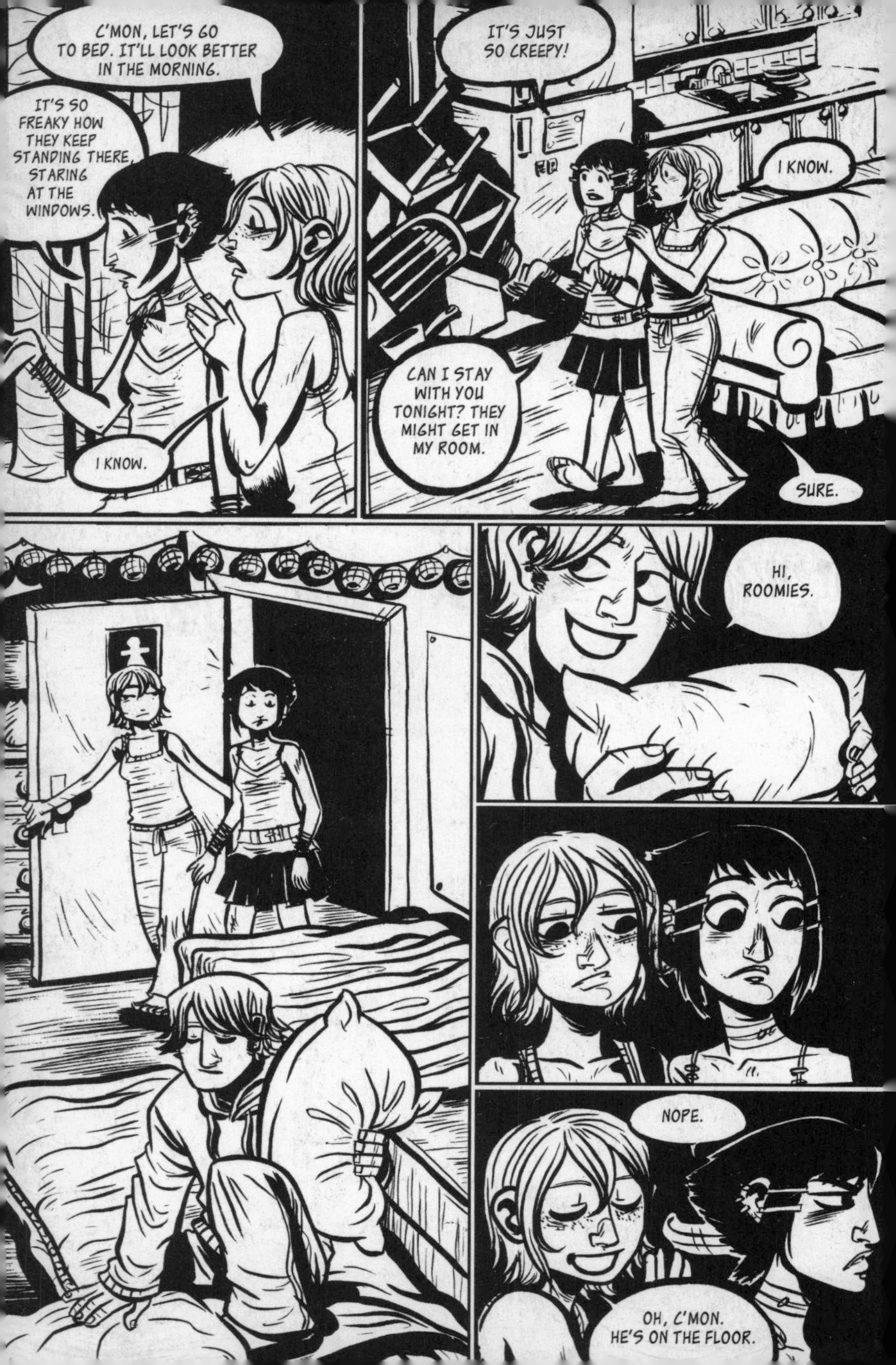
C'MON, LET'S GO TO BED. IT'LL LOOK BETTER IN THE MORNING.
IT'S SO FREAKY HOW THEY KEEP STANDING THERE, STARING AT THE WINDOWS.
I KNOW.
IT'S JUST SO CREEPY!
I KNOW.
CAN I STAY WITH YOU TONIGHT? THEY MIGHT GET IN MY ROOM.
SURE.
HI, ROOMIES.
NOPE.
OH, C'MON. HE'S ON THE FLOOR.

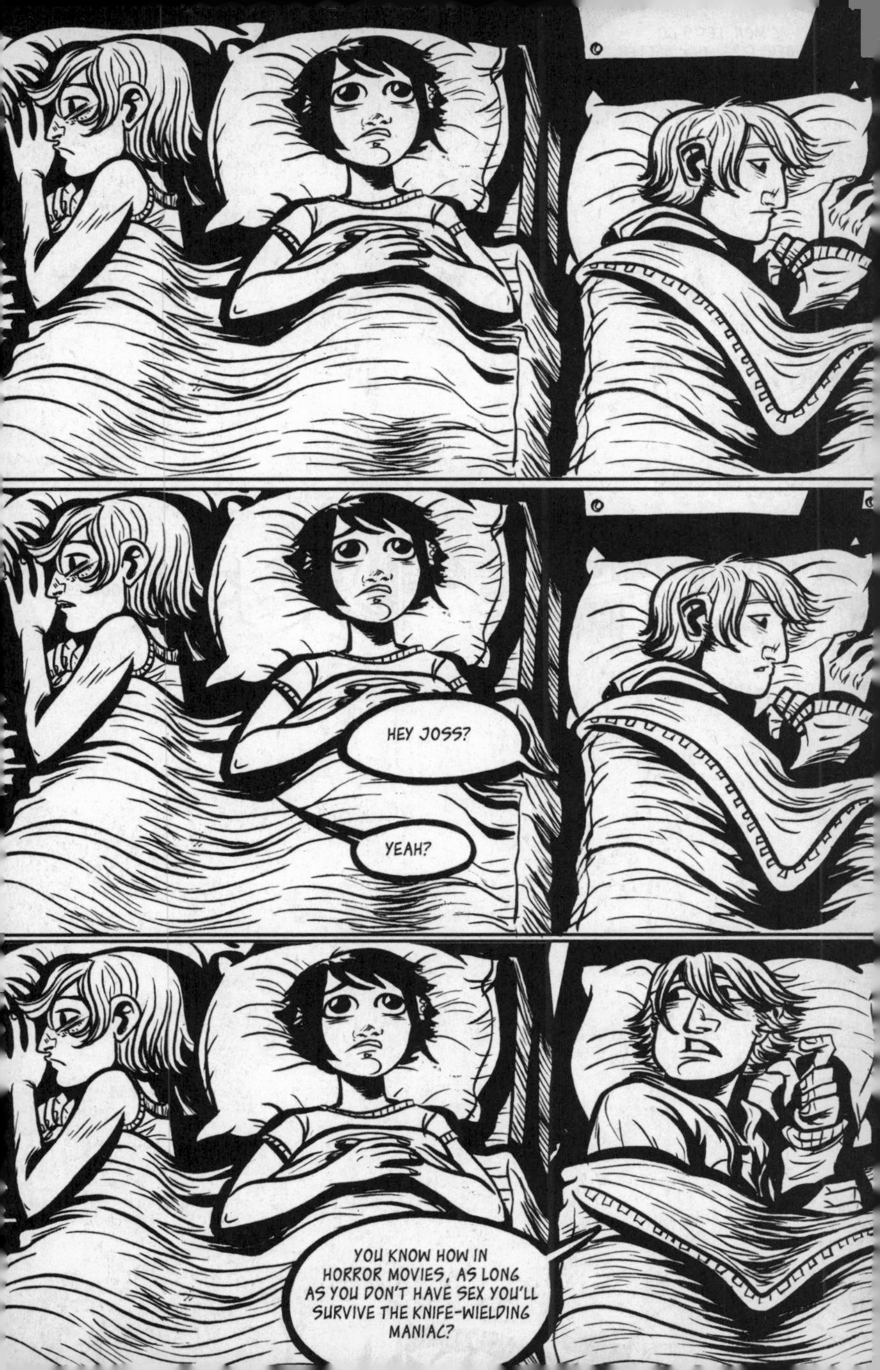
HEY JOSS?
YEAH?
YOU KNOW HOW IN HORROR MOVIES, AS LONG AS YOU DON'T HAVE SEX YOU'LL SURVIVE THE KNIFE-WIELDING MANIAC?

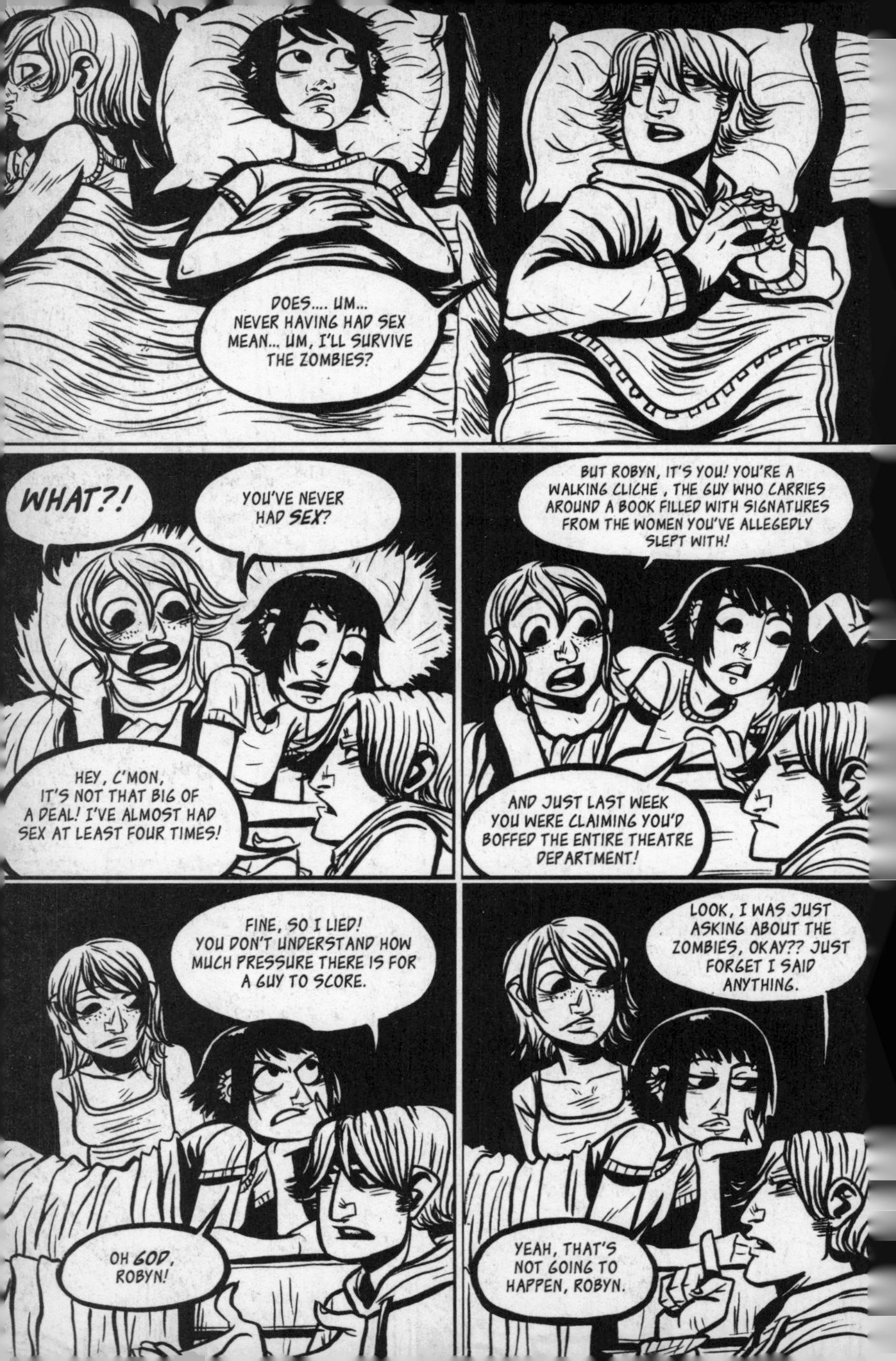
DOES.... UM...
NEVER HAVING HAD SEX
MEAN... UM, I'LL SURVIVE
THE ZOMBIES?
WHAT?!
YOU'VE NEVER
HAD SEX?
HEY, C'MON,
IT'S NOT THAT BIG OF
A DEAL! I'VE ALMOST HAD
SEX AT LEAST FOUR TIMES!
BUT ROBYN, IT'S YOU! YOU'RE A
WALKING CLICHE , THE GUY WHO CARRIES
AROUND A BOOK FILLED WITH SIGNATURES
FROM THE WOMEN YOU'VE ALLEGEDLY
SLEPT WITH!
AND JUST LAST WEEK
YOU WERE CLAIMING YOU'D
BOFFED THE ENTIRE THEATRE
DEPARTMENT!
FINE, SO I LIED!
YOU DON'T UNDERSTAND HOW
MUCH PRESSURE THERE IS FOR
A GUY TO SCORE.
OH GOD,
ROBYN!
LOOK, I WAS JUST
ASKING ABOUT THE
ZOMBIES, OKAY?? JUST
FORGET I SAID
ANYTHING.
YEAH, THAT'S
NOT GOING TO
HAPPEN, ROBYN.

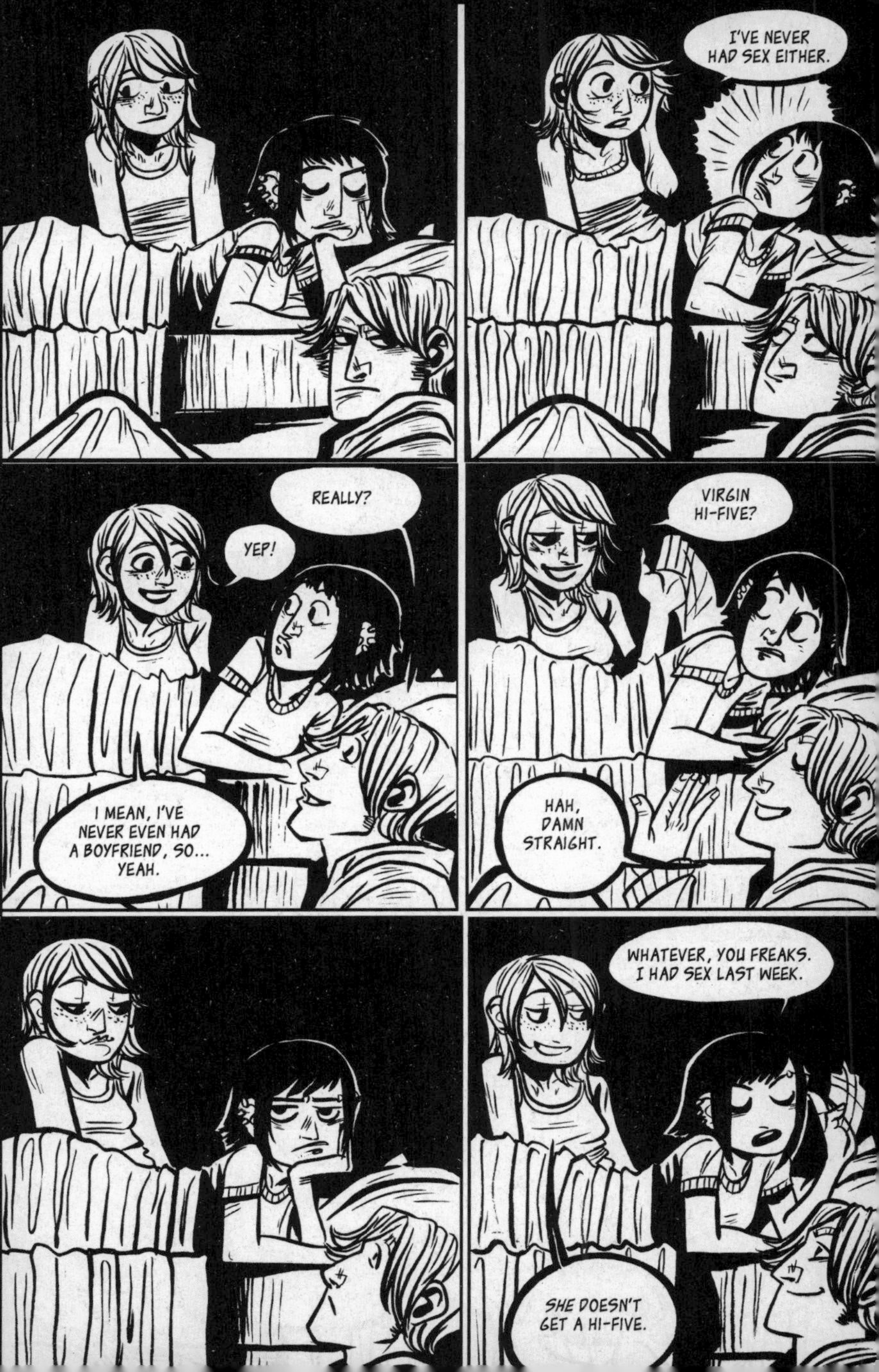
I'VE NEVER HAD SEX EITHER.
REALLY?
YEP!
I MEAN, I'VE NEVER EVEN HAD A BOYFRIEND, SO... YEAH.
VIRGIN HI-FIVE?
HAH, DAMN STRAIGHT.
WHATEVER, YOU FREAKS. I HAD SEX LAST WEEK.
SHE DOESN'T GET A HI-FIVE.

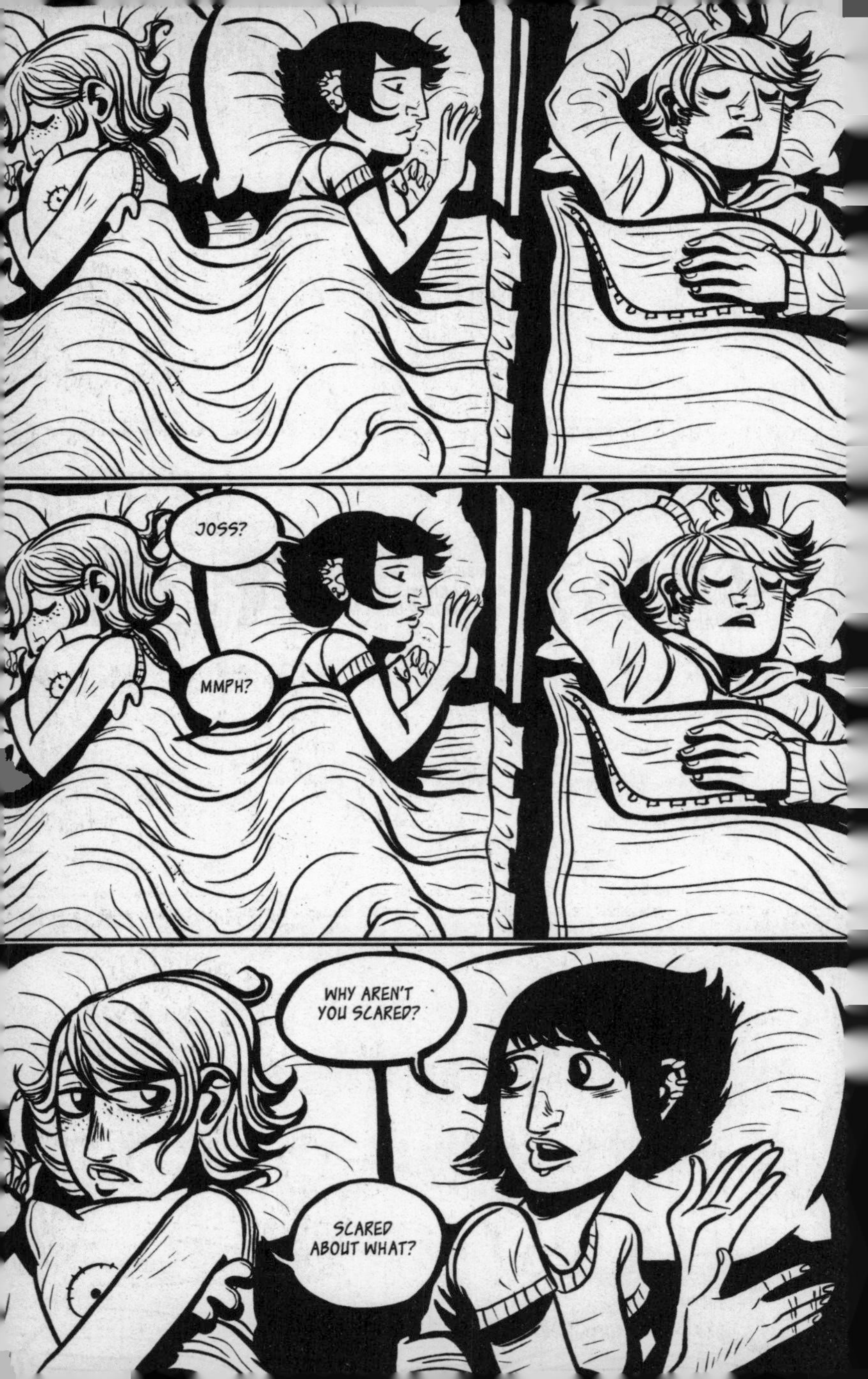
JOSS?
MMPH?
WHY AREN'T YOU SCARED?
SCARED ABOUT WHAT?

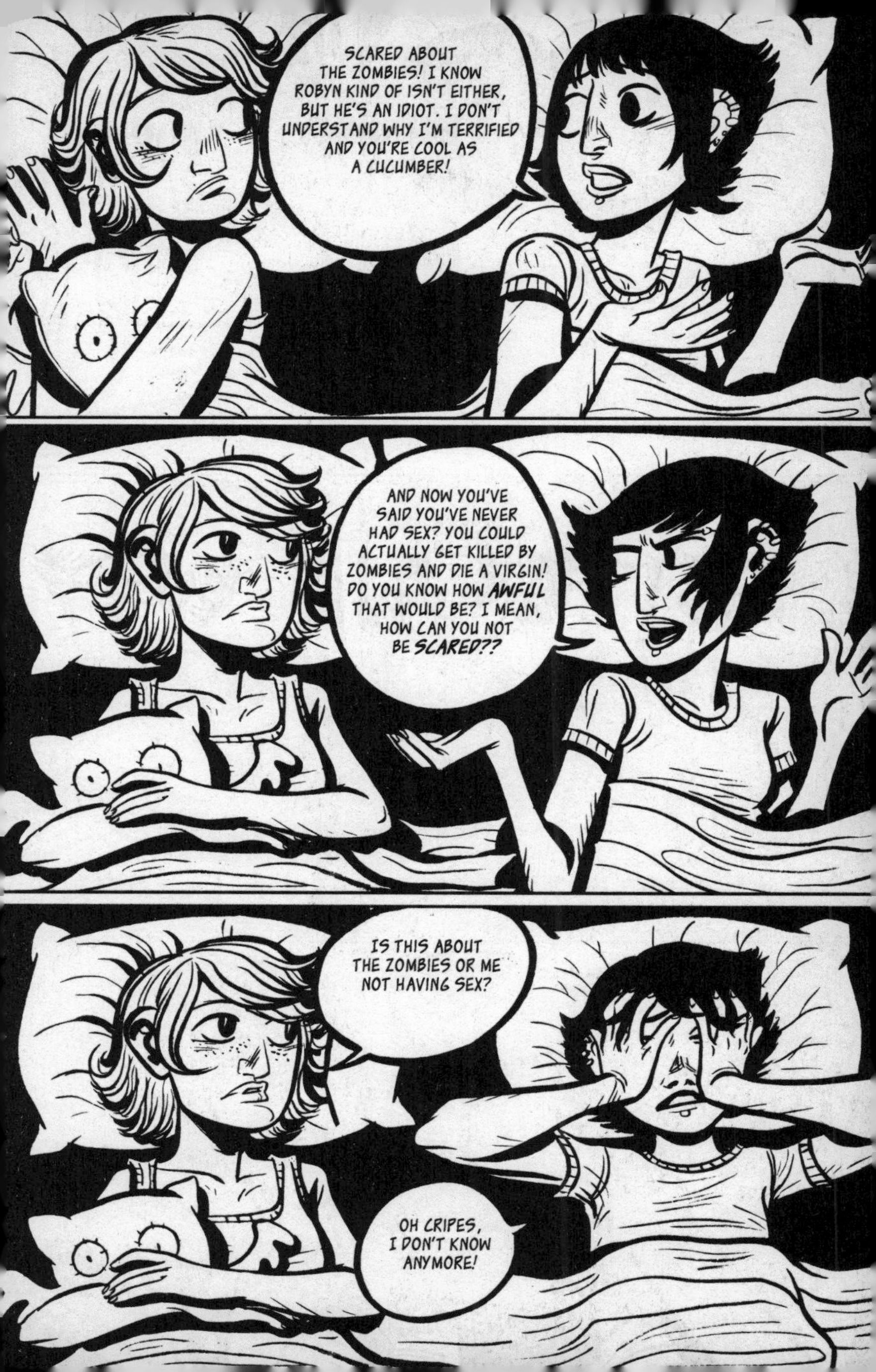
SCARED ABOUT THE ZOMBIES! I KNOW ROBYN KIND OF ISN'T EITHER, BUT HE'S AN IDIOT. I DON'T UNDERSTAND WHY I'M TERRIFIED AND YOU'RE COOL AS A CUCUMBER!
AND NOW YOU'VE SAID YOU'VE NEVER HAD SEX? YOU COULD ACTUALLY GET KILLED BY ZOMBIES AND DIE A VIRGIN! DO YOU KNOW HOW AWFUL THAT WOULD BE? I MEAN, HOW CAN YOU NOT BE SCARED??
IS THIS ABOUT THE ZOMBIES OR ME NOT HAVING SEX?
OH CRIPES, I DON'T KNOW ANYMORE!

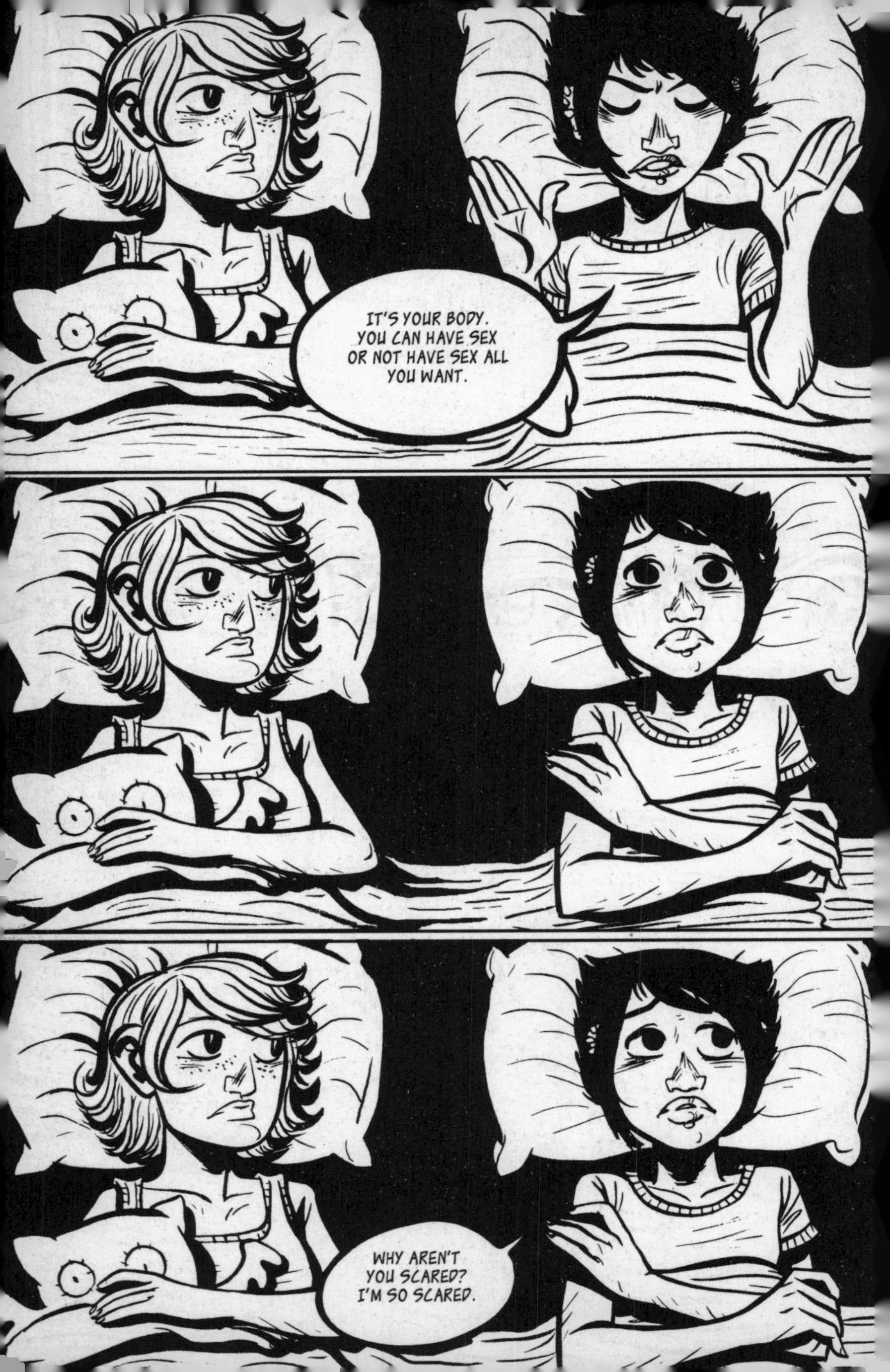
IT'S YOUR BODY. YOU CAN HAVE SEX OR NOT HAVE SEX ALL YOU WANT.
WHY AREN'T YOU SCARED? I'M SO SCARED.

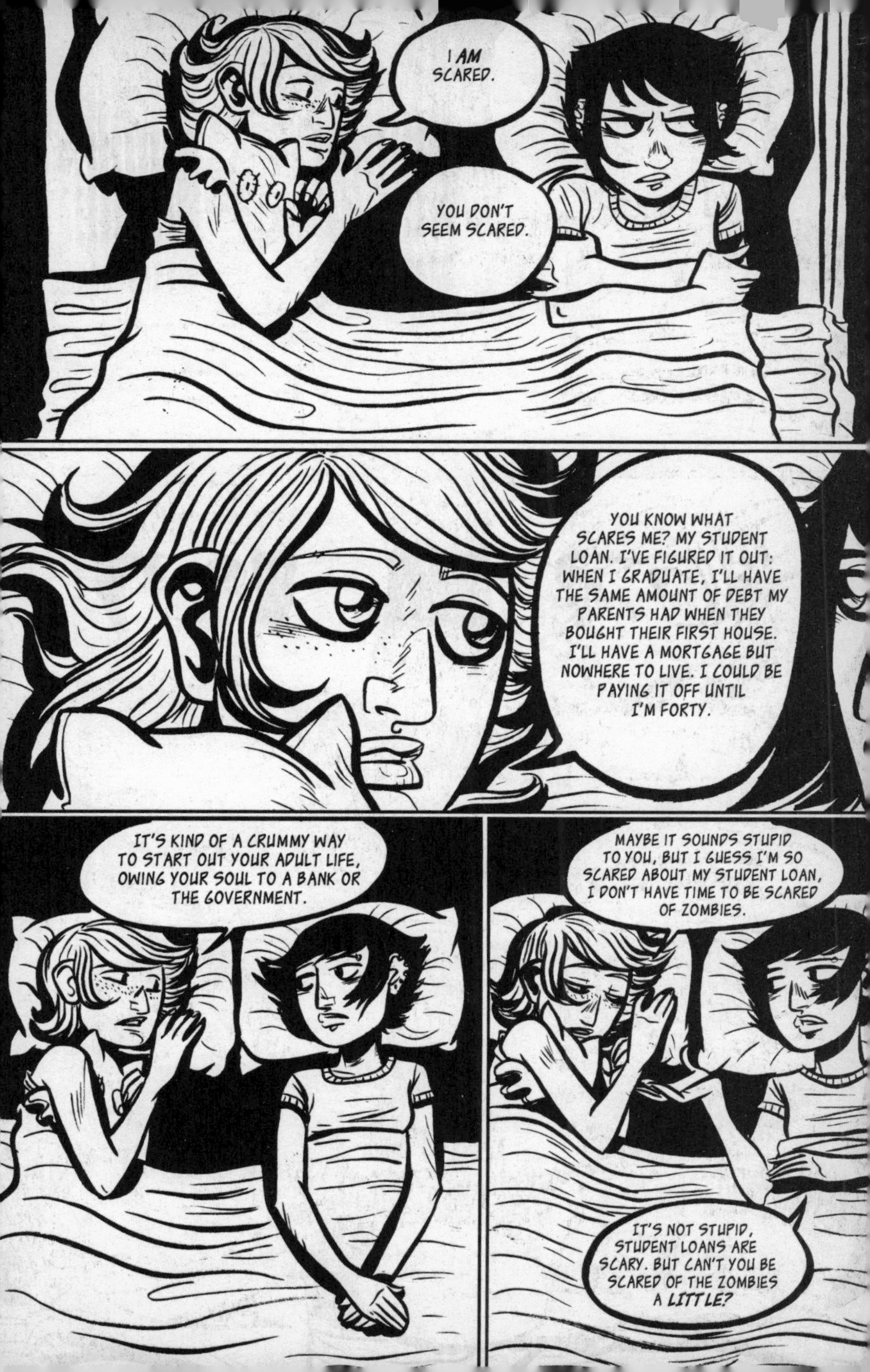
I AM SCARED.
YOU DON'T SEEM SCARED.
YOU KNOW WHAT SCARES ME? MY STUDENT LOAN. I'VE FIGURED IT OUT: WHEN I GRADUATE, I'LL HAVE THE SAME AMOUNT OF DEBT MY PARENTS HAD WHEN THEY BOUGHT THEIR FIRST HOUSE. I'LL HAVE A MORTGAGE BUT NOWHERE TO LIVE. I COULD BE PAYING IT OFF UNTIL I'M FORTY.
IT'S KIND OF A CRUMMY WAY TO START OUT YOUR ADULT LIFE, OWING YOUR SOUL TO A BANK OR THE GOVERNMENT.
MAYBE IT SOUNDS STUPID TO YOU, BUT I GUESS I'M SO SCARED ABOUT MY STUDENT LOAN, I DON'T HAVE TIME TO BE SCARED OF ZOMBIES.
IT'S NOT STUPID, STUDENT LOANS ARE SCARY. BUT CAN'T YOU BE SCARED OF THE ZOMBIES A LITTLE?

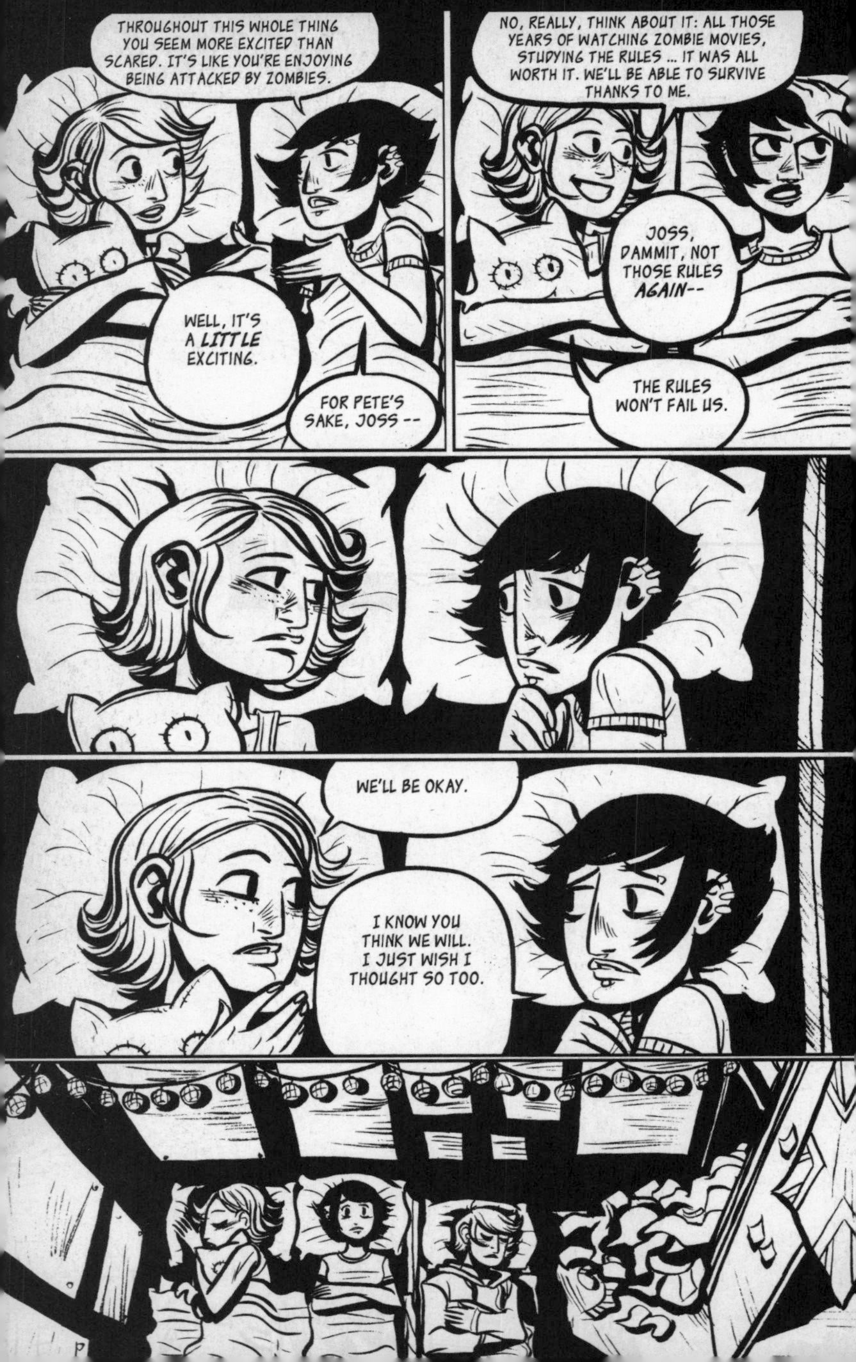
THROUGHOUT THIS WHOLE THING YOU SEEM MORE EXCITED THAN SCARED. IT'S LIKE YOU'RE ENJOYING BEING ATTACKED BY ZOMBIES.
WELL, IT'S A LITTLE EXCITING.
FOR PETE'S SAKE, JOSS --
NO, REALLY, THINK ABOUT IT: ALL THOSE YEARS OF WATCHING ZOMBIE MOVIES, STUDYING THE RULES ... IT WAS ALL WORTH IT. WE'LL BE ABLE TO SURVIVE THANKS TO ME.
JOSS, DAMMIT, NOT THOSE RULES AGAIN--
THE RULES WON'T FAIL US.
WE'LL BE OKAY.
I KNOW YOU THINK WE WILL. I JUST WISH I THOUGHT SO TOO.

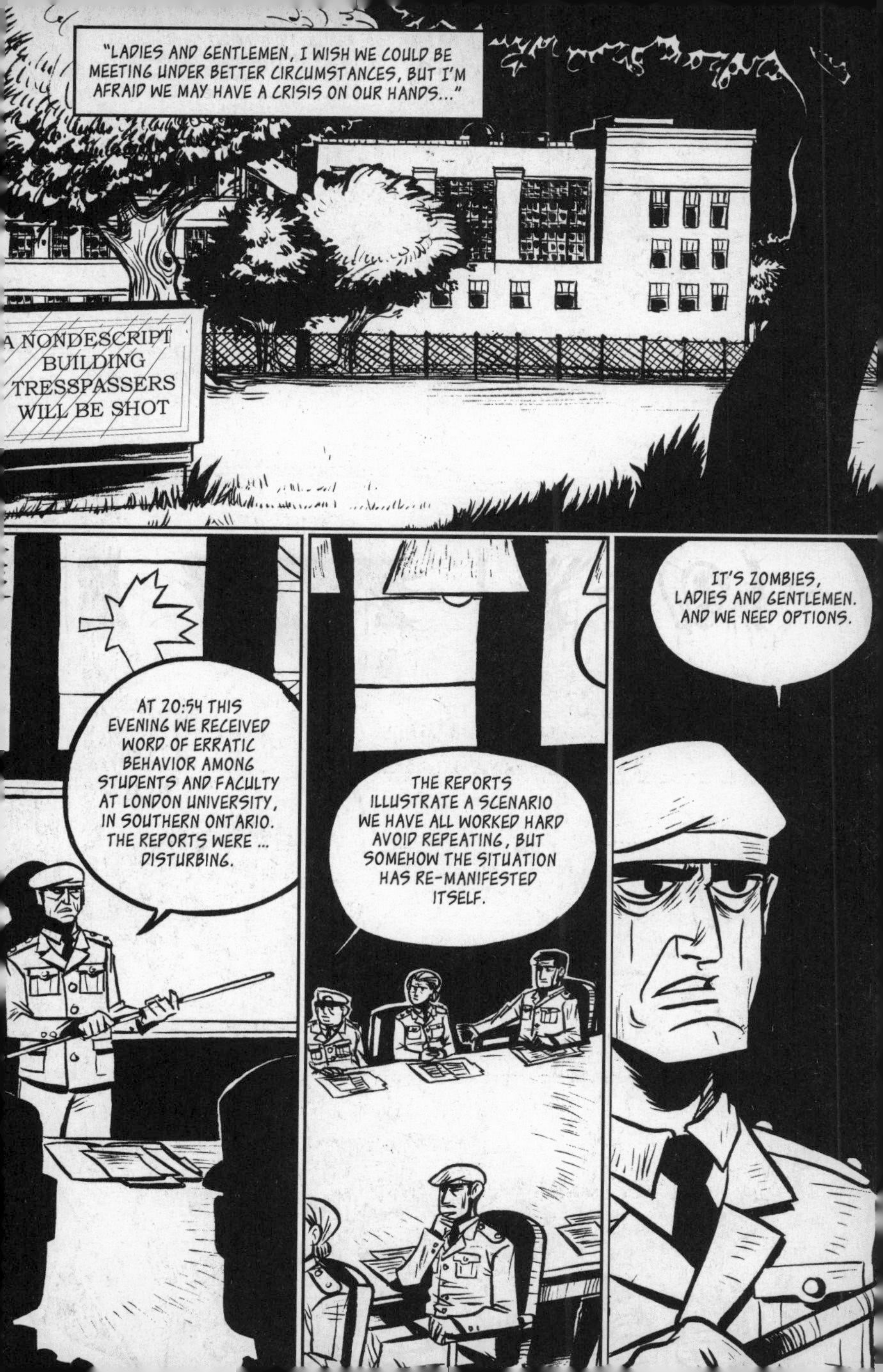
"LADIES AND GENTLEMEN, I WISH WE COULD BE MEETING UNDER BETTER CIRCUMSTANCES, BUT I'M AFRAID WE MAY HAVE A CRISIS ON OUR HANDS..."
A NONDESCRIPT BUILDING TRESSPASSERS WILL BE SHOT
AT 20:54 THIS EVENING WE RECEIVED WORD OF ERRATIC BEHAVIOR AMONG STUDENTS AND FACULTY AT LONDON UNIVERSITY, IN SOUTHERN ONTARIO. THE REPORTS WERE ... DISTURBING.
THE REPORTS ILLUSTRATE A SCENARIO WE HAVE ALL WORKED HARD AVOID REPEATING, BUT SOMEHOW THE SITUATION HAS RE-MANIFESTED ITSELF.
IT'S ZOMBIES, LADIES AND GENTLEMEN. AND WE NEED OPTIONS.

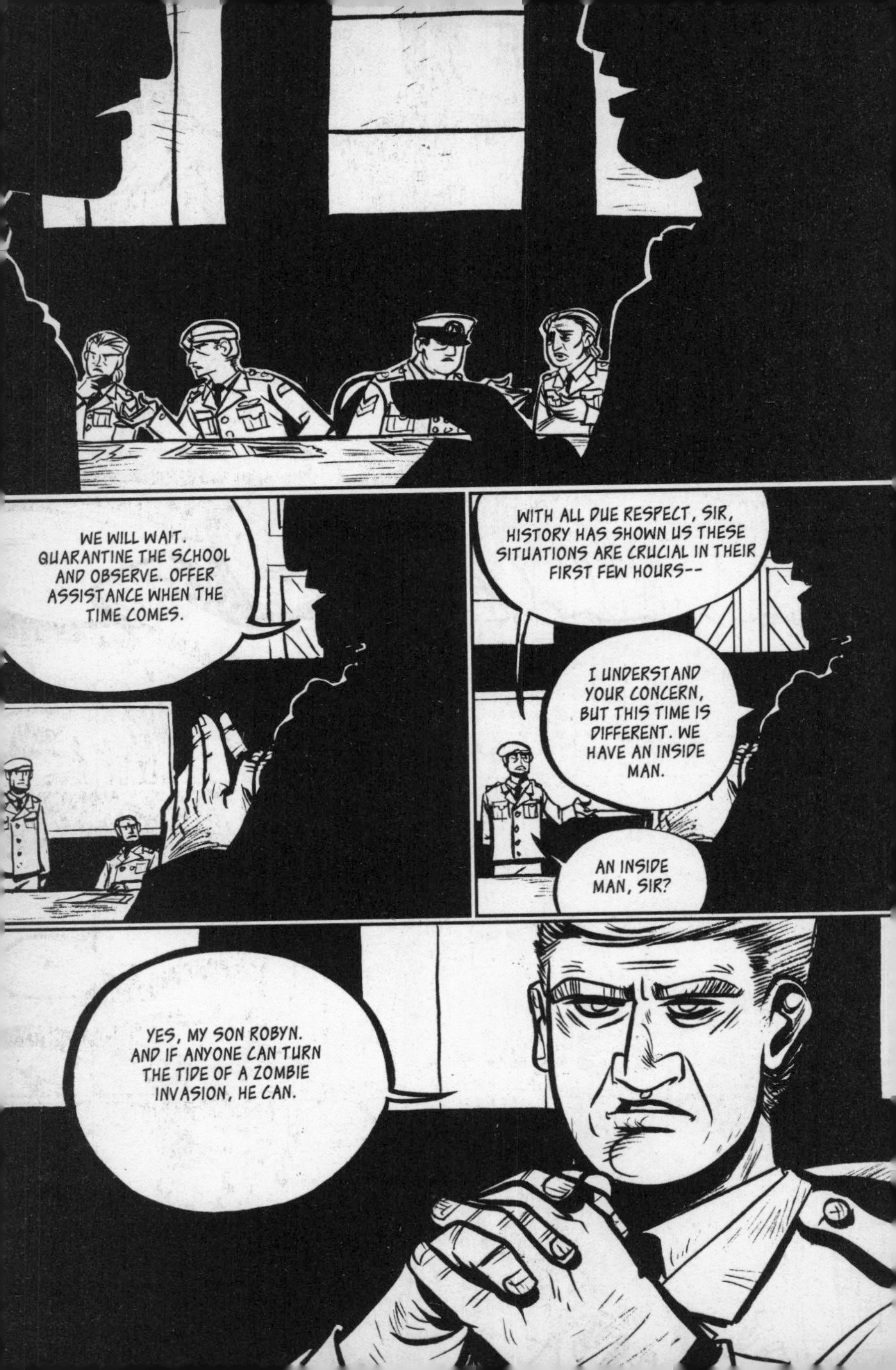
WE WILL WAIT. QUARANTINE THE SCHOOL AND OBSERVE. OFFER ASSISTANCE WHEN THE TIME COMES.
WITH ALL DUE RESPECT, SIR, HISTORY HAS SHOWN US THESE SITUATIONS ARE CRUCIAL IN THEIR FIRST FEW HOURS--
I UNDERSTAND YOUR CONCERN, BUT THIS TIME IS DIFFERENT. WE HAVE AN INSIDE MAN.
AN INSIDE MAN, SIR?
YES, MY SON ROBYN. AND IF ANYONE CAN TURN THE TIDE OF A ZOMBIE INVASION, HE CAN.

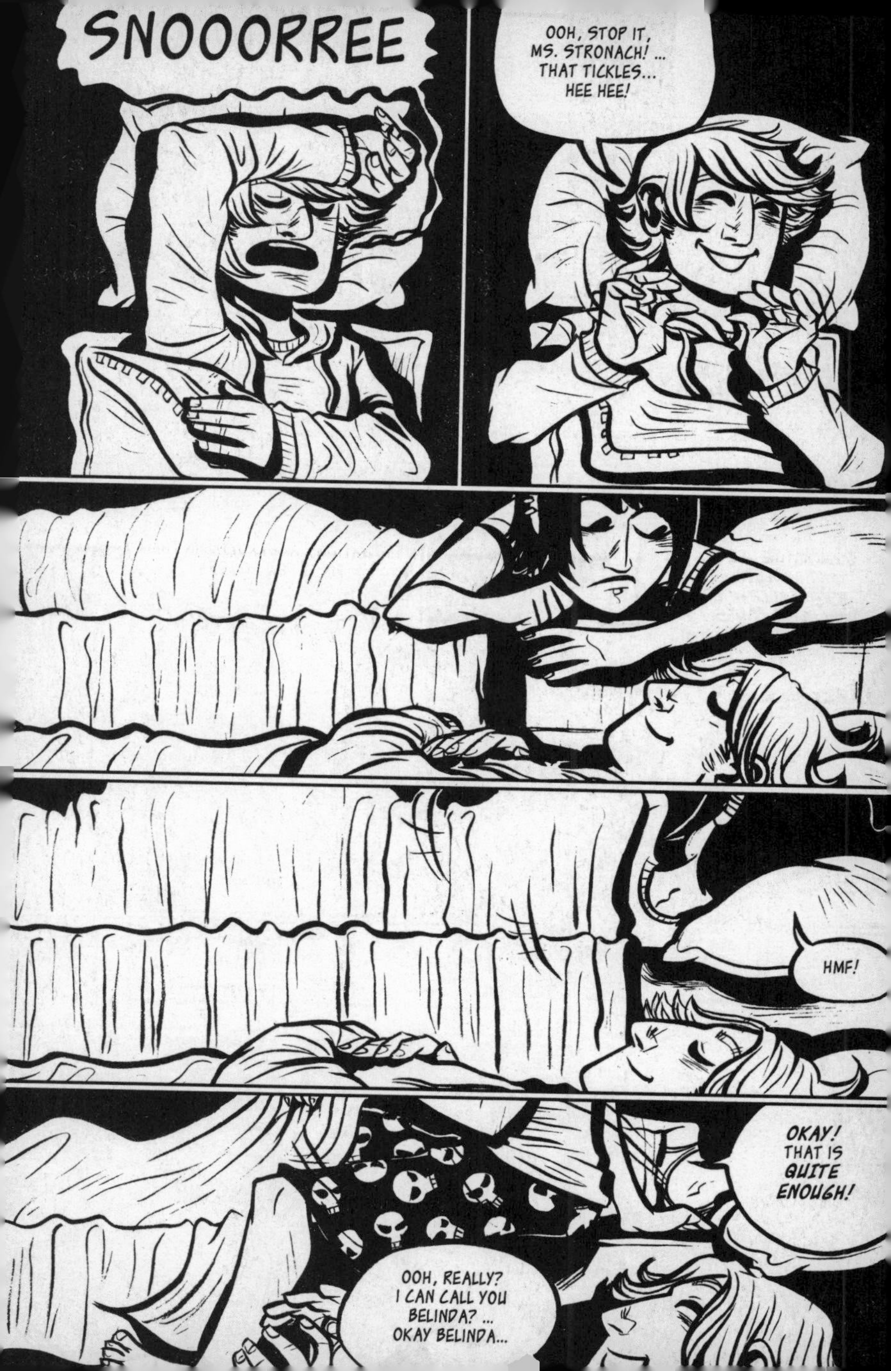
SNOOORREE
OOH, STOP IT, MS. STRONACH! ... THAT TICKLES... HEE HEE!
HMF!
OKAY! THAT IS QUITE ENOUGH!
OOH, REALLY? I CAN CALL YOU BELINDA? ... OKAY BELINDA...

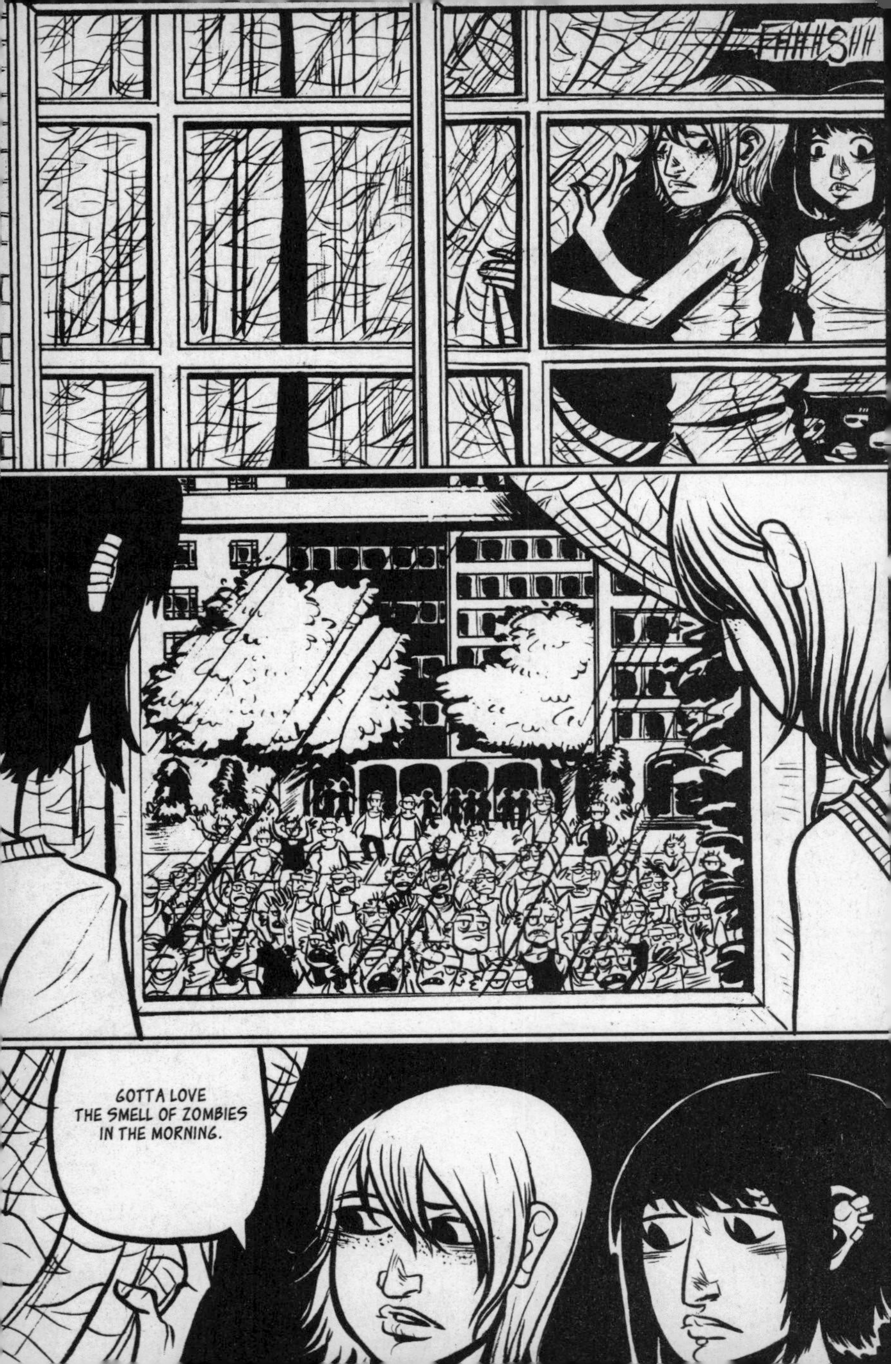
FWHHSHH
GOTTA LOVE THE SMELL OF ZOMBIES IN THE MORNING.

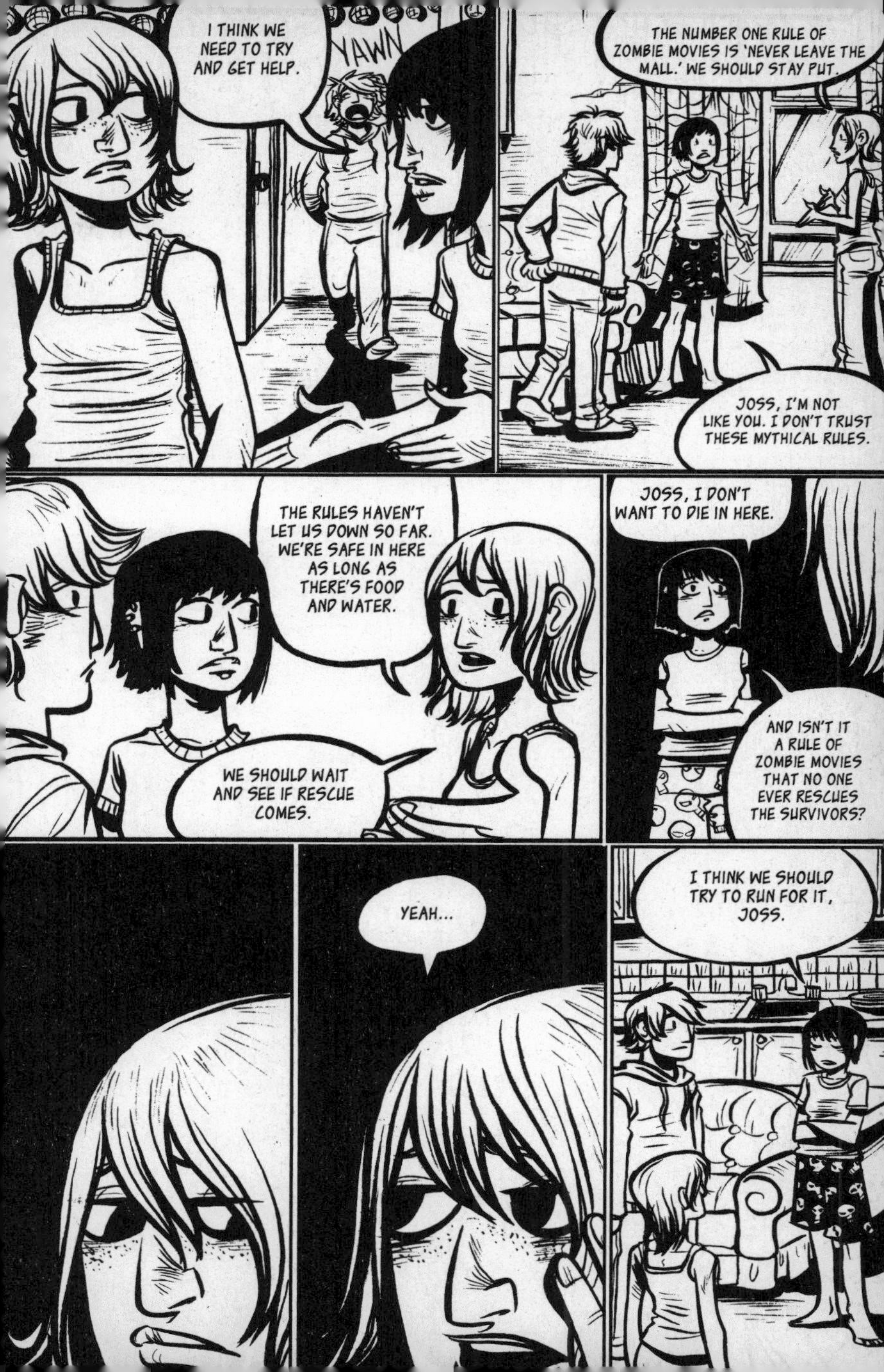
I THINK WE NEED TO TRY AND GET HELP.
YAWN
THE NUMBER ONE RULE OF ZOMBIE MOVIES IS 'NEVER LEAVE THE MALL.' WE SHOULD STAY PUT.
JOSS, I'M NOT LIKE YOU. I DON'T TRUST THESE MYTHICAL RULES.
THE RULES HAVEN'T LET US DOWN SO FAR. WE'RE SAFE IN HERE AS LONG AS THERE'S FOOD AND WATER.
WE SHOULD WAIT AND SEE IF RESCUE COMES.
JOSS, I DON'T WANT TO DIE IN HERE.
AND ISN'T IT A RULE OF ZOMBIE MOVIES THAT NO ONE EVER RESCUES THE SURVIVORS?
YEAH...
I THINK WE SHOULD TRY TO RUN FOR IT, JOSS.

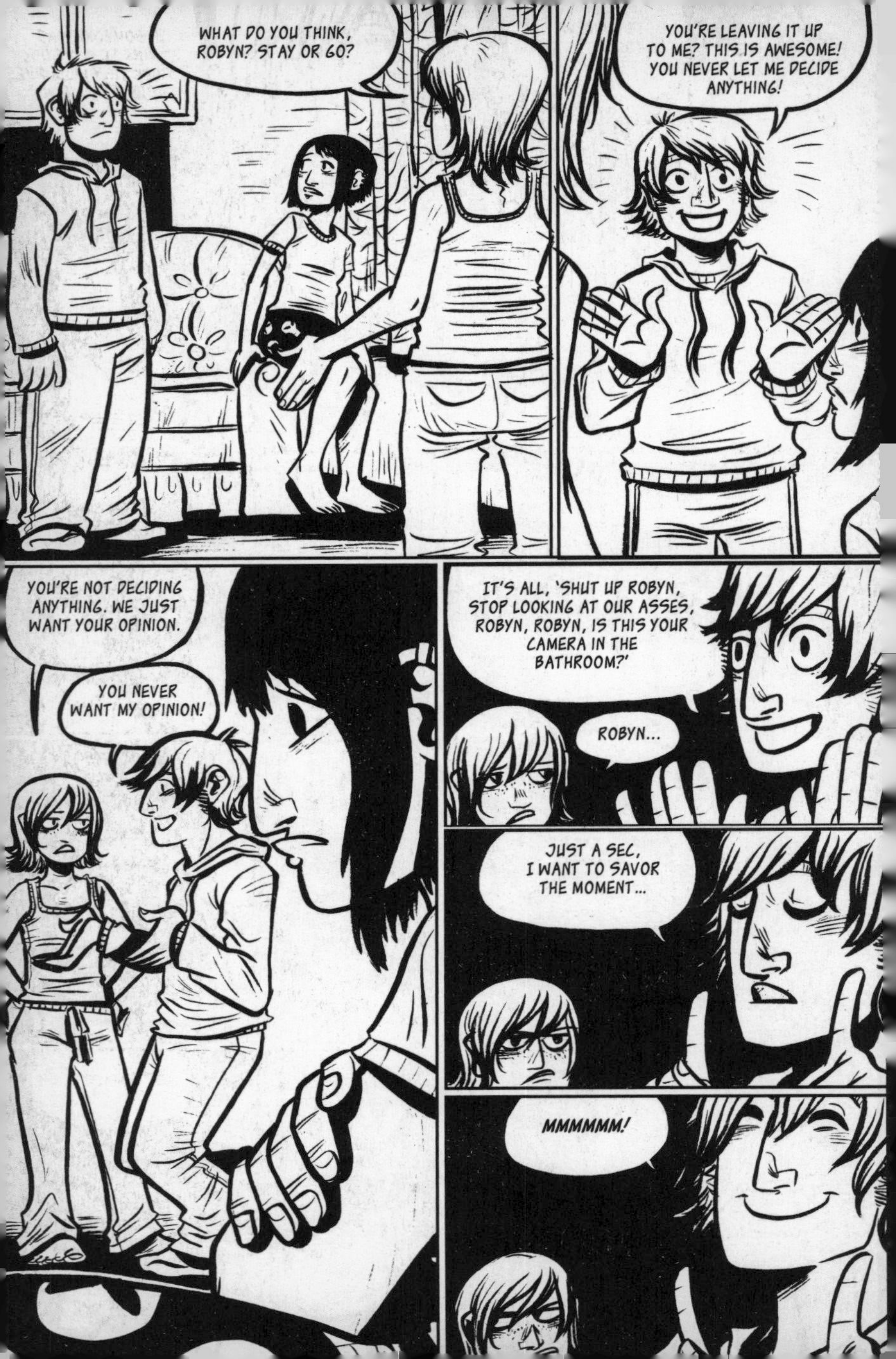
WHAT DO YOU THINK, ROBYN? STAY OR GO?
YOU'RE LEAVING IT UP TO ME? THIS IS AWESOME! YOU NEVER LET ME DECIDE ANYTHING!
YOU'RE NOT DECIDING ANYTHING. WE JUST WANT YOUR OPINION.
YOU NEVER WANT MY OPINION!
IT'S ALL, 'SHUT UP ROBYN, STOP LOOKING AT OUR ASSES, ROBYN, ROBYN, IS THIS YOUR CAMERA IN THE BATHROOM?'
ROBYN...
JUST A SEC, I WANT TO SAVOR THE MOMENT...
MMMMMM!

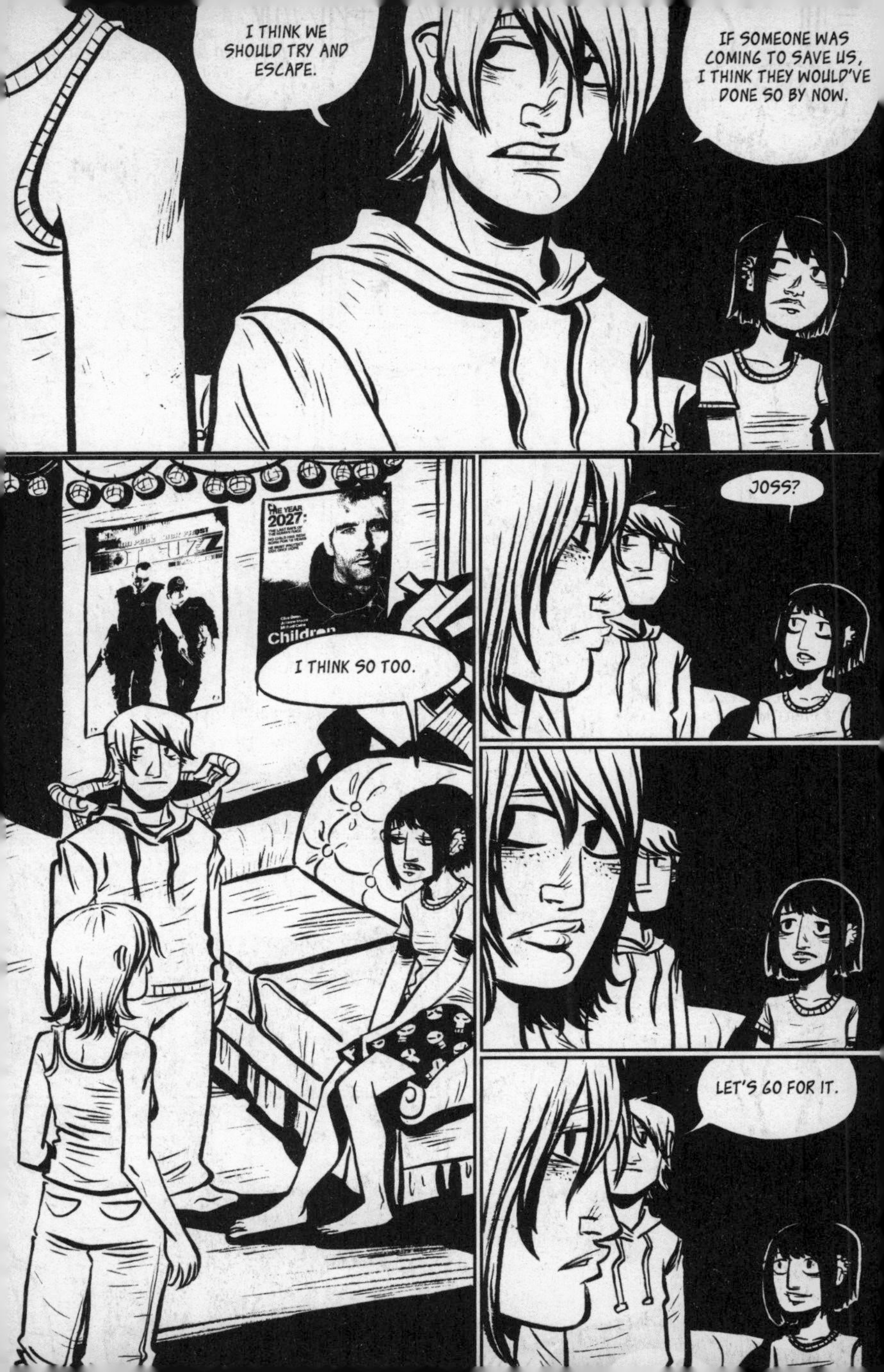
I THINK WE SHOULD TRY AND ESCAPE.
IF SOMEONE WAS COMING TO SAVE US, I THINK THEY WOULD'VE DONE SO BY NOW.
THE YEAR 2027:
Children
I THINK SO TOO.
JOSS?
LET'S GO FOR IT.

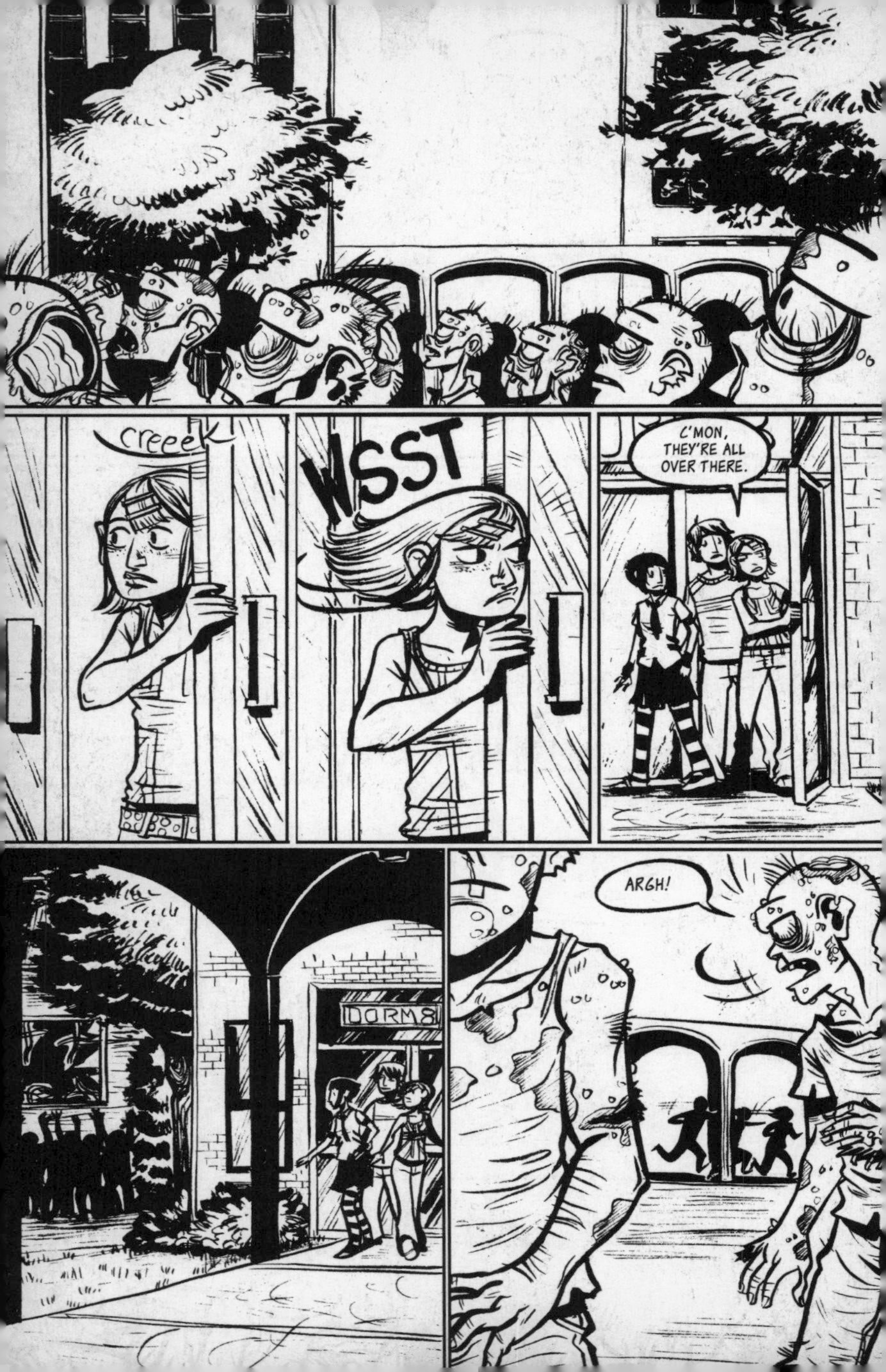
creeek
WSST
C'MON, THEY'RE ALL OVER THERE.
DORM 8
ARGH!

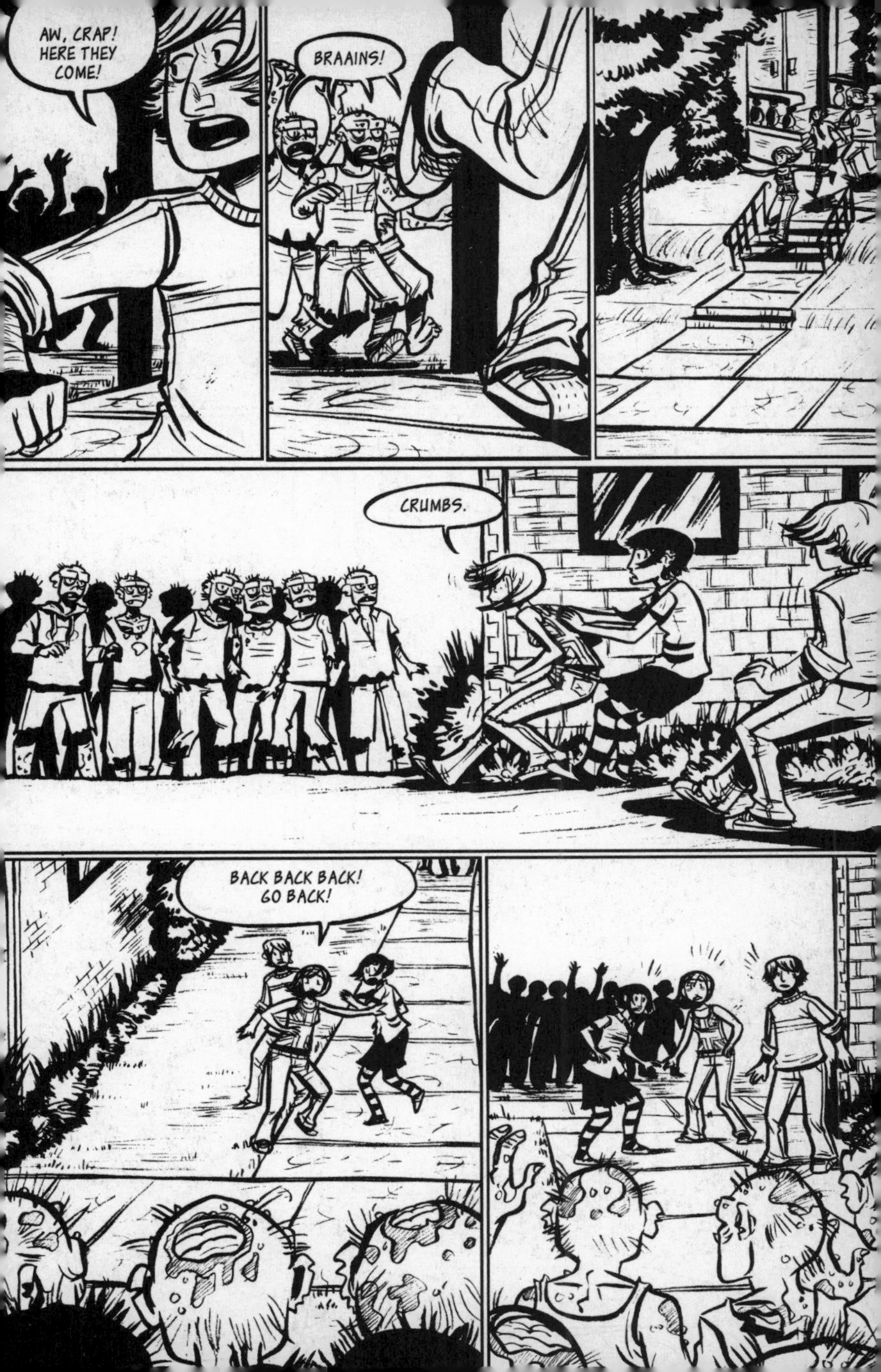
AW, CRAP! HERE THEY COME!
BRAAINS!
CRUMBS.
BACK BACK BACK! GO BACK!

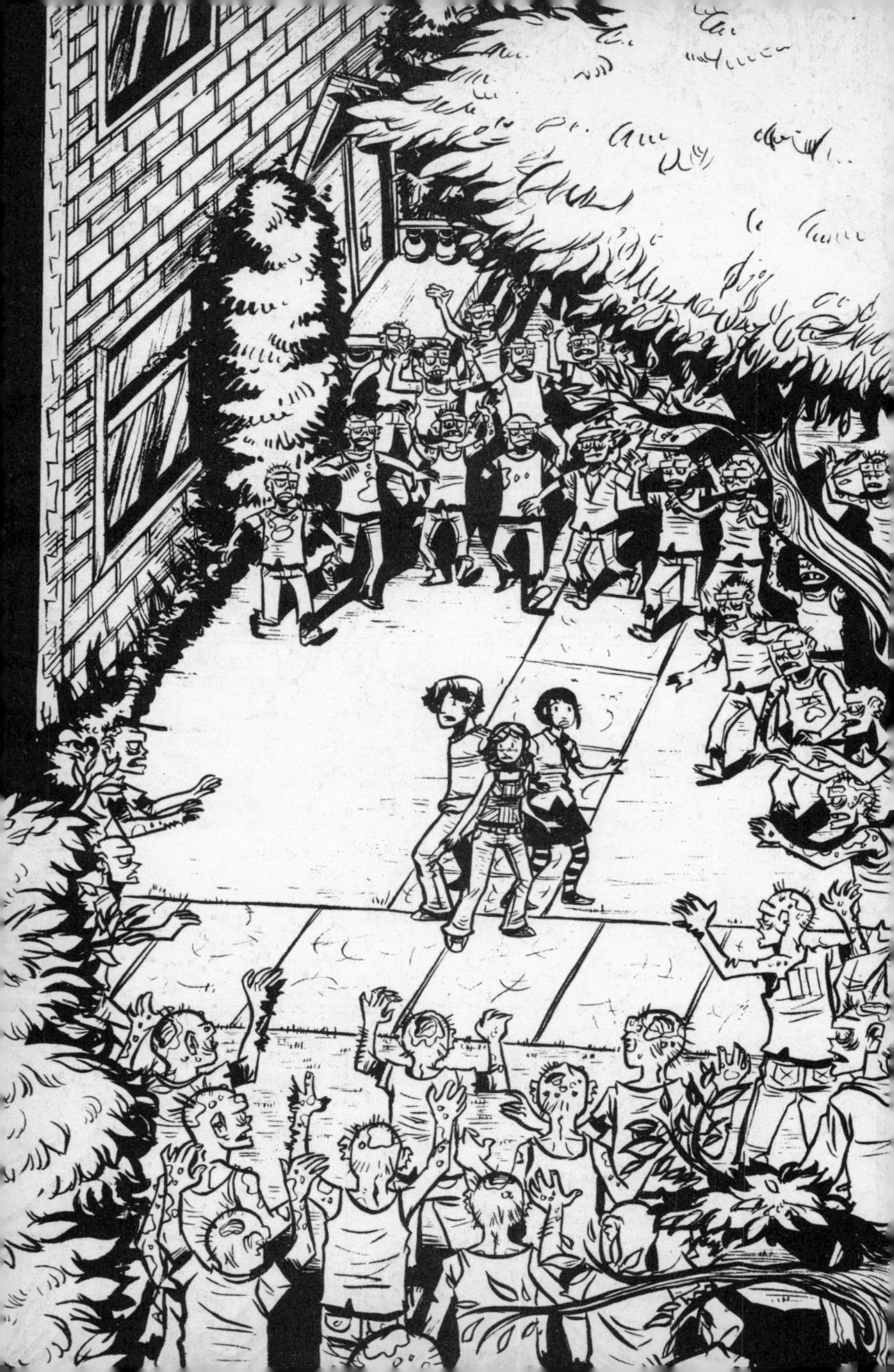

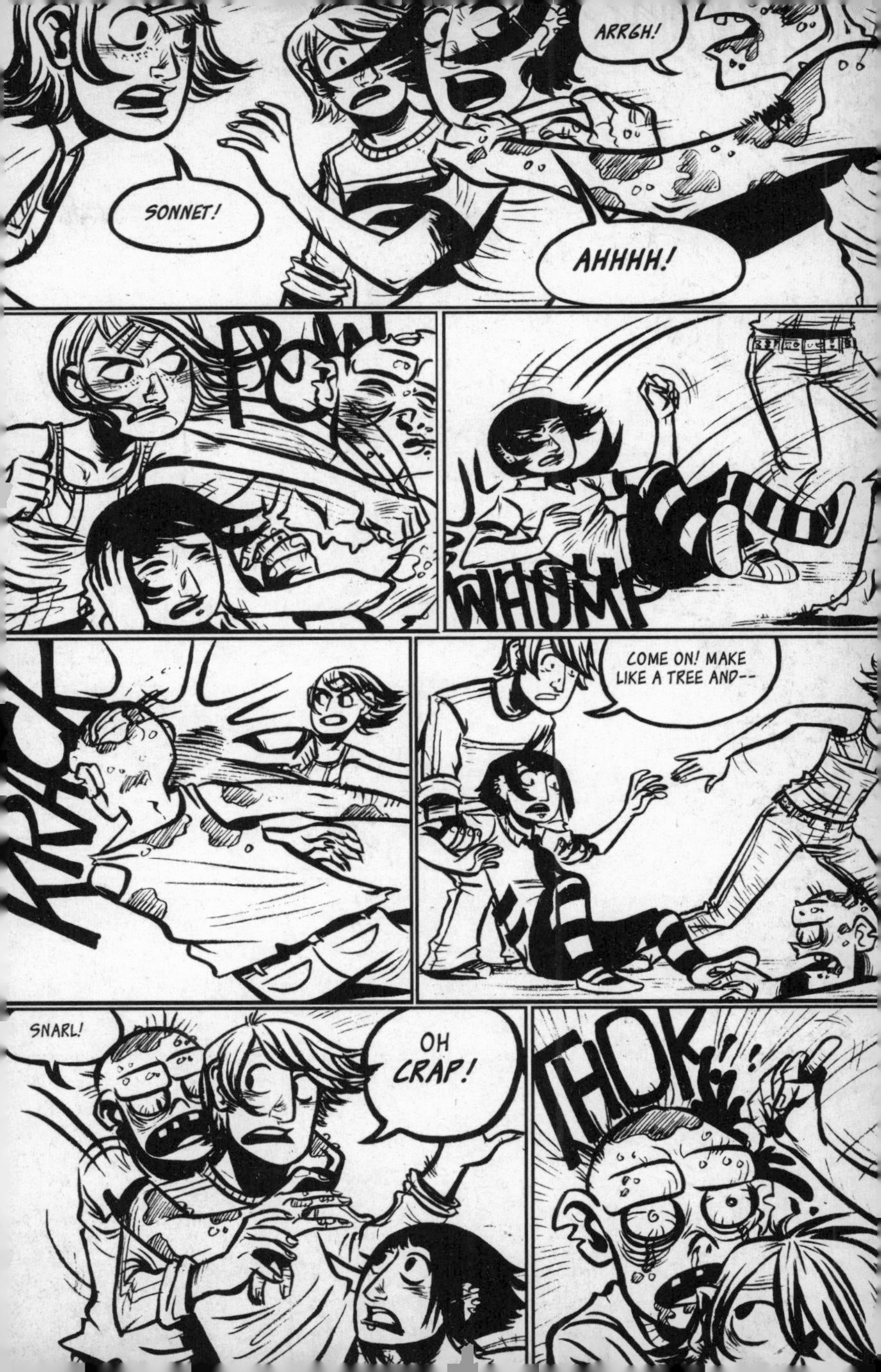
ARRGH!
SONNET!
AHHHH!
POW
WHOMP
KRAK
COME ON! MAKE LIKE A TREE AND--
SNARL!
OH CRAP!
THOK

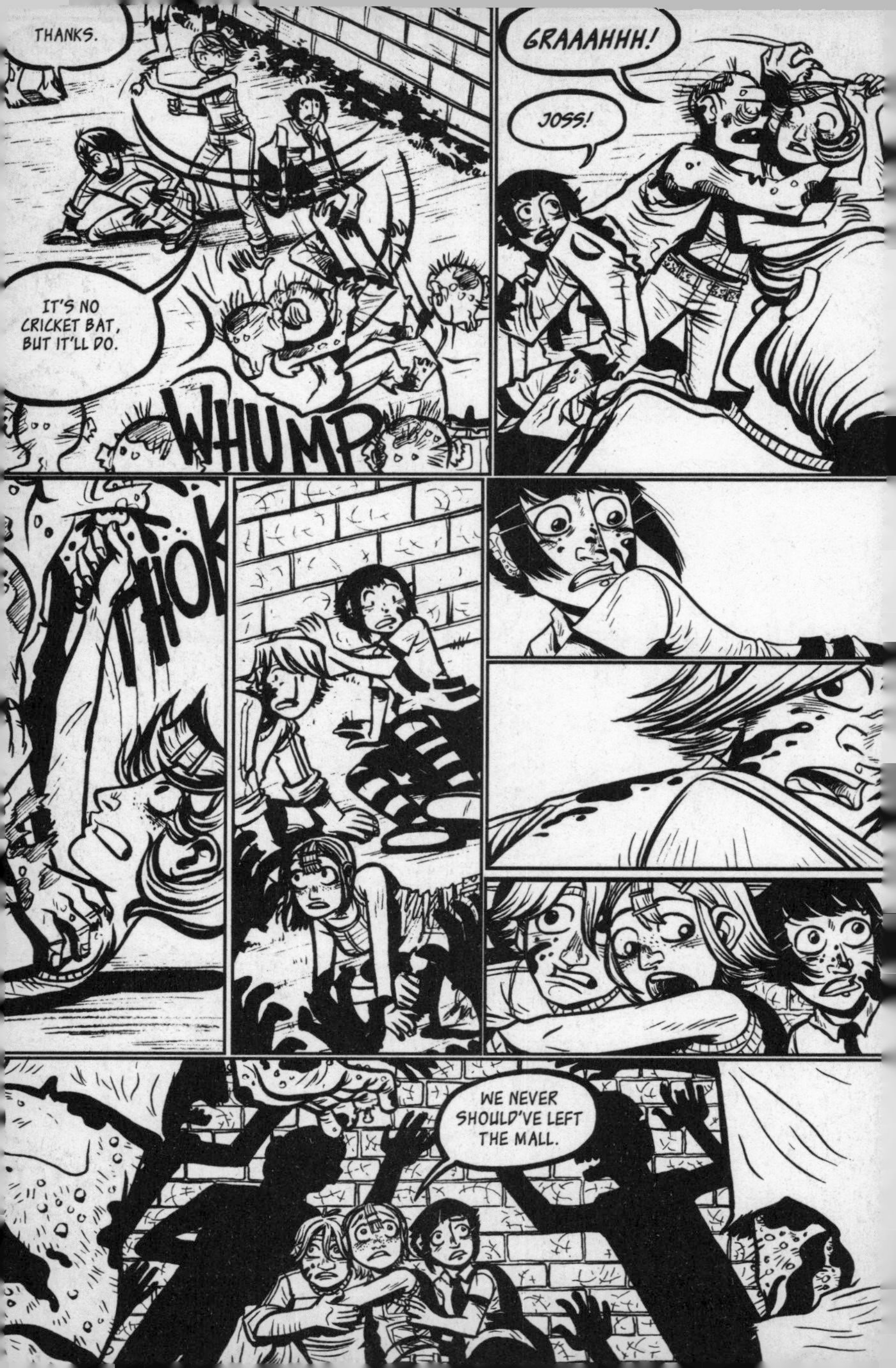
THANKS.
IT'S NO CRICKET BAT, BUT IT'LL DO.
WHUMP
GRAAAHHH!
JOSS!
THOK
WE NEVER SHOULD'VE LEFT THE MALL.

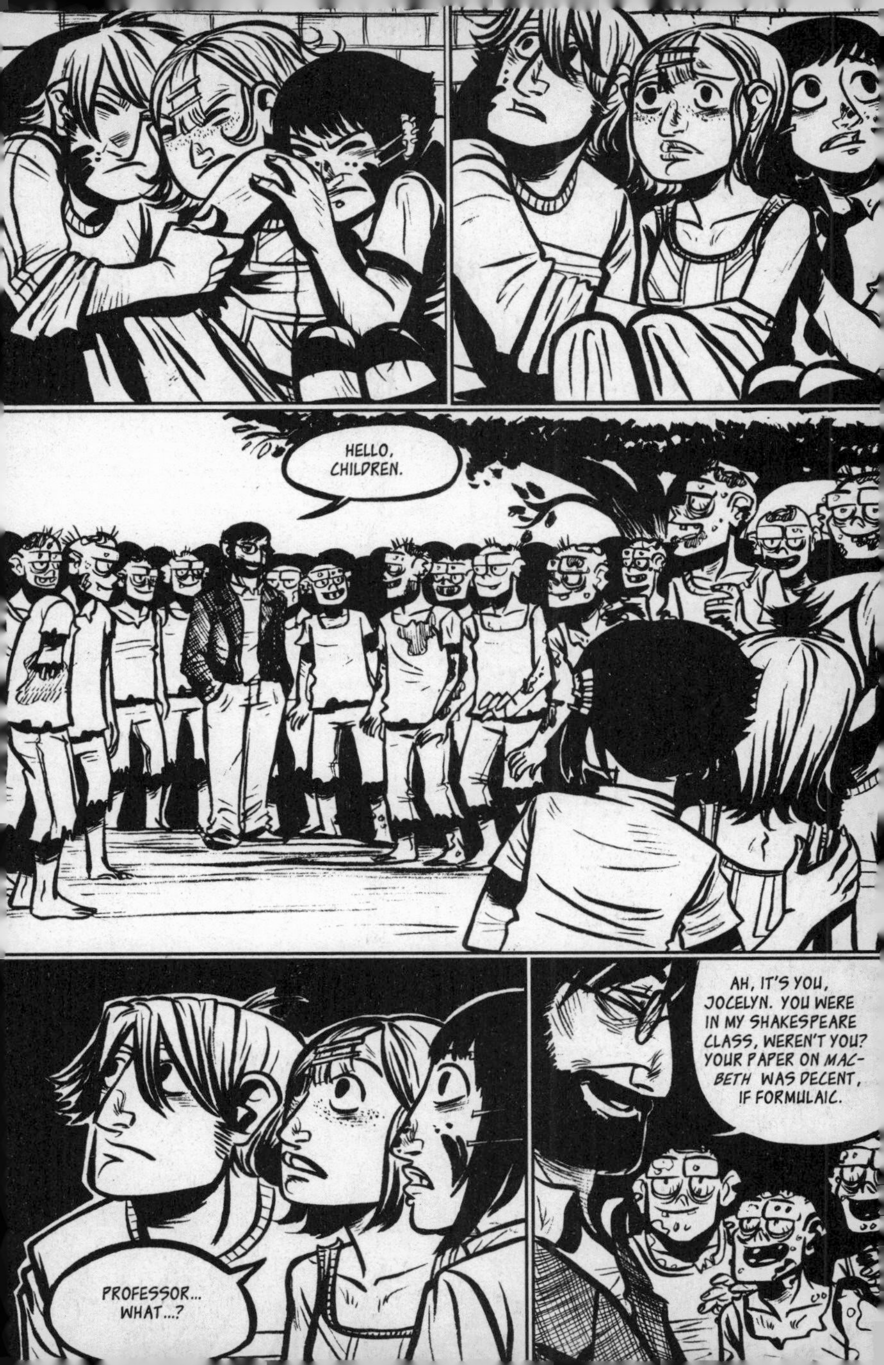
HELLO, CHILDREN.
PROFESSOR... WHAT...?
AH, IT'S YOU, JOCELYN. YOU WERE IN MY SHAKESPEARE CLASS, WEREN'T YOU? YOUR PAPER ON *MACBETH* WAS DECENT, IF FORMULAIC.

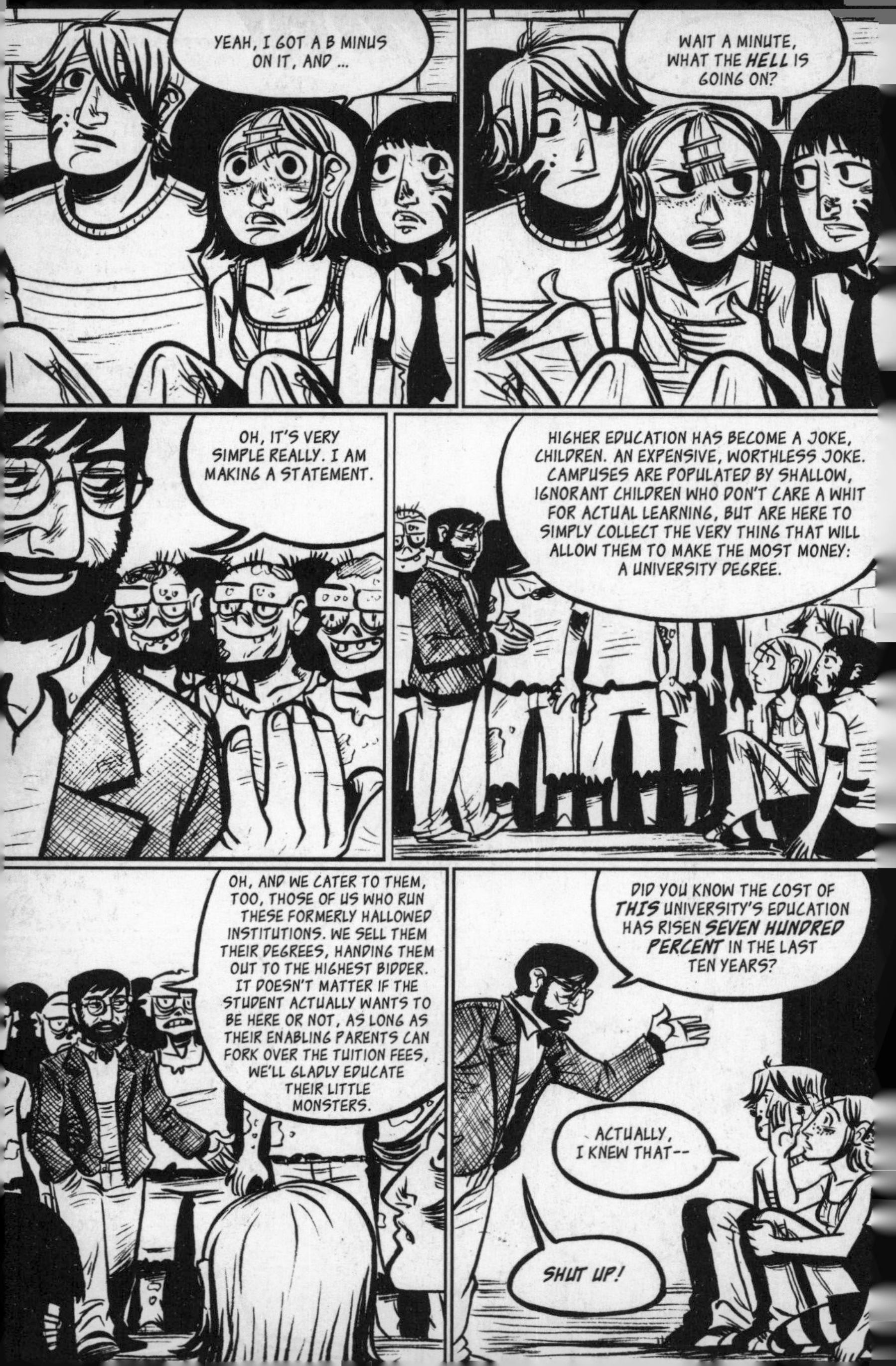
YEAH, I GOT A B MINUS ON IT, AND ...
WAIT A MINUTE, WHAT THE HELL IS GOING ON?
OH, IT'S VERY SIMPLE REALLY. I AM MAKING A STATEMENT.
HIGHER EDUCATION HAS BECOME A JOKE, CHILDREN. AN EXPENSIVE, WORTHLESS JOKE. CAMPUSES ARE POPULATED BY SHALLOW, IGNORANT CHILDREN WHO DON'T CARE A WHIT FOR ACTUAL LEARNING, BUT ARE HERE TO SIMPLY COLLECT THE VERY THING THAT WILL ALLOW THEM TO MAKE THE MOST MONEY: A UNIVERSITY DEGREE.
OH, AND WE CATER TO THEM, TOO, THOSE OF US WHO RUN THESE FORMERLY HALLOWED INSTITUTIONS. WE SELL THEM THEIR DEGREES, HANDING THEM OUT TO THE HIGHEST BIDDER. IT DOESN'T MATTER IF THE STUDENT ACTUALLY WANTS TO BE HERE OR NOT, AS LONG AS THEIR ENABLING PARENTS CAN FORK OVER THE TUITION FEES, WE'LL GLADLY EDUCATE THEIR LITTLE MONSTERS.
DID YOU KNOW THE COST OF THIS UNIVERSITY'S EDUCATION HAS RISEN SEVEN HUNDRED PERCENT IN THE LAST TEN YEARS?
ACTUALLY, I KNEW THAT--
SHUT UP!

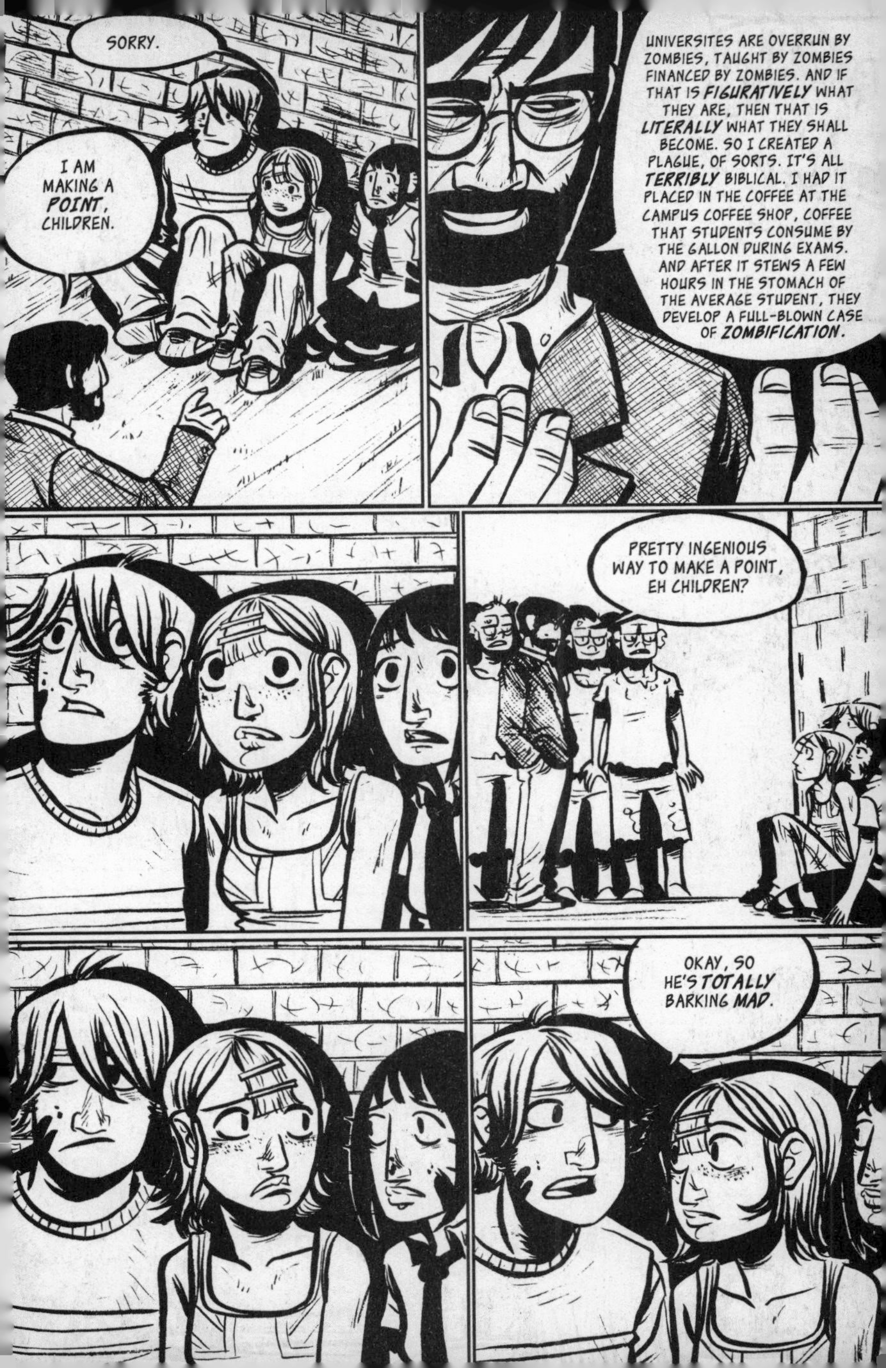
SORRY.
I AM MAKING A *POINT*, CHILDREN.
UNIVERSITES ARE OVERRUN BY ZOMBIES, TAUGHT BY ZOMBIES FINANCED BY ZOMBIES. AND IF THAT IS *FIGURATIVELY* WHAT THEY ARE, THEN THAT IS *LITERALLY* WHAT THEY SHALL BECOME. SO I CREATED A PLAGUE, OF SORTS. IT'S ALL *TERRIBLY* BIBLICAL. I HAD IT PLACED IN THE COFFEE AT THE CAMPUS COFFEE SHOP, COFFEE THAT STUDENTS CONSUME BY THE GALLON DURING EXAMS. AND AFTER IT STEWS A FEW HOURS IN THE STOMACH OF THE AVERAGE STUDENT, THEY DEVELOP A FULL-BLOWN CASE OF *ZOMBIFICATION*.
PRETTY INGENIOUS WAY TO MAKE A POINT, EH CHILDREN?
OKAY, SO HE'S *TOTALLY* BARKING *MAD*.

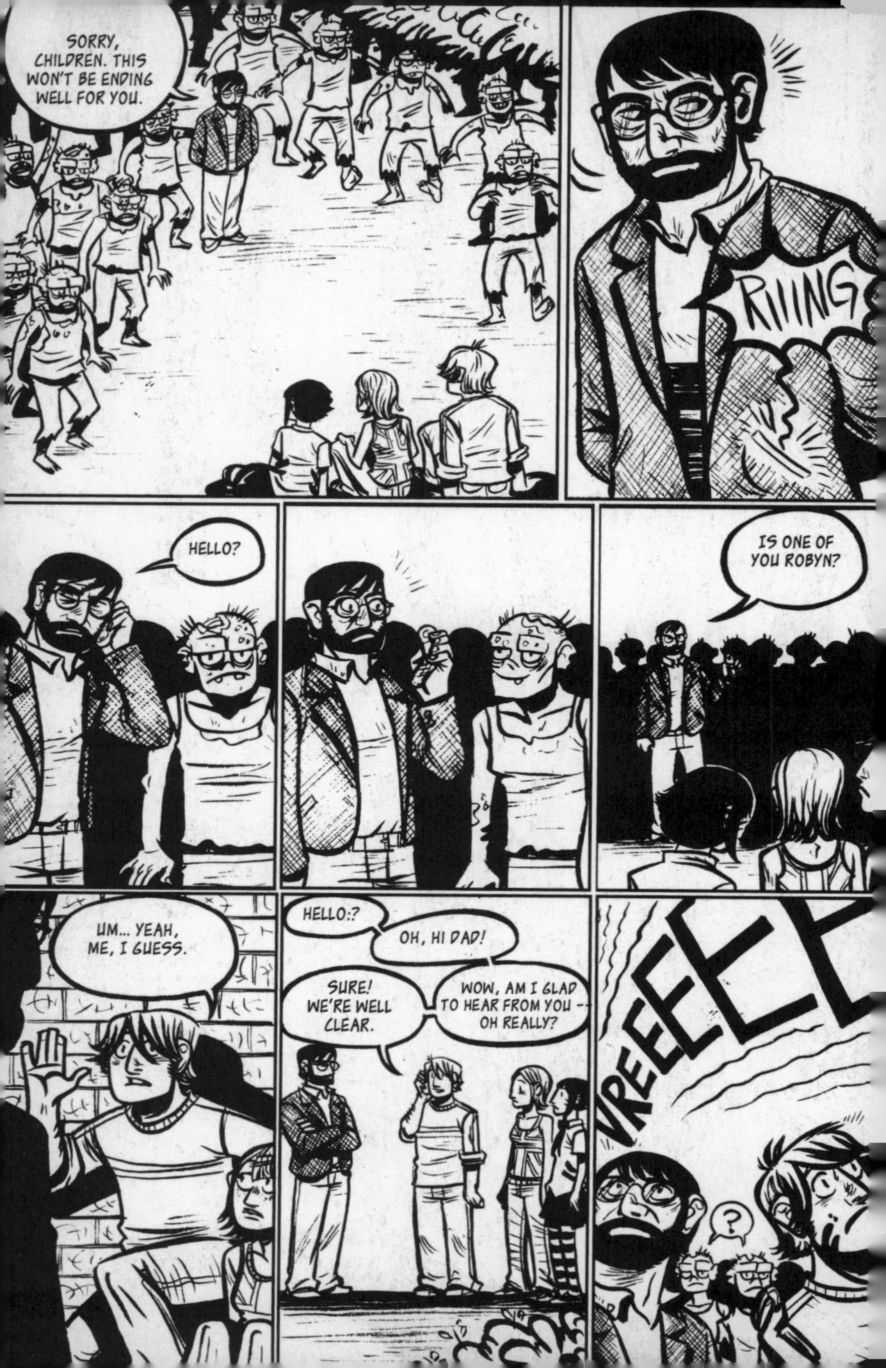
SORRY, CHILDREN. THIS WON'T BE ENDING WELL FOR YOU.
RIIING
HELLO?
IS ONE OF YOU ROBYN?
UM... YEAH, ME, I GUESS.
HELLO:?
OH, HI DAD!
WOW, AM I GLAD TO HEAR FROM YOU -- OH REALLY?
SURE! WE'RE WELL CLEAR.
VREEEEEE
?

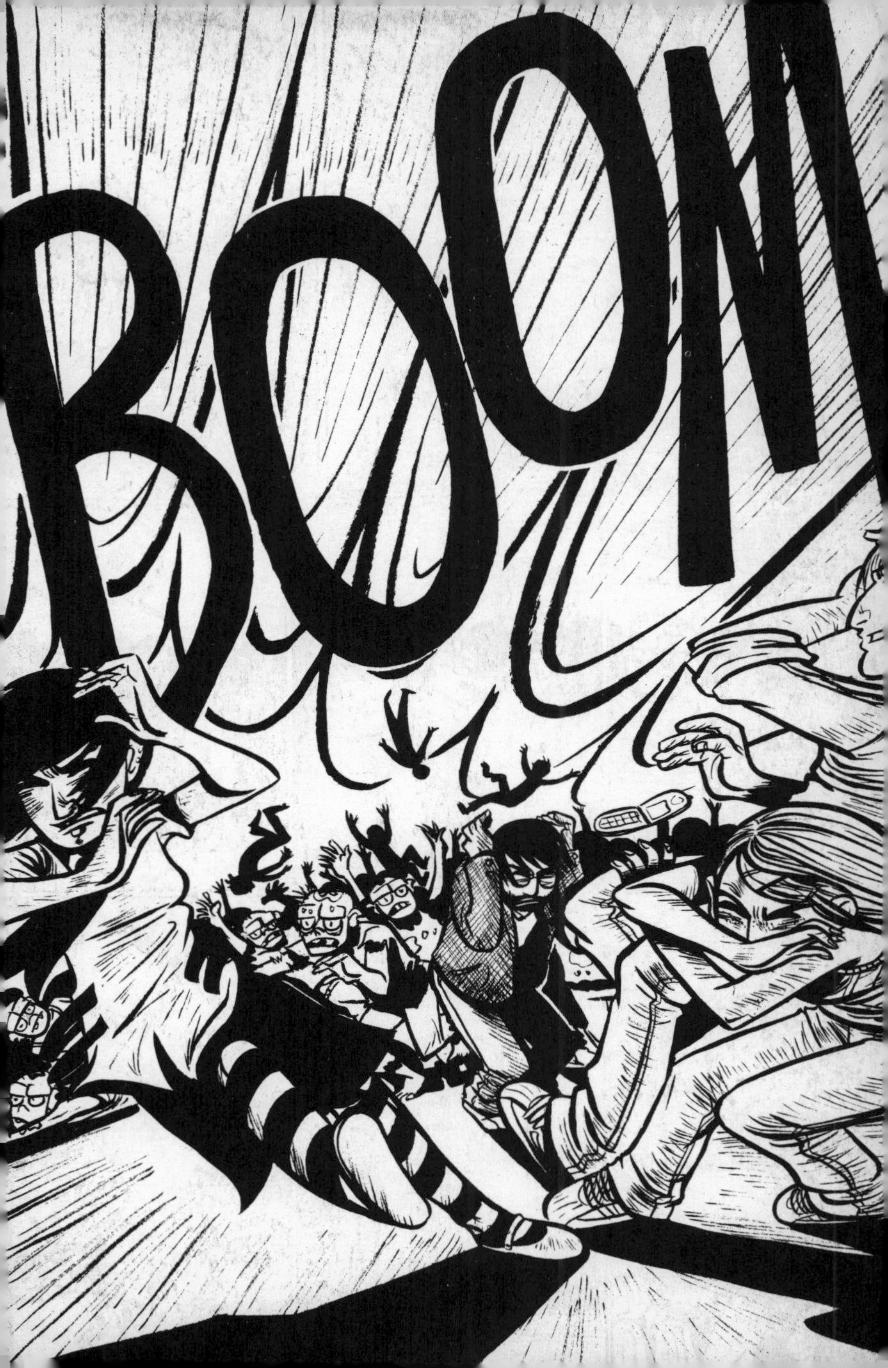
BOOM

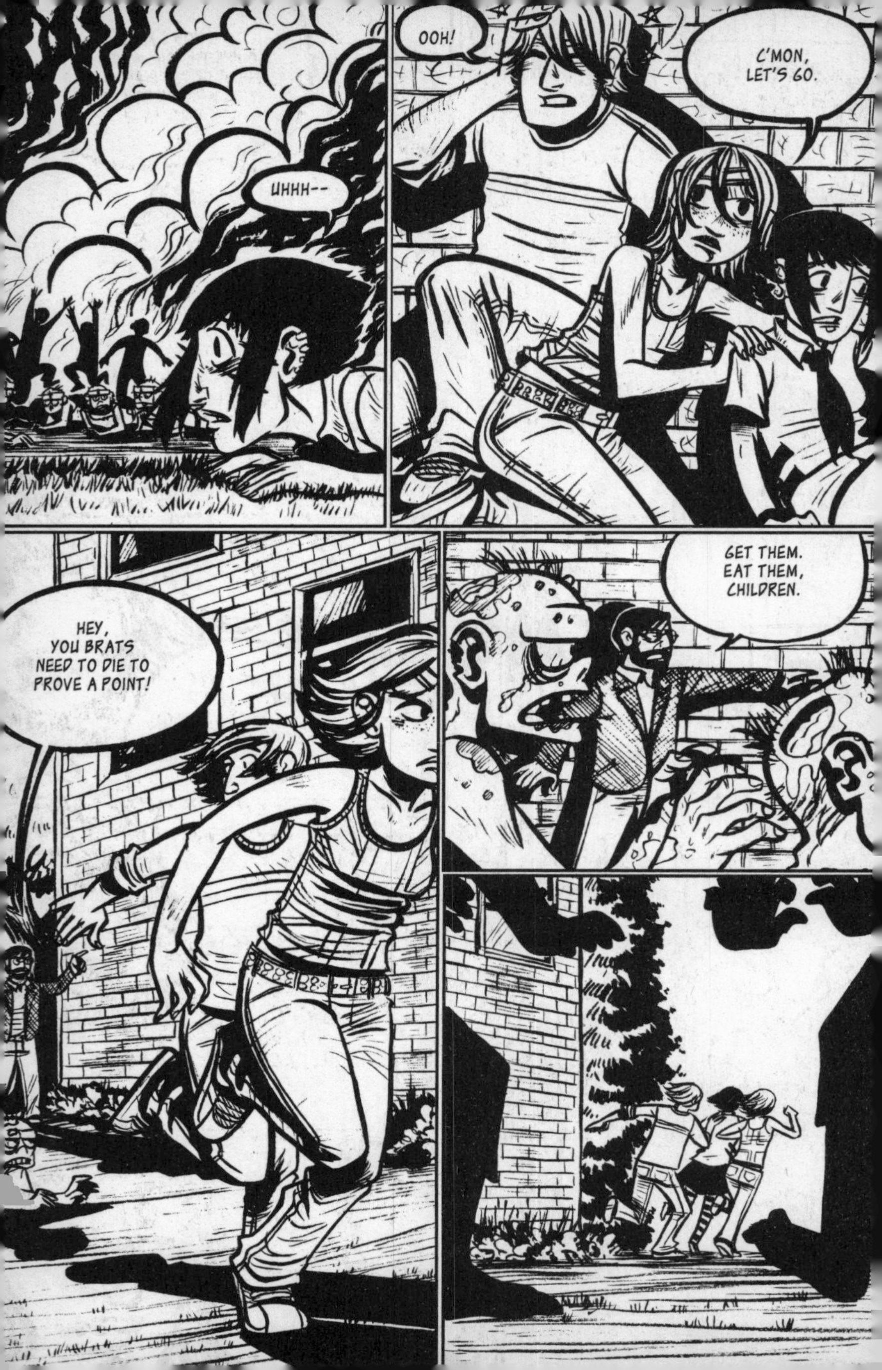
UHHH--
OOH!
C'MON, LET'S GO.
HEY, YOU BRATS NEED TO DIE TO PROVE A POINT!
GET THEM. EAT THEM, CHILDREN.

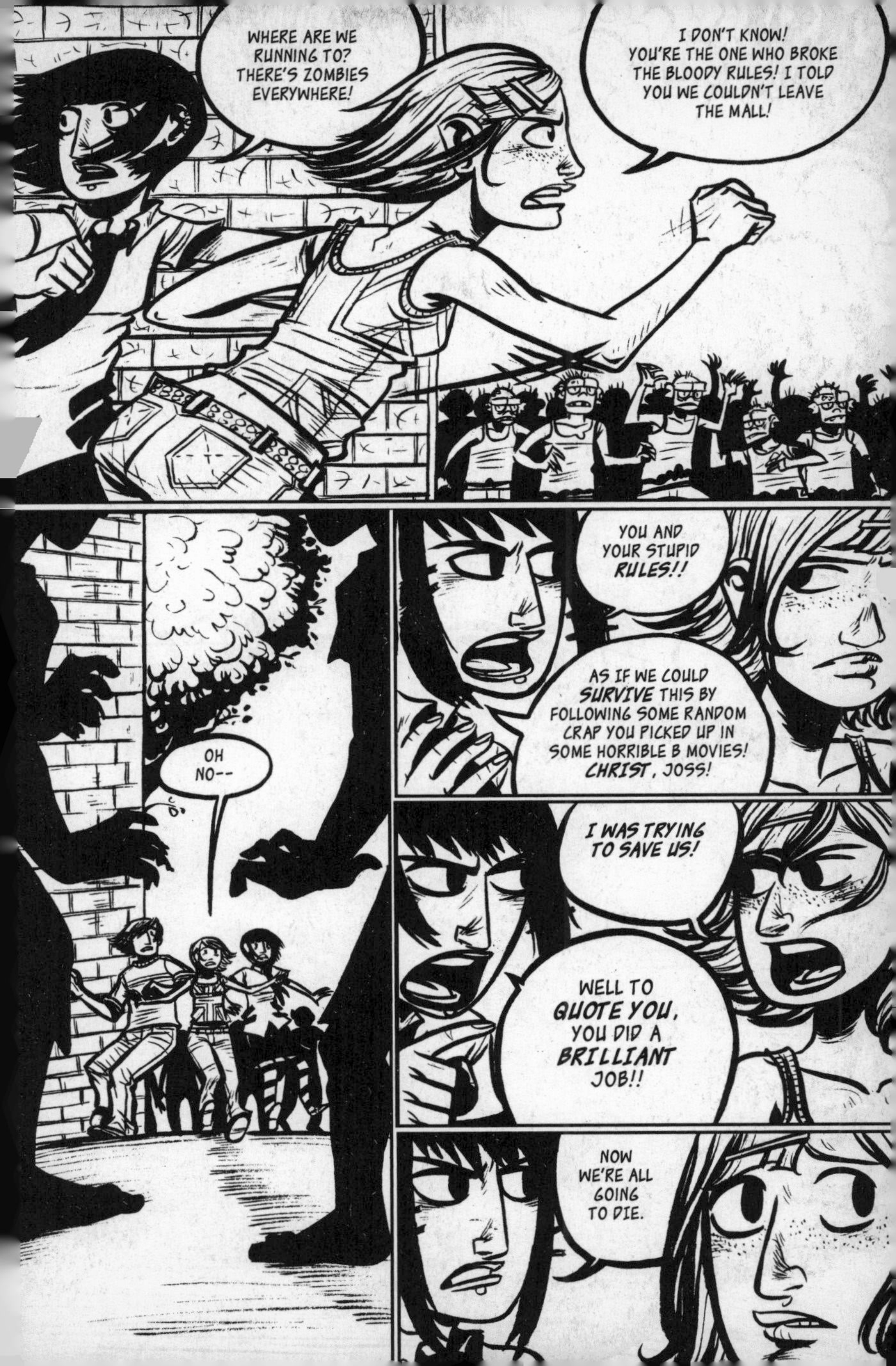
WHERE ARE WE RUNNING TO? THERE'S ZOMBIES EVERYWHERE!
I DON'T KNOW! YOU'RE THE ONE WHO BROKE THE BLOODY RULES! I TOLD YOU WE COULDN'T LEAVE THE MALL!
OH NO--
YOU AND YOUR STUPID RULES!!
AS IF WE COULD SURVIVE THIS BY FOLLOWING SOME RANDOM CRAP YOU PICKED UP IN SOME HORRIBLE B MOVIES! CHRIST, JOSS!
I WAS TRYING TO SAVE US!
WELL TO QUOTE YOU, YOU DID A BRILLIANT JOB!!
NOW WE'RE ALL GOING TO DIE.

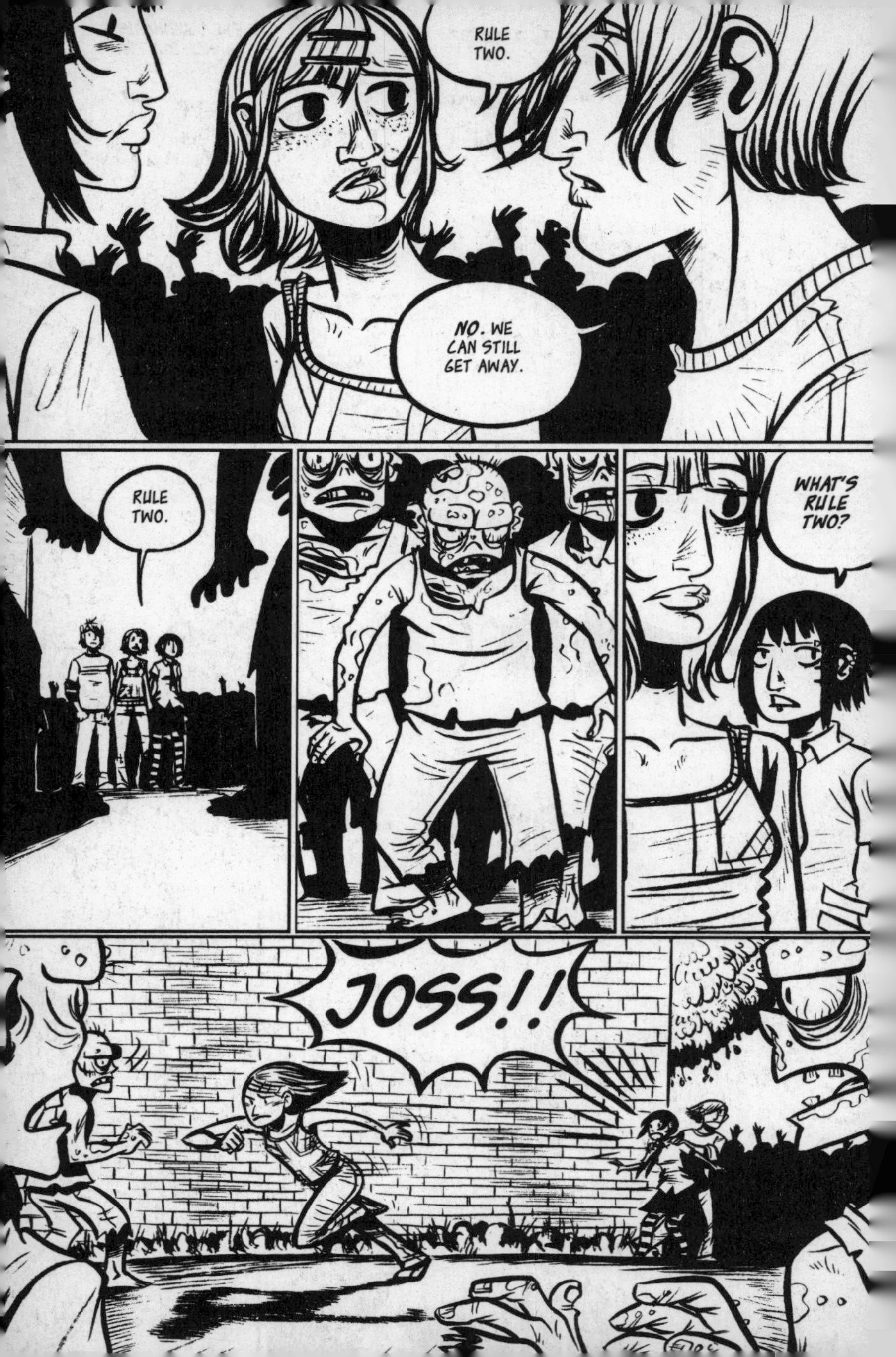
RULE TWO.
NO. WE CAN STILL GET AWAY.
RULE TWO.
WHAT'S RULE TWO?
JOSS!!

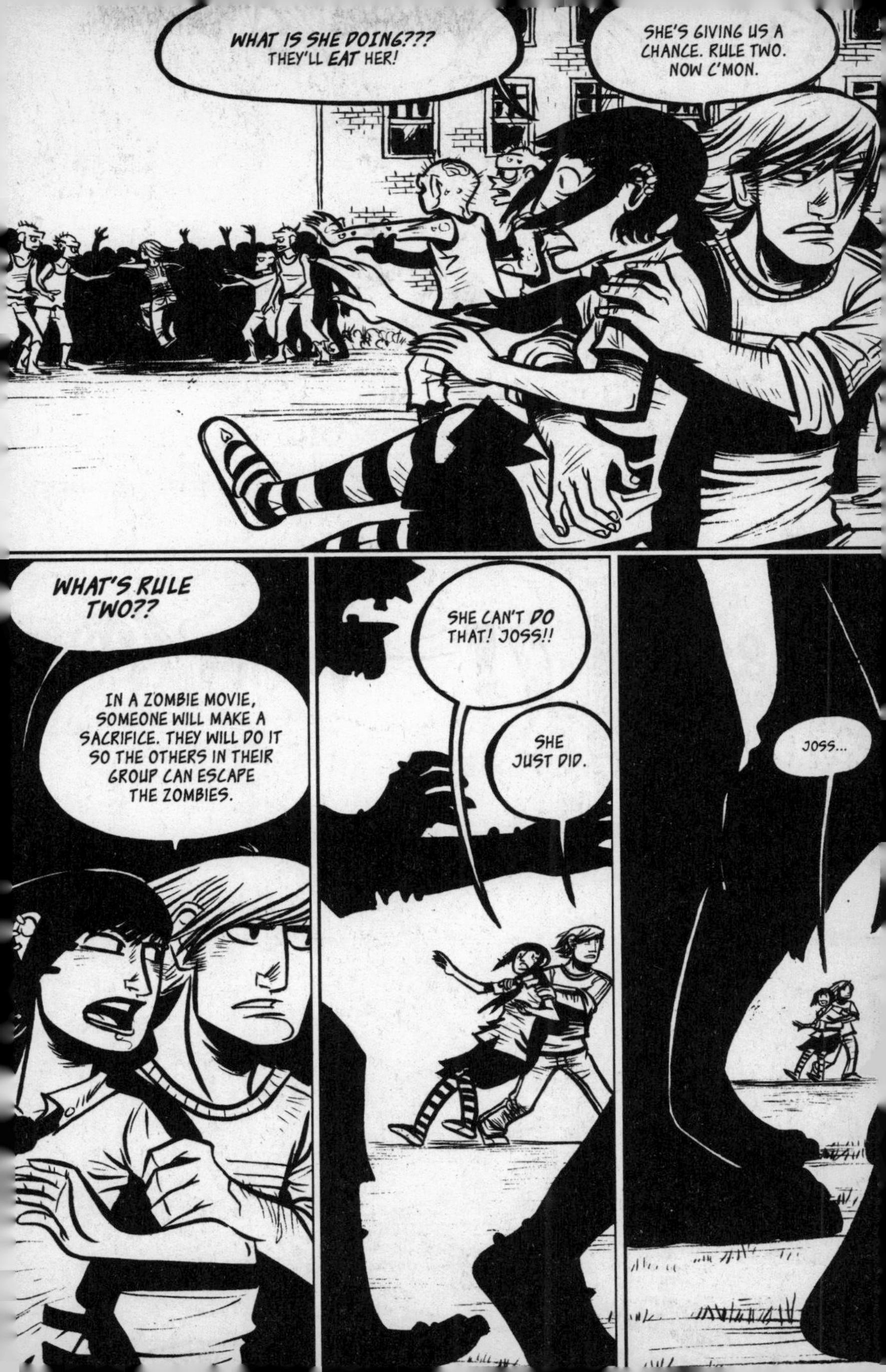
WHAT IS SHE DOING??? THEY'LL EAT HER!
SHE'S GIVING US A CHANCE. RULE TWO. NOW C'MON.
WHAT'S RULE TWO??
IN A ZOMBIE MOVIE, SOMEONE WILL MAKE A SACRIFICE. THEY WILL DO IT SO THE OTHERS IN THEIR GROUP CAN ESCAPE THE ZOMBIES.
SHE CAN'T DO THAT! JOSS!!
SHE JUST DID.
JOSS...

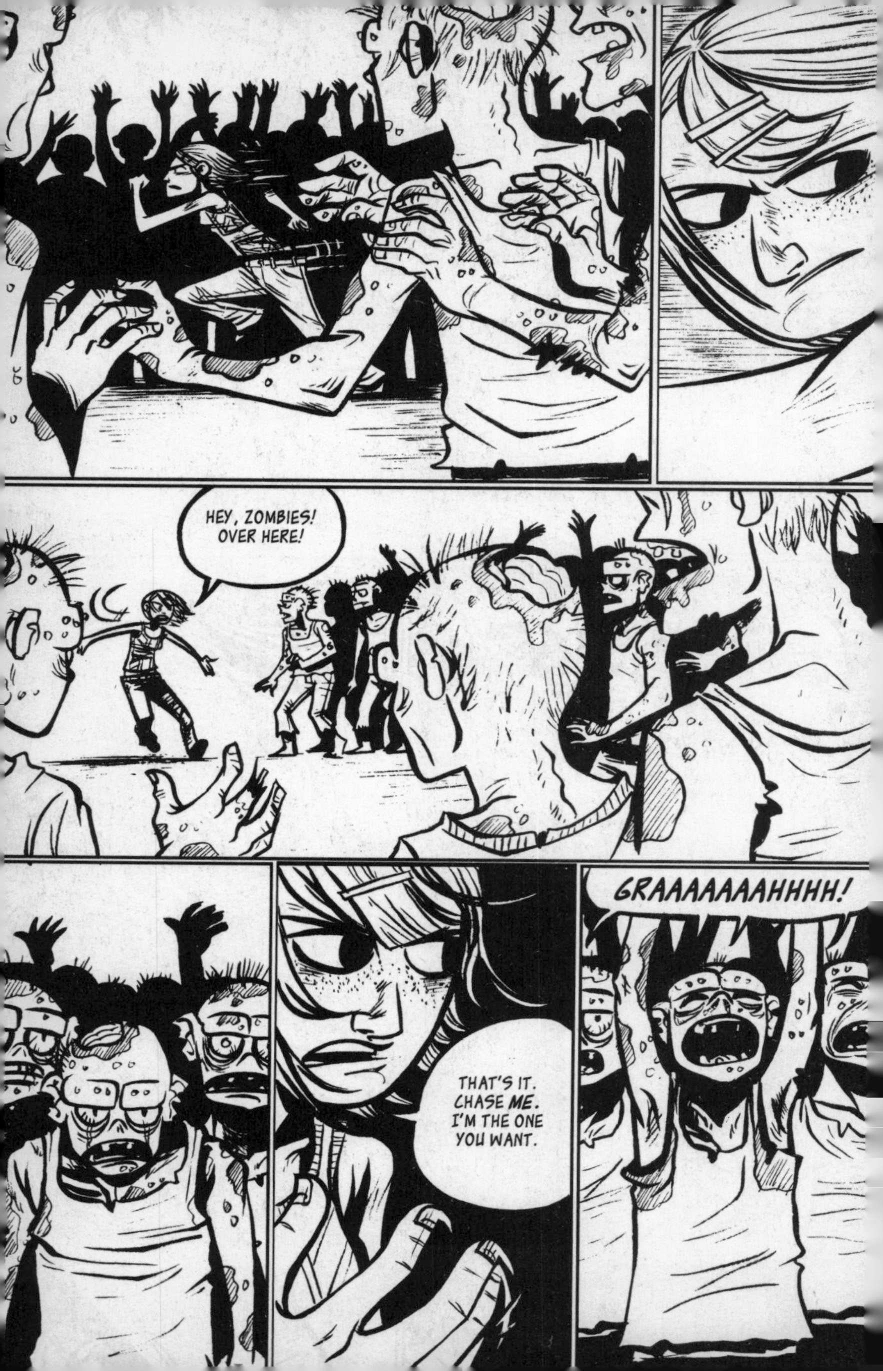
HEY, ZOMBIES! OVER HERE!
THAT'S IT. CHASE ME. I'M THE ONE YOU WANT.
GRAAAAAAAHHHH!

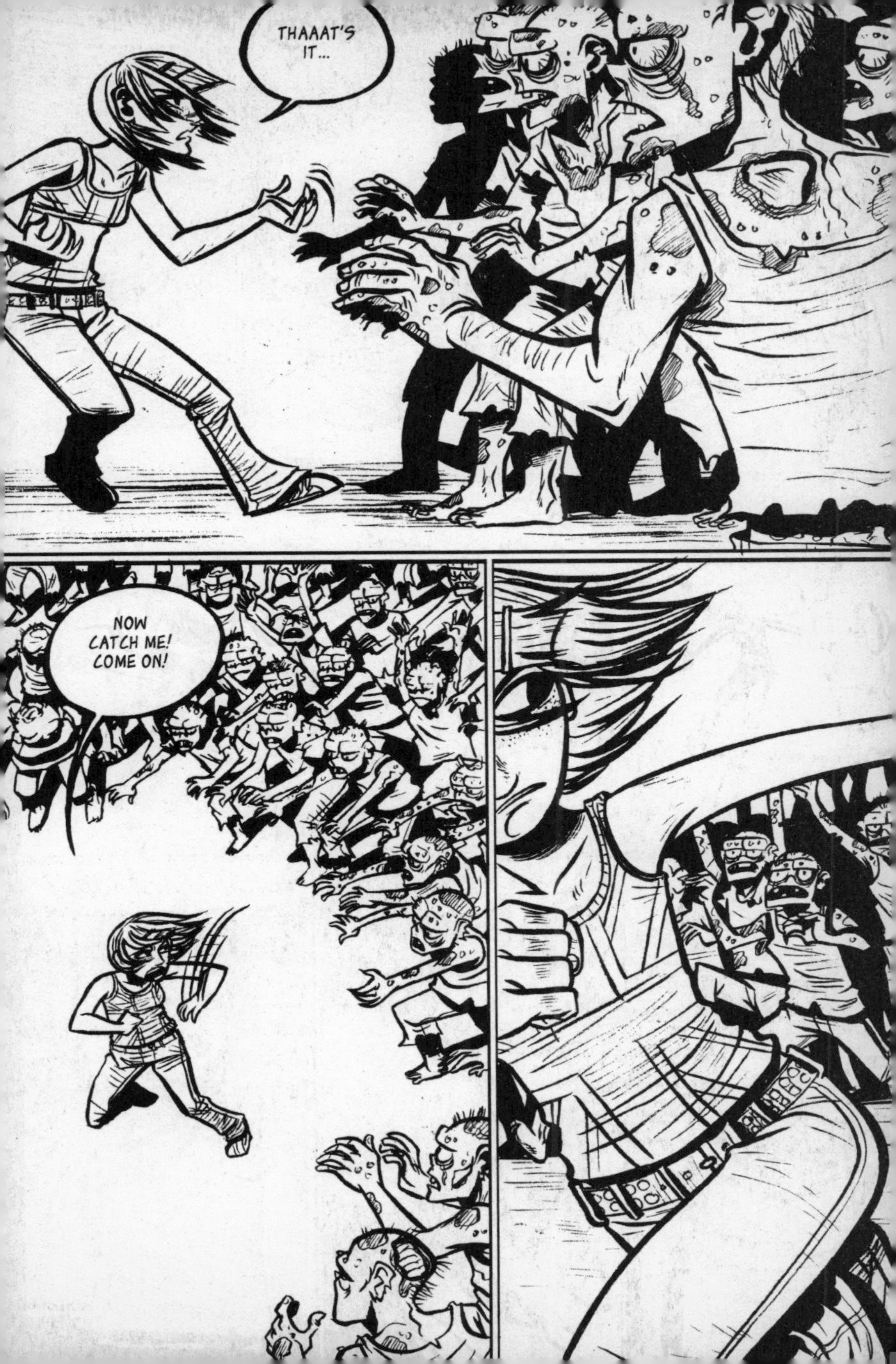
THAAAT'S IT...
NOW CATCH ME! COME ON!

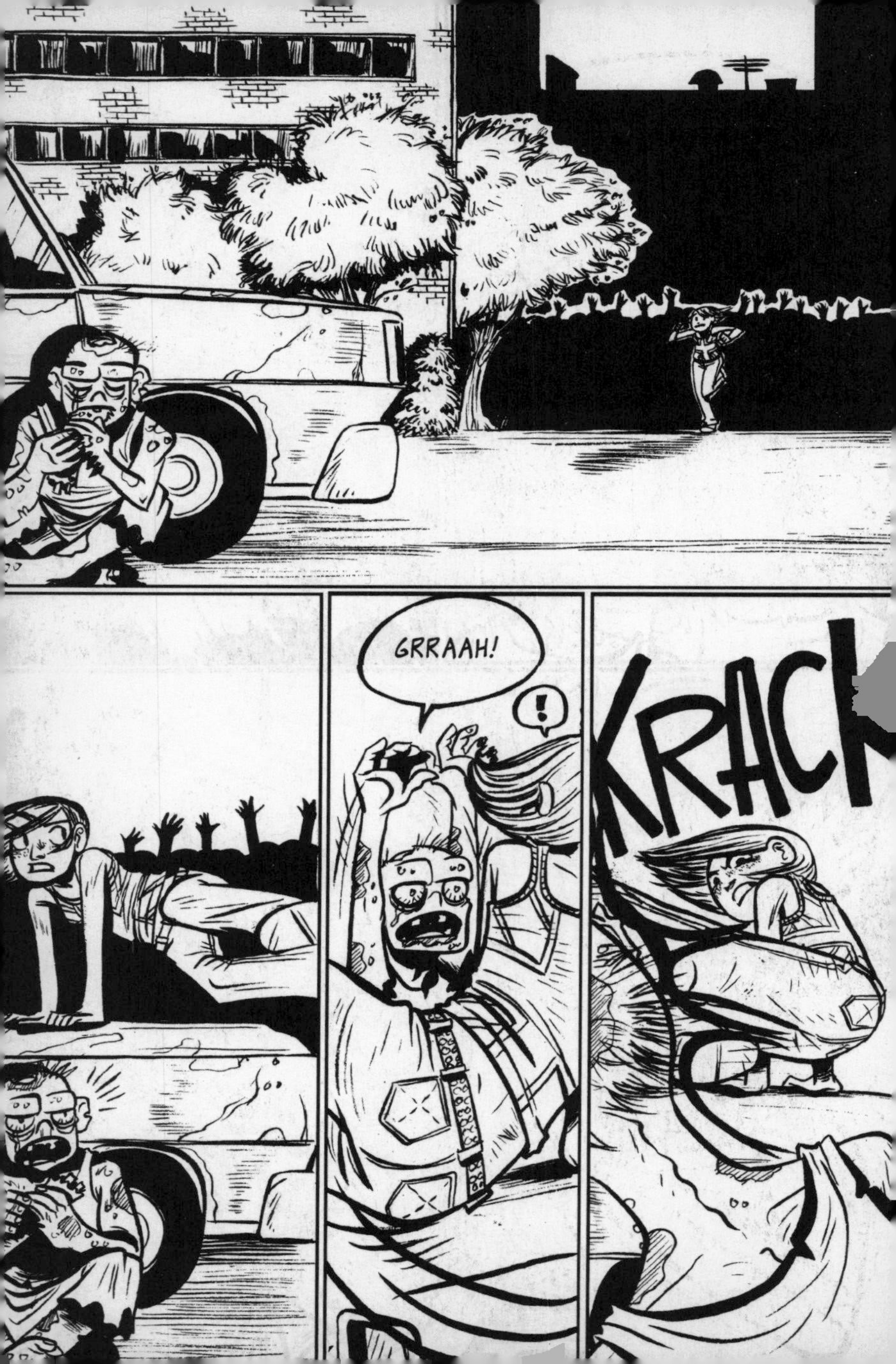
GRRAAH!
!
KRACK

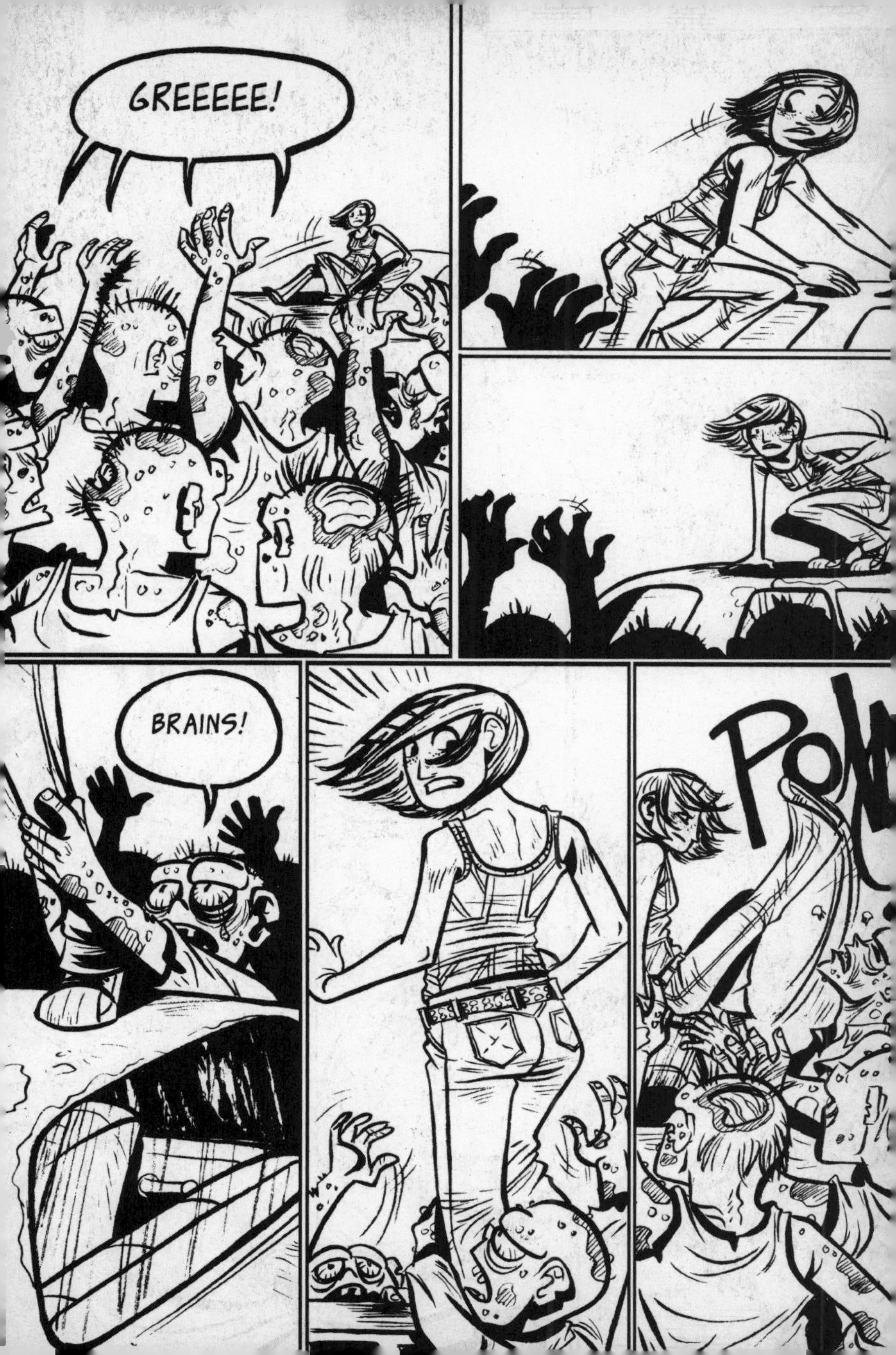
GREEEEE!
BRAINS!
PO

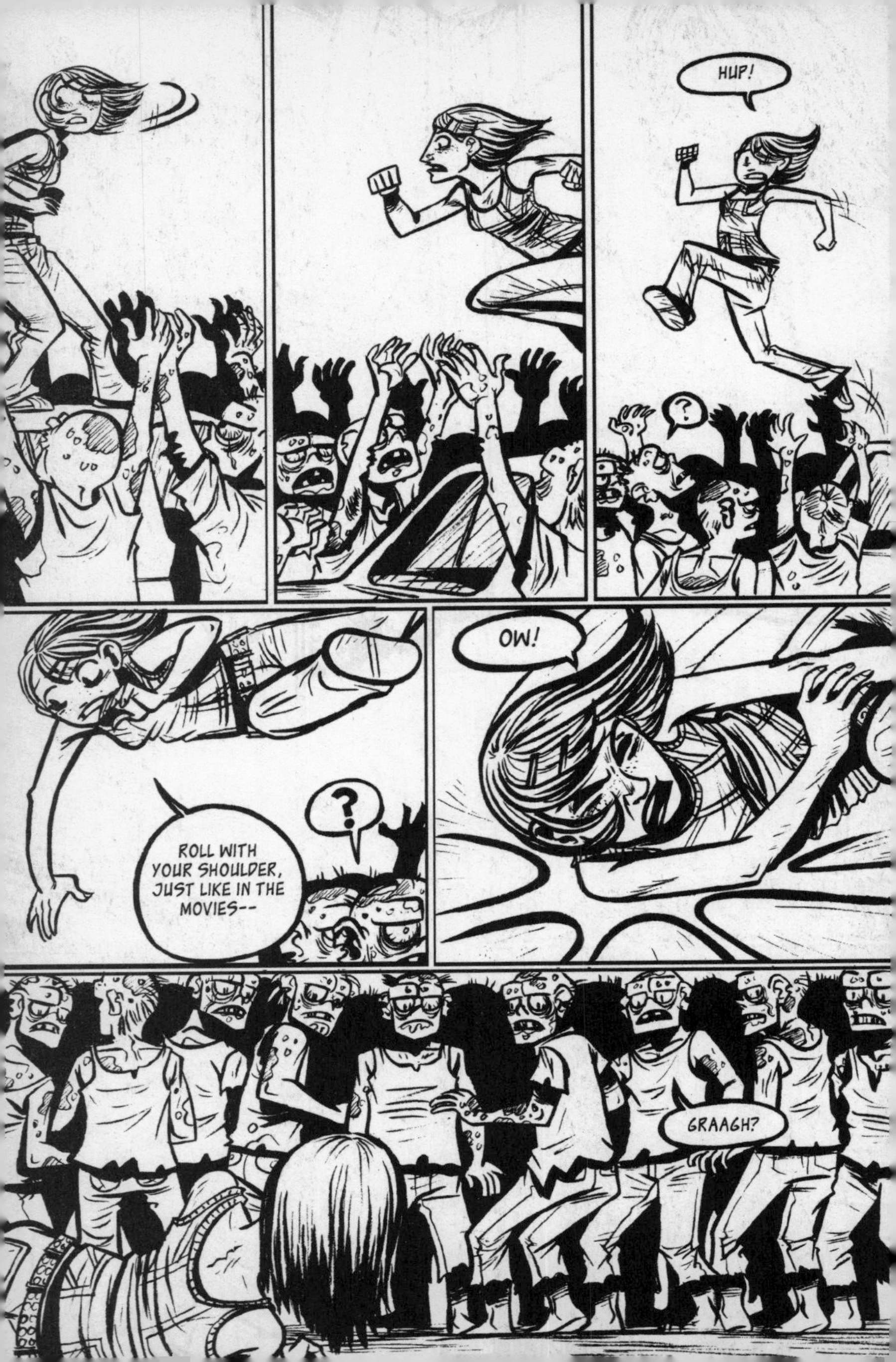
HUP!
?
ROLL WITH YOUR SHOULDER, JUST LIKE IN THE MOVIES--
?
OW!
GRAAGH?

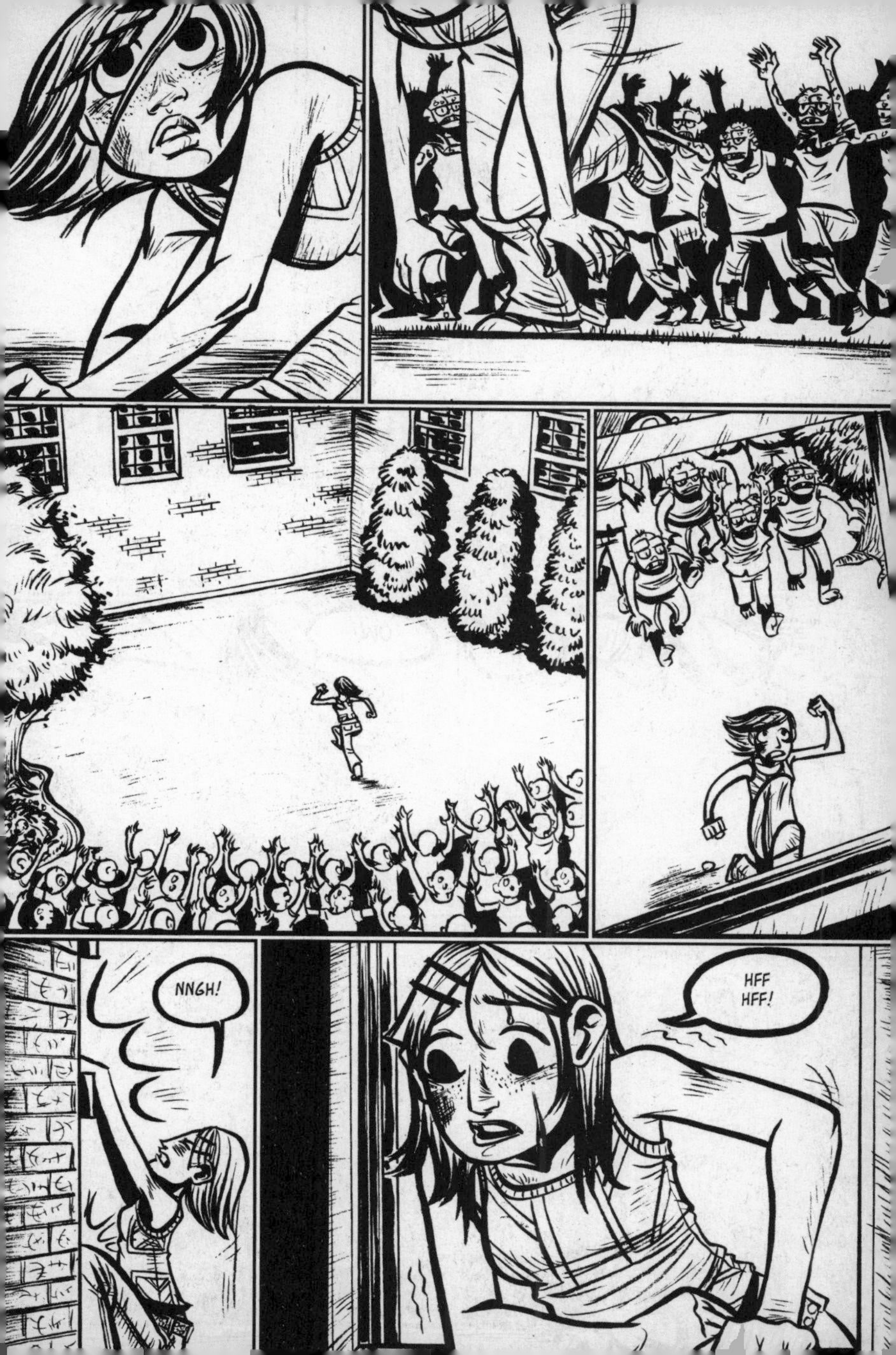
NNGH!
HFF HFF!

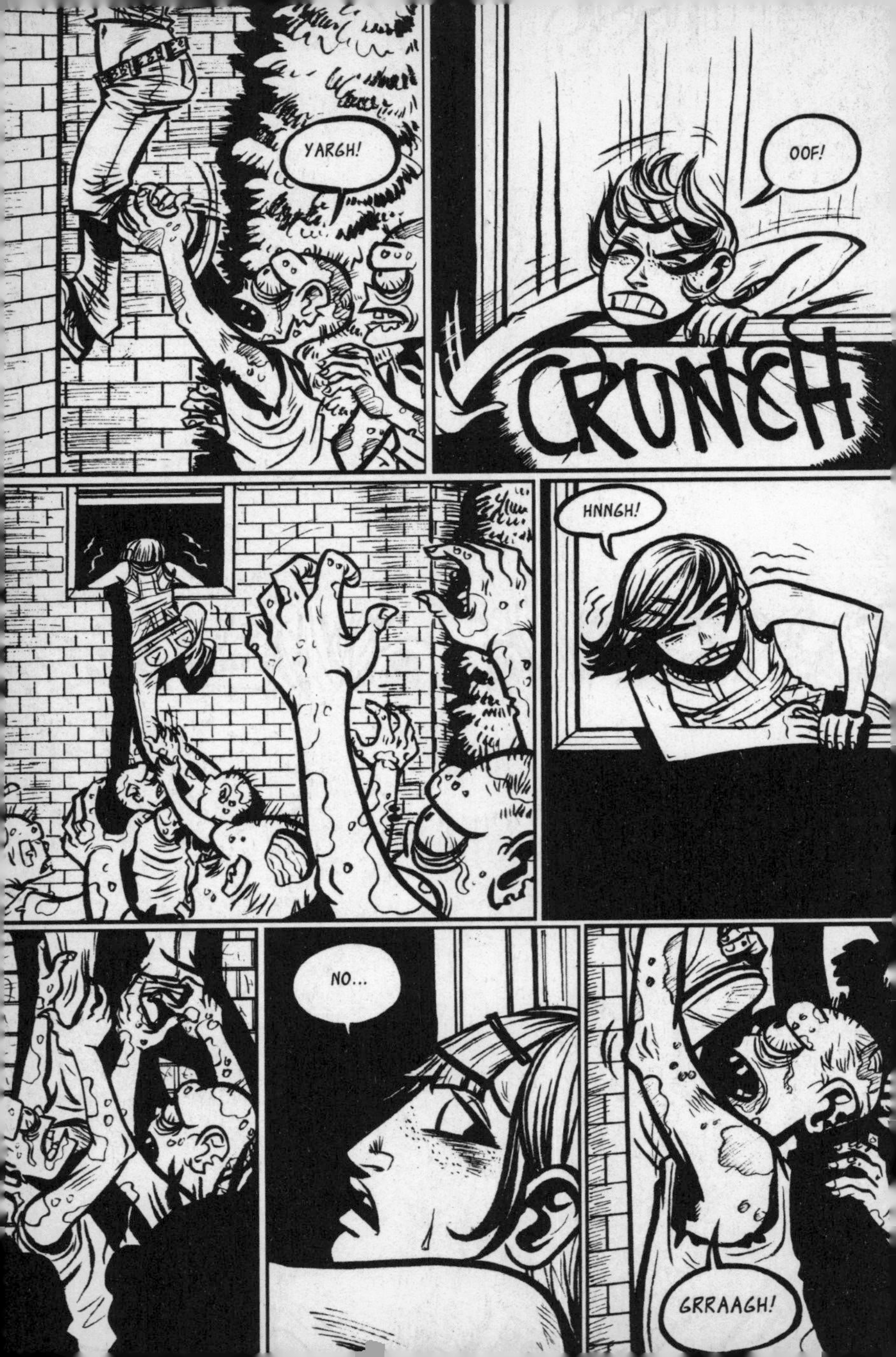
YARGH!
OOF!
CRUNCH
HNNGH!
NO...
GRRAAGH!

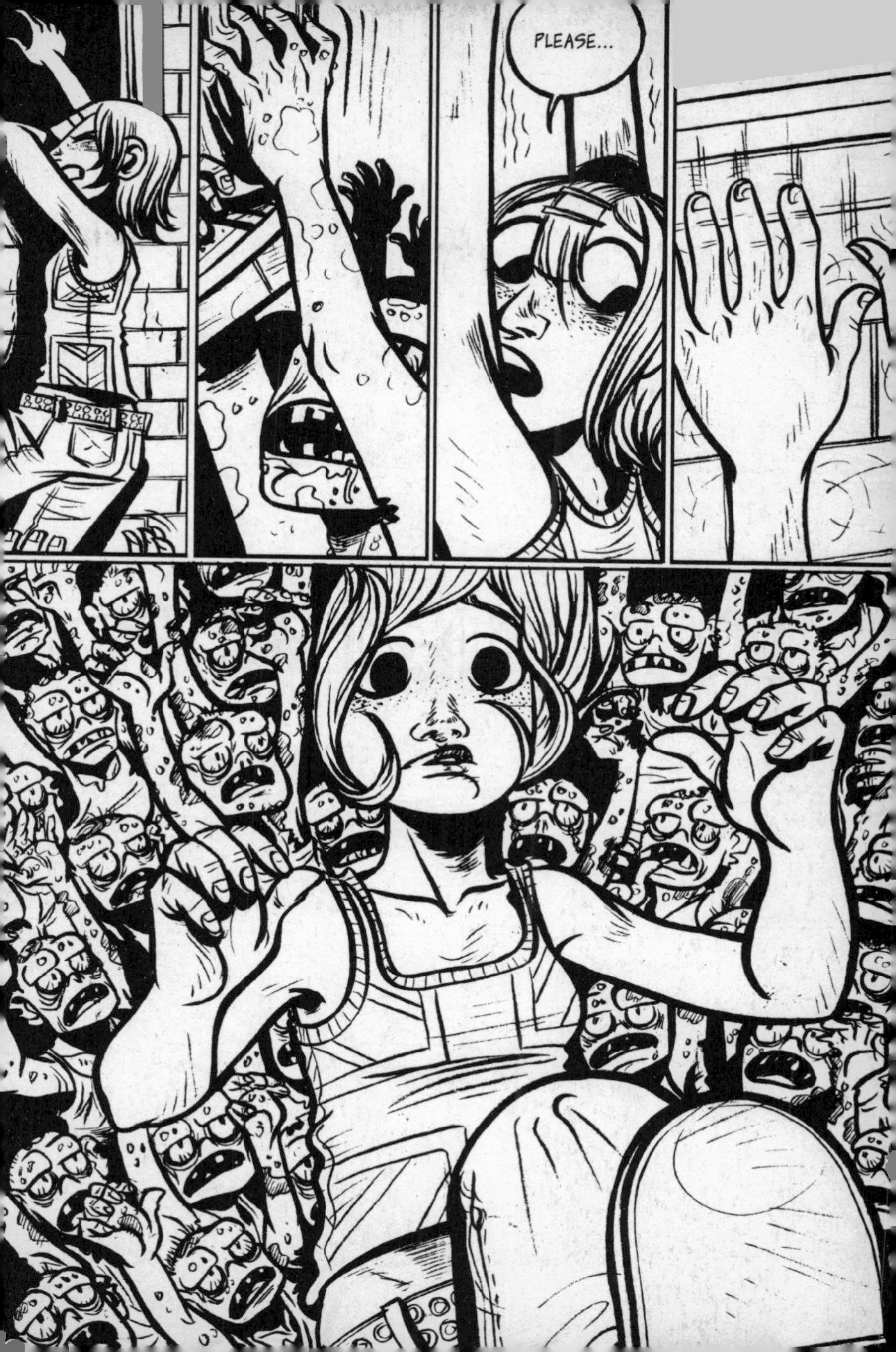
PLEASE...

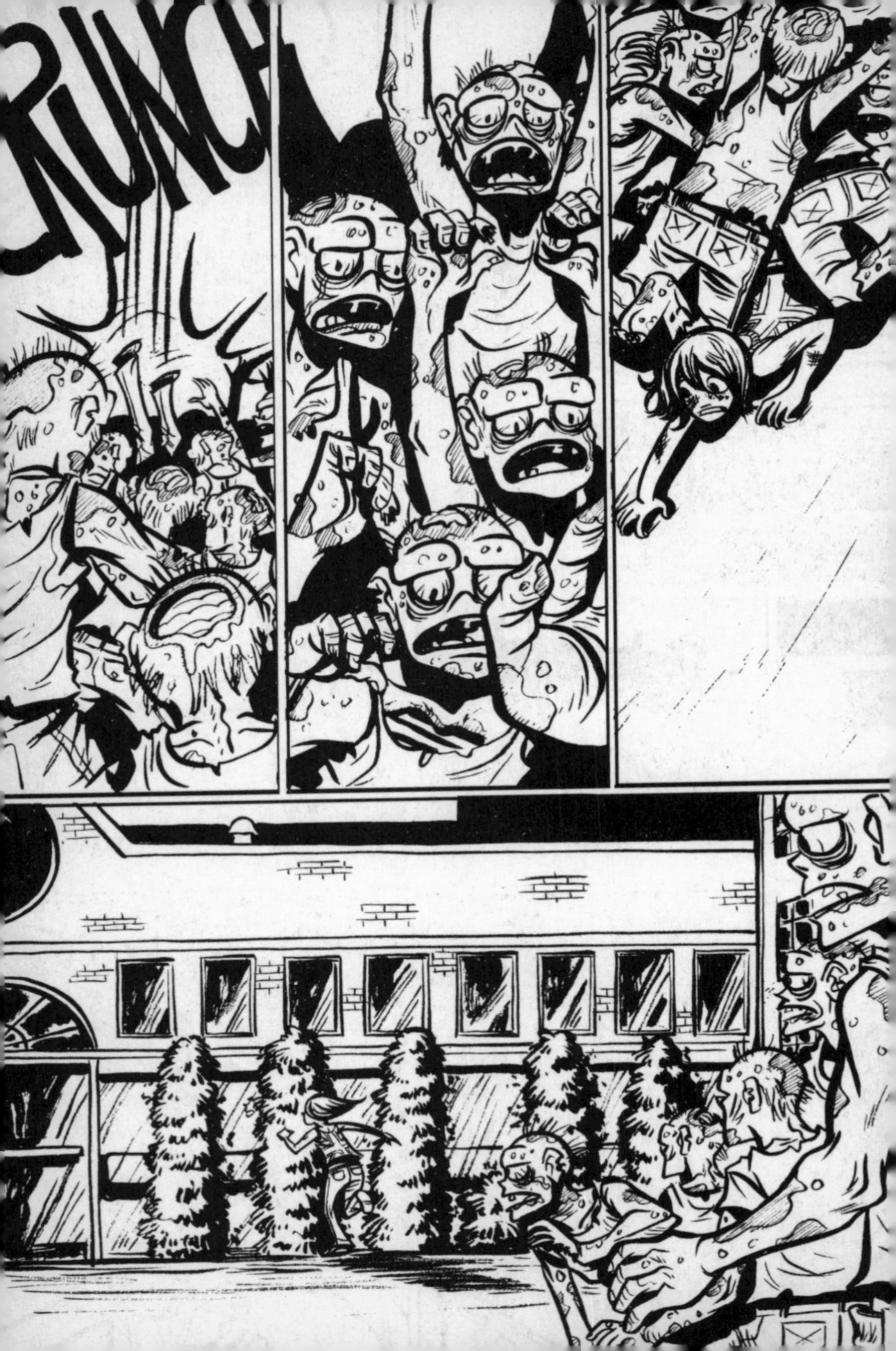

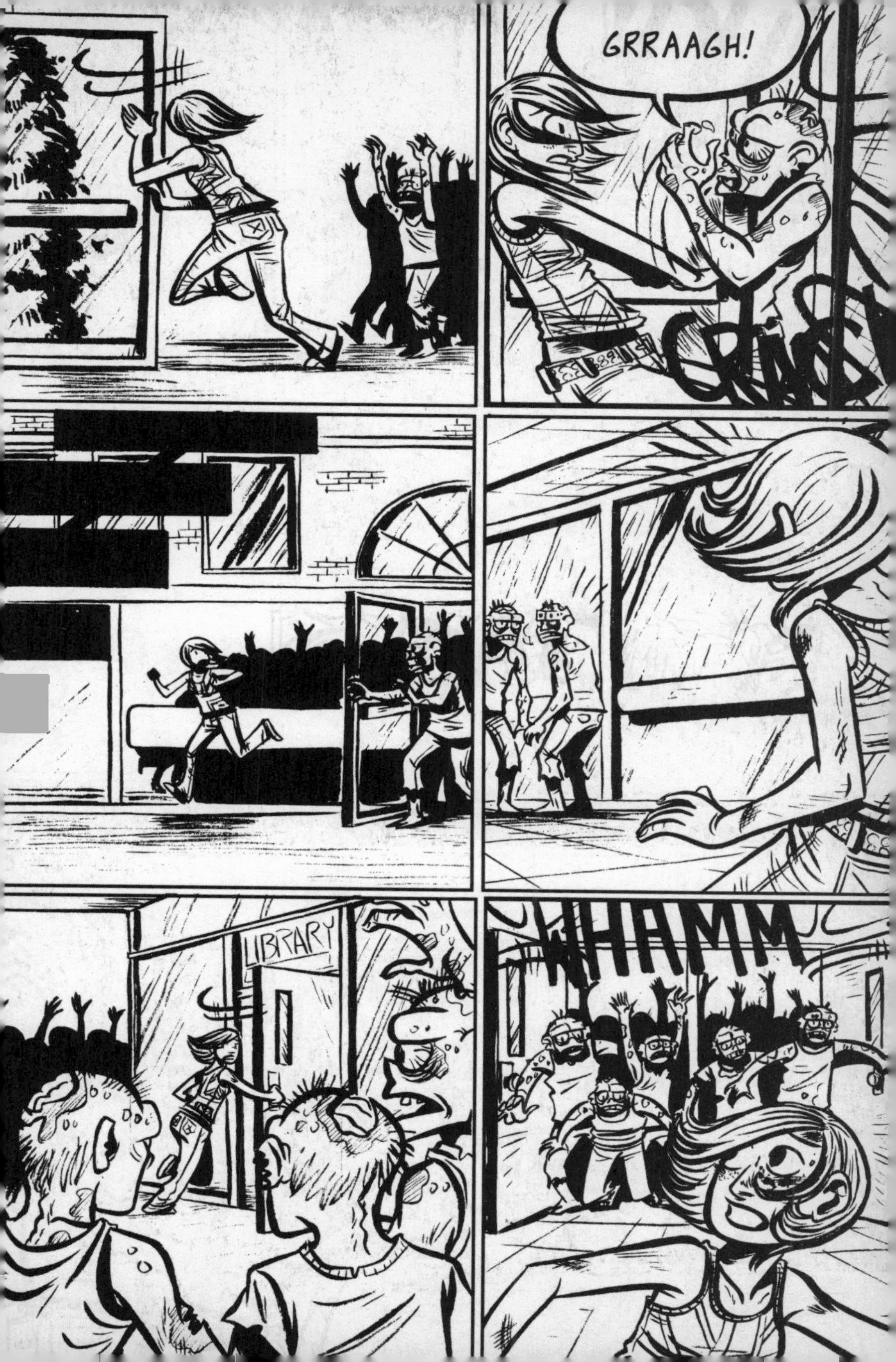
GRRAAGH!
LIBRARY
WHAMM

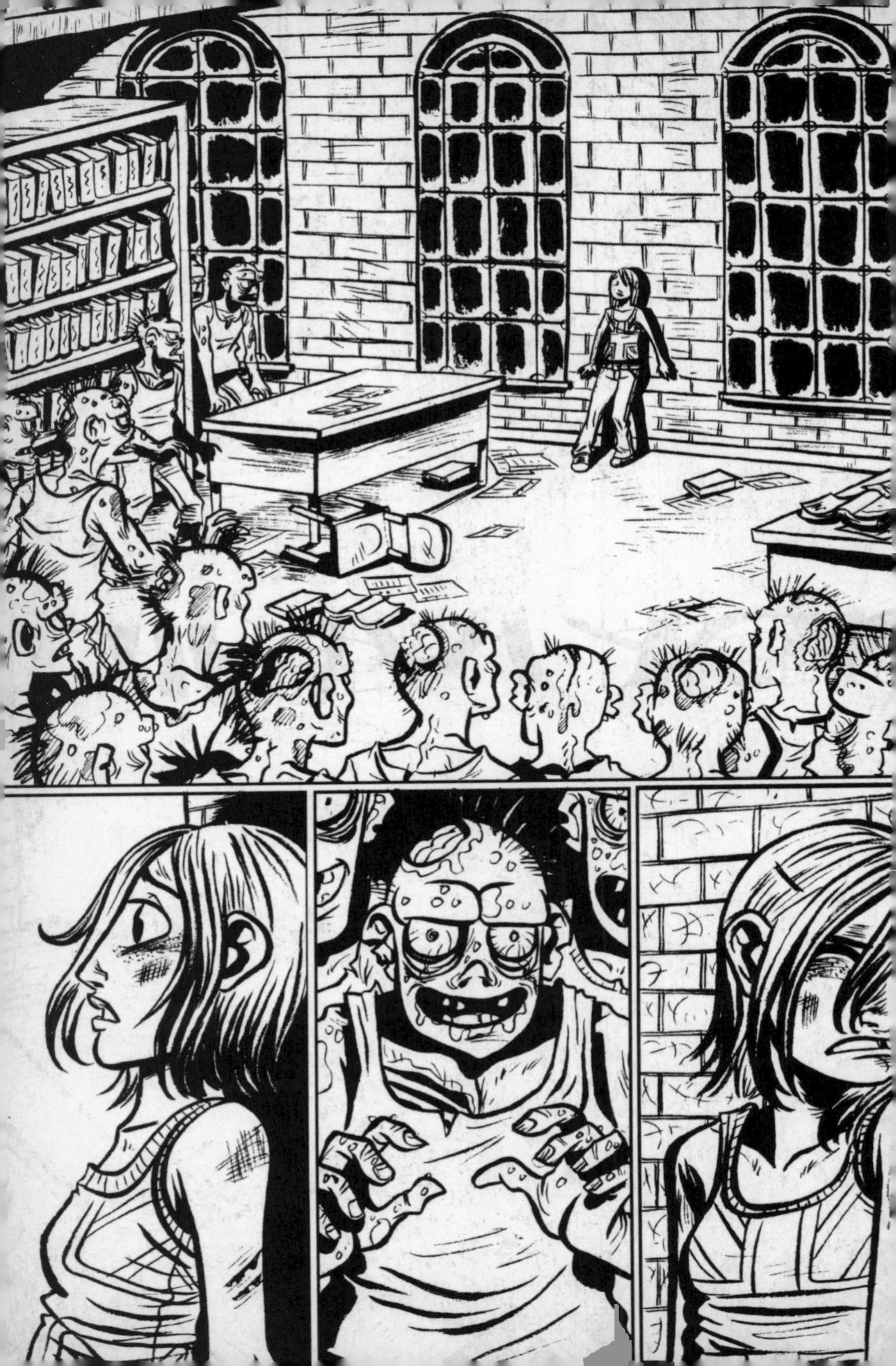

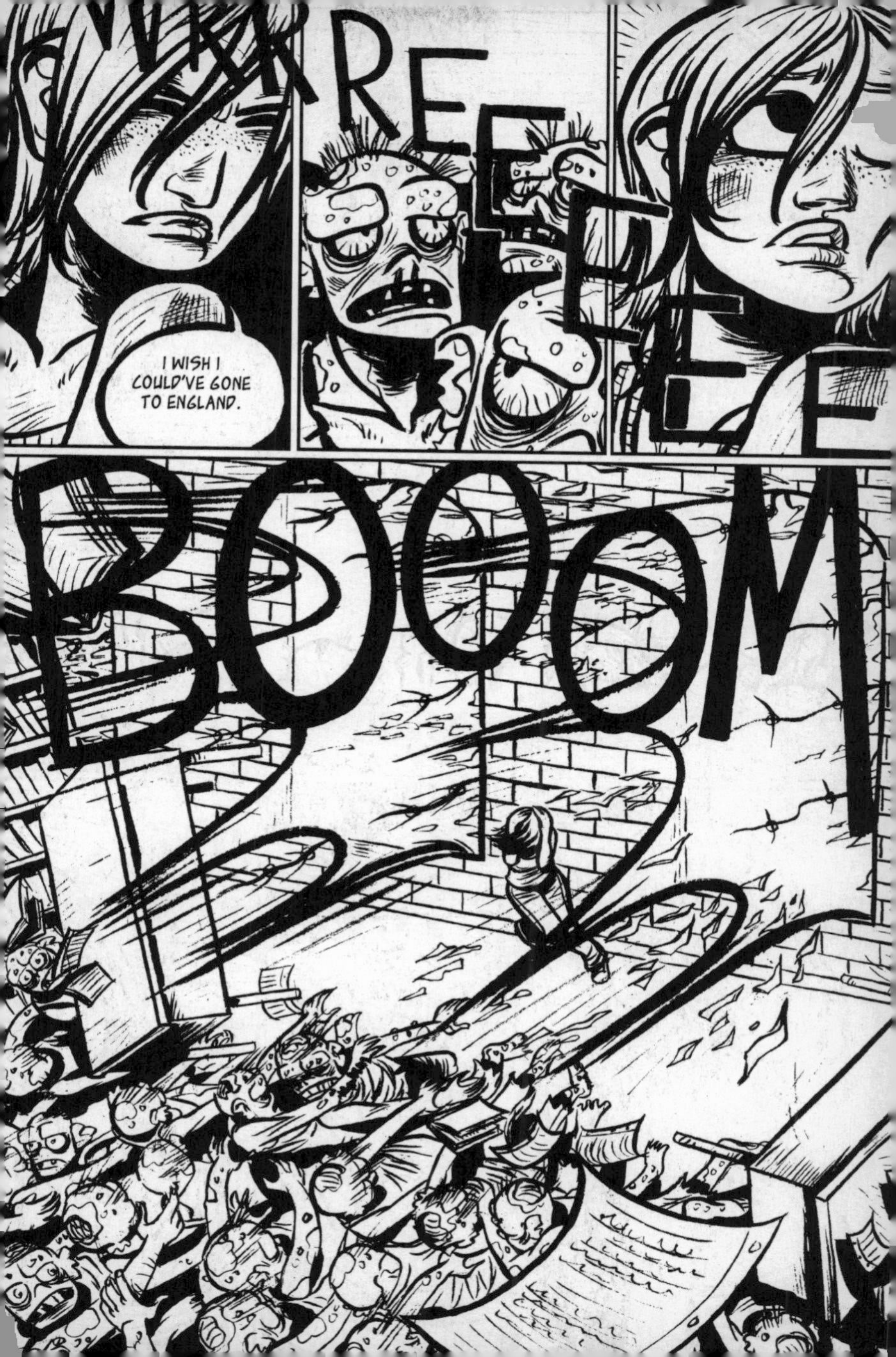
I WISH I COULD'VE GONE TO ENGLAND.
BOOOM

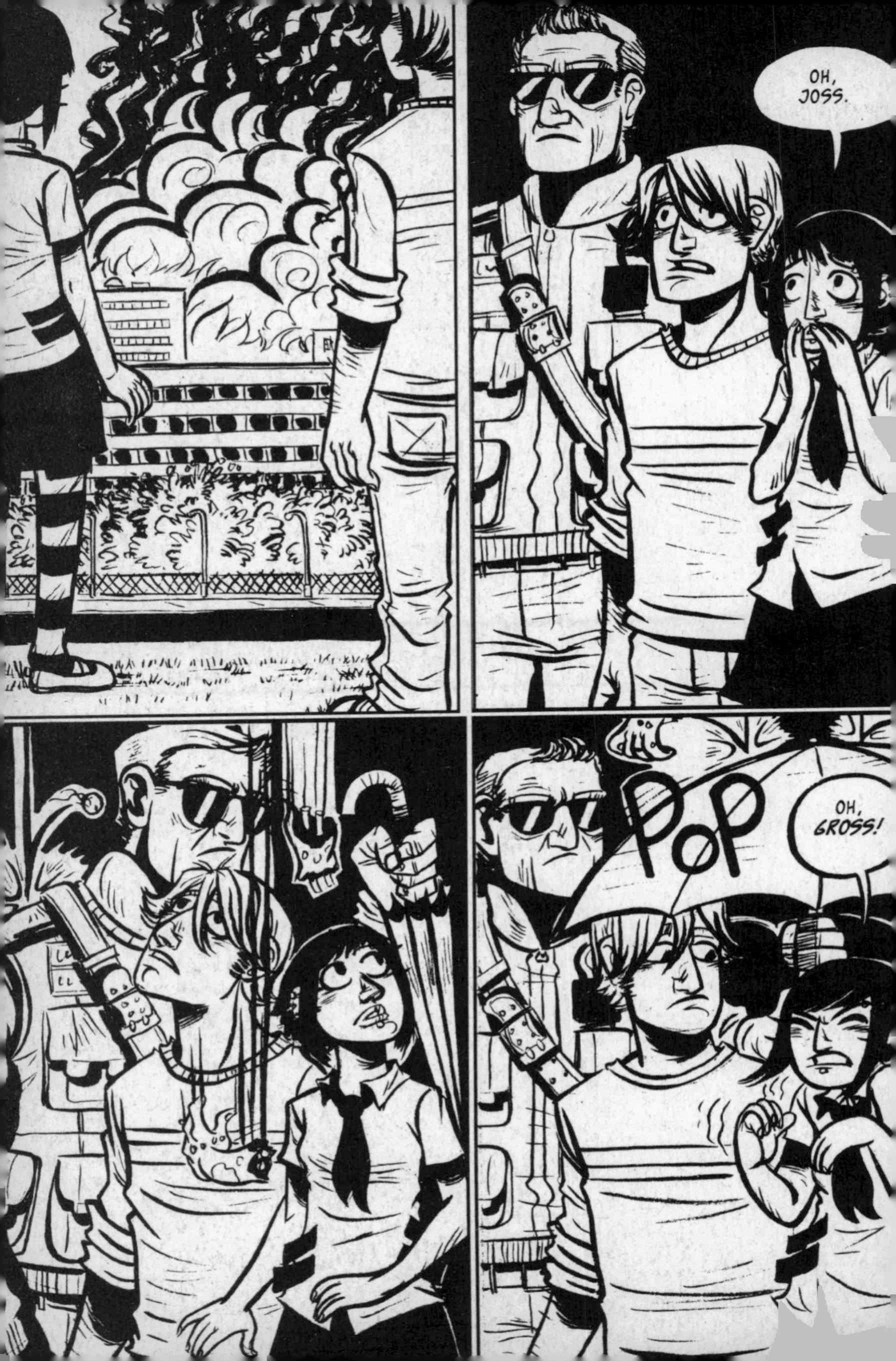
OH, JOSS.
POP
OH, GROSS!

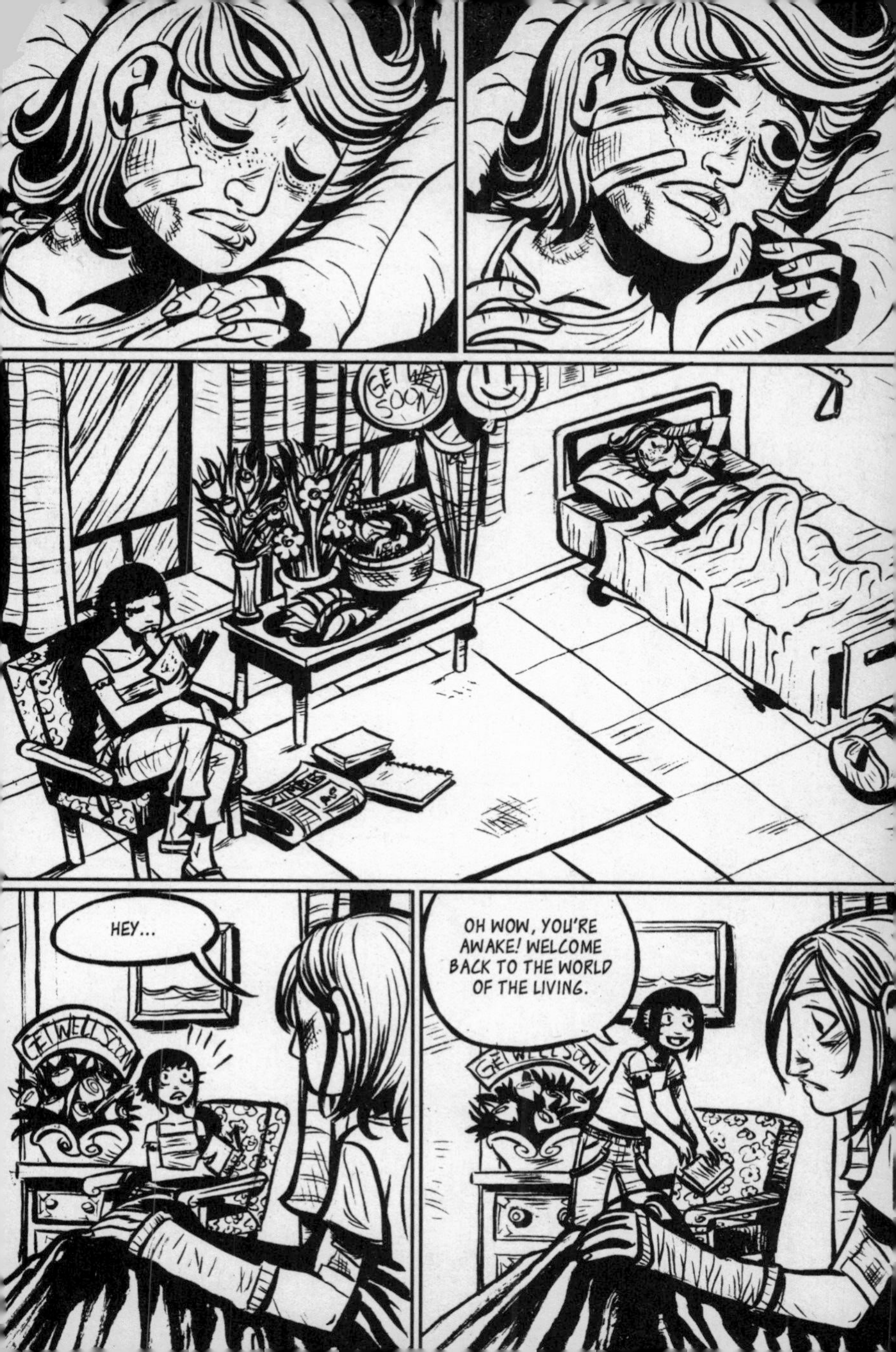
GET WELL SOON
HEY...
GET WELL SOON
OH WOW, YOU'RE AWAKE! WELCOME BACK TO THE WORLD OF THE LIVING.
GET WELL SOON

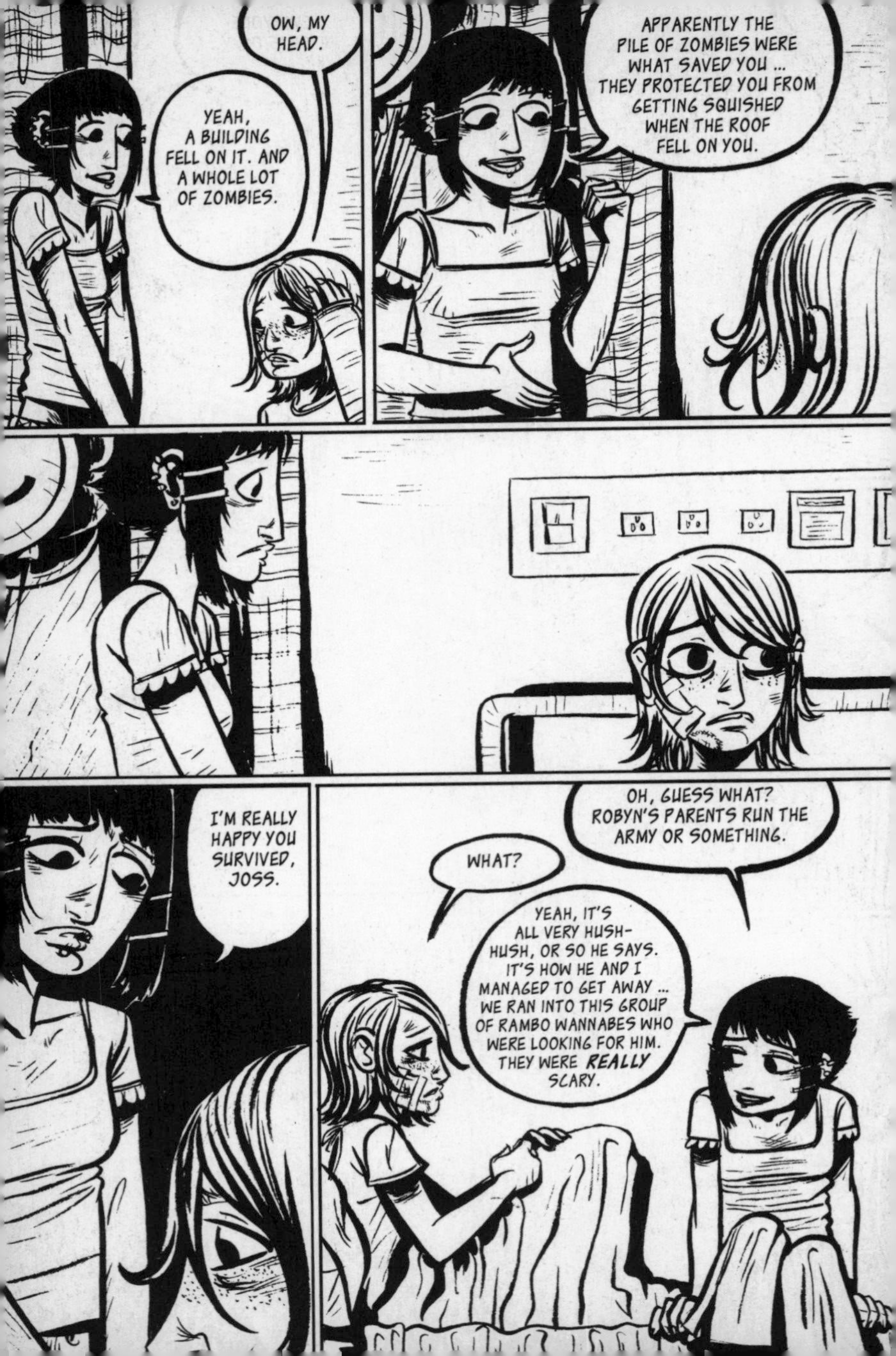
OW, MY HEAD.
YEAH, A BUILDING FELL ON IT. AND A WHOLE LOT OF ZOMBIES.
APPARENTLY THE PILE OF ZOMBIES WERE WHAT SAVED YOU ... THEY PROTECTED YOU FROM GETTING SQUISHED WHEN THE ROOF FELL ON YOU.
I'M REALLY HAPPY YOU SURVIVED, JOSS.
OH, GUESS WHAT? ROBYN'S PARENTS RUN THE ARMY OR SOMETHING.
WHAT?
YEAH, IT'S ALL VERY HUSH-HUSH, OR SO HE SAYS. IT'S HOW HE AND I MANAGED TO GET AWAY ... WE RAN INTO THIS GROUP OF RAMBO WANNABES WHO WERE LOOKING FOR HIM. THEY WERE *REALLY* SCARY.

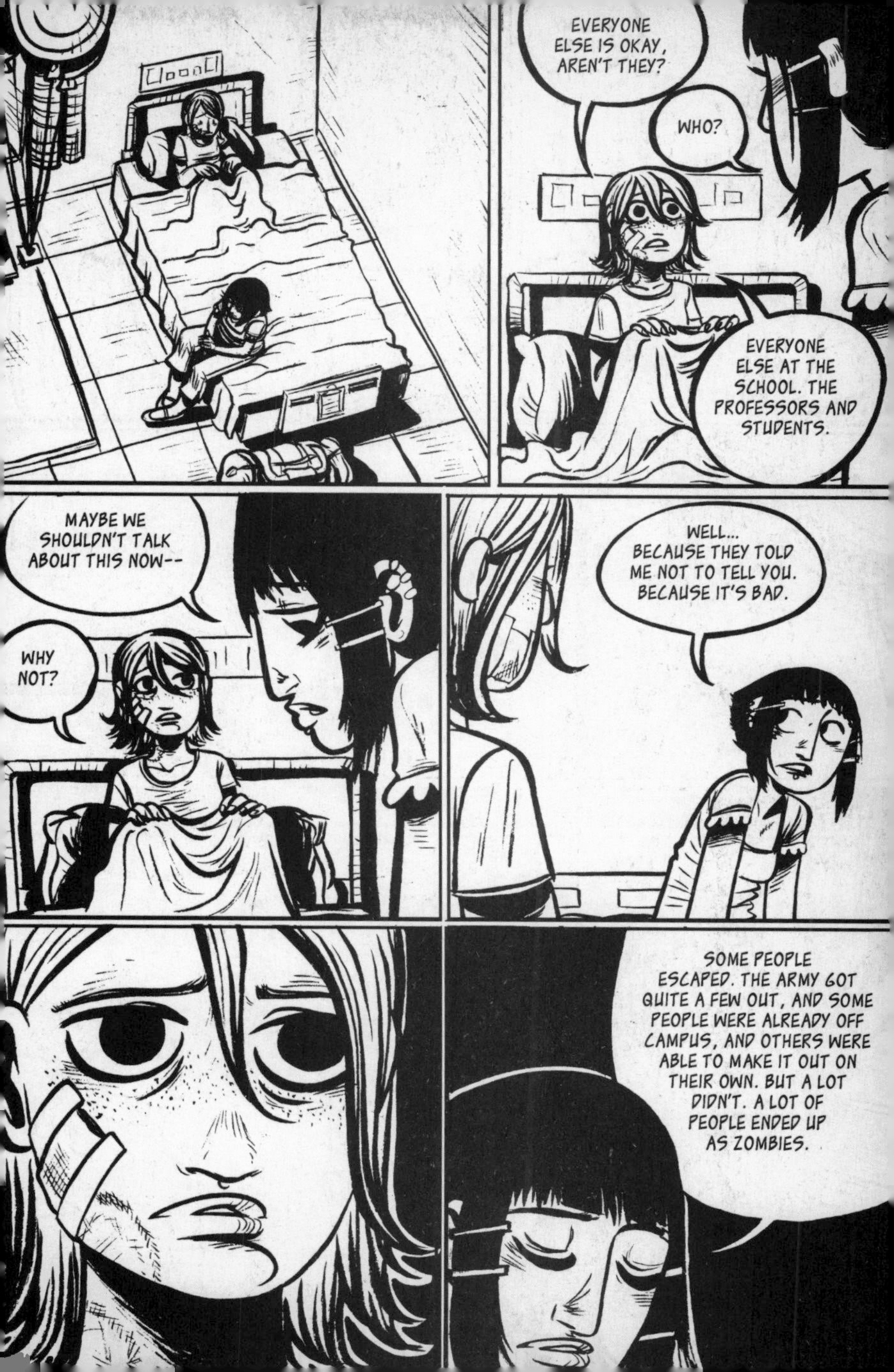
EVERYONE ELSE IS OKAY, AREN'T THEY?
WHO?
EVERYONE ELSE AT THE SCHOOL. THE PROFESSORS AND STUDENTS.
MAYBE WE SHOULDN'T TALK ABOUT THIS NOW--
WHY NOT?
WELL... BECAUSE THEY TOLD ME NOT TO TELL YOU. BECAUSE IT'S BAD.
SOME PEOPLE ESCAPED. THE ARMY GOT QUITE A FEW OUT, AND SOME PEOPLE WERE ALREADY OFF CAMPUS, AND OTHERS WERE ABLE TO MAKE IT OUT ON THEIR OWN. BUT A LOT DIDN'T. A LOT OF PEOPLE ENDED UP AS ZOMBIES.

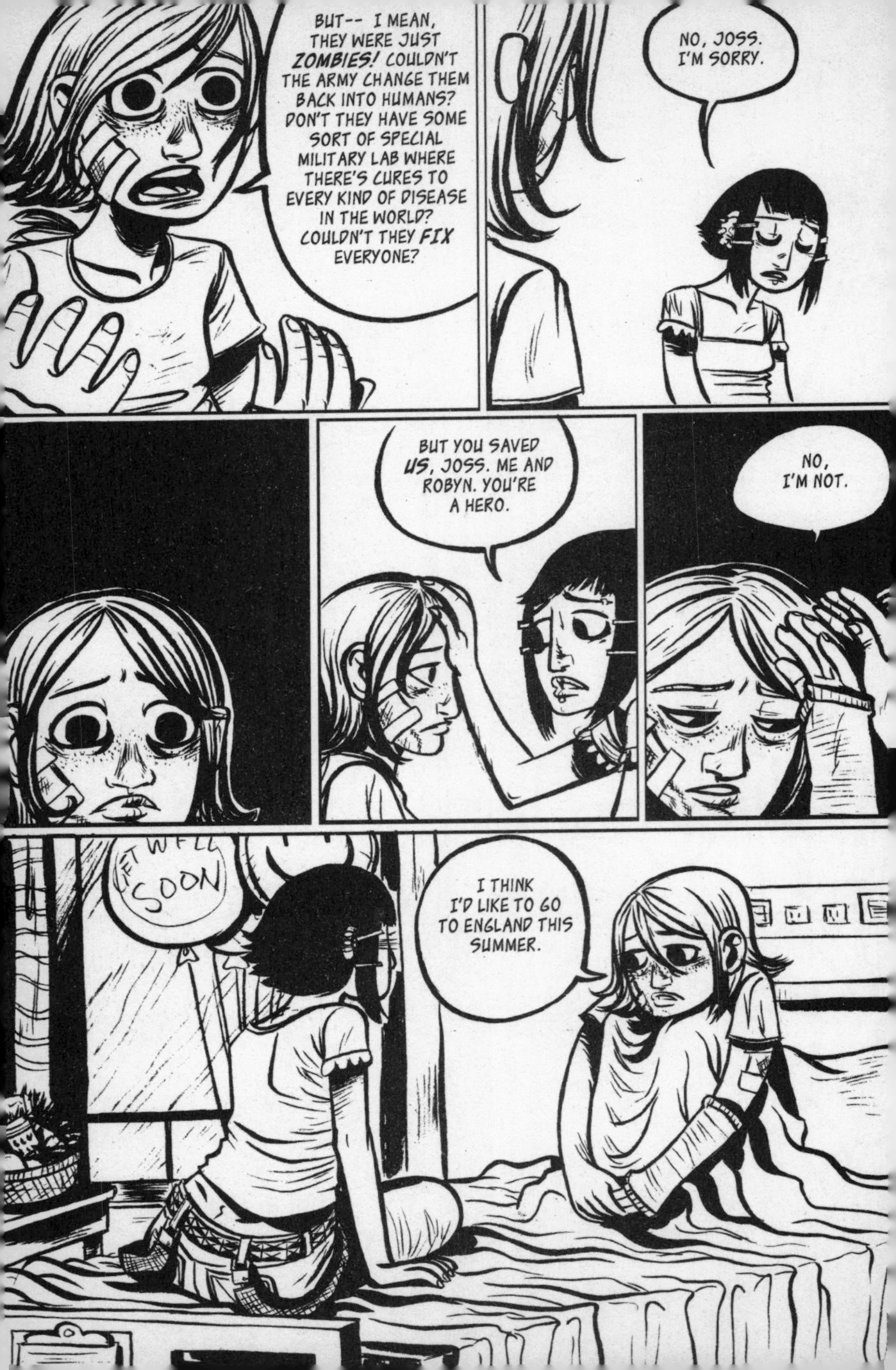
BUT-- I MEAN, THEY WERE JUST ZOMBIES! COULDN'T THE ARMY CHANGE THEM BACK INTO HUMANS? DON'T THEY HAVE SOME SORT OF SPECIAL MILITARY LAB WHERE THERE'S CURES TO EVERY KIND OF DISEASE IN THE WORLD? COULDN'T THEY FIX EVERYONE?
NO, JOSS. I'M SORRY.
BUT YOU SAVED US, JOSS. ME AND ROBYN. YOU'RE A HERO.
NO, I'M NOT.
SOON
I THINK I'D LIKE TO GO TO ENGLAND THIS SUMMER.

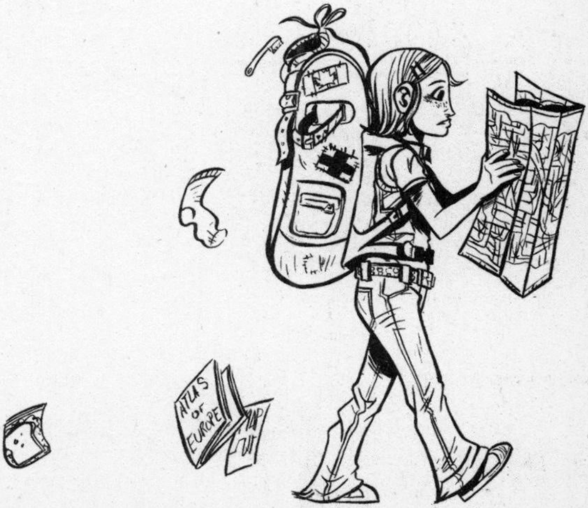
ATLAS OF EUROPE

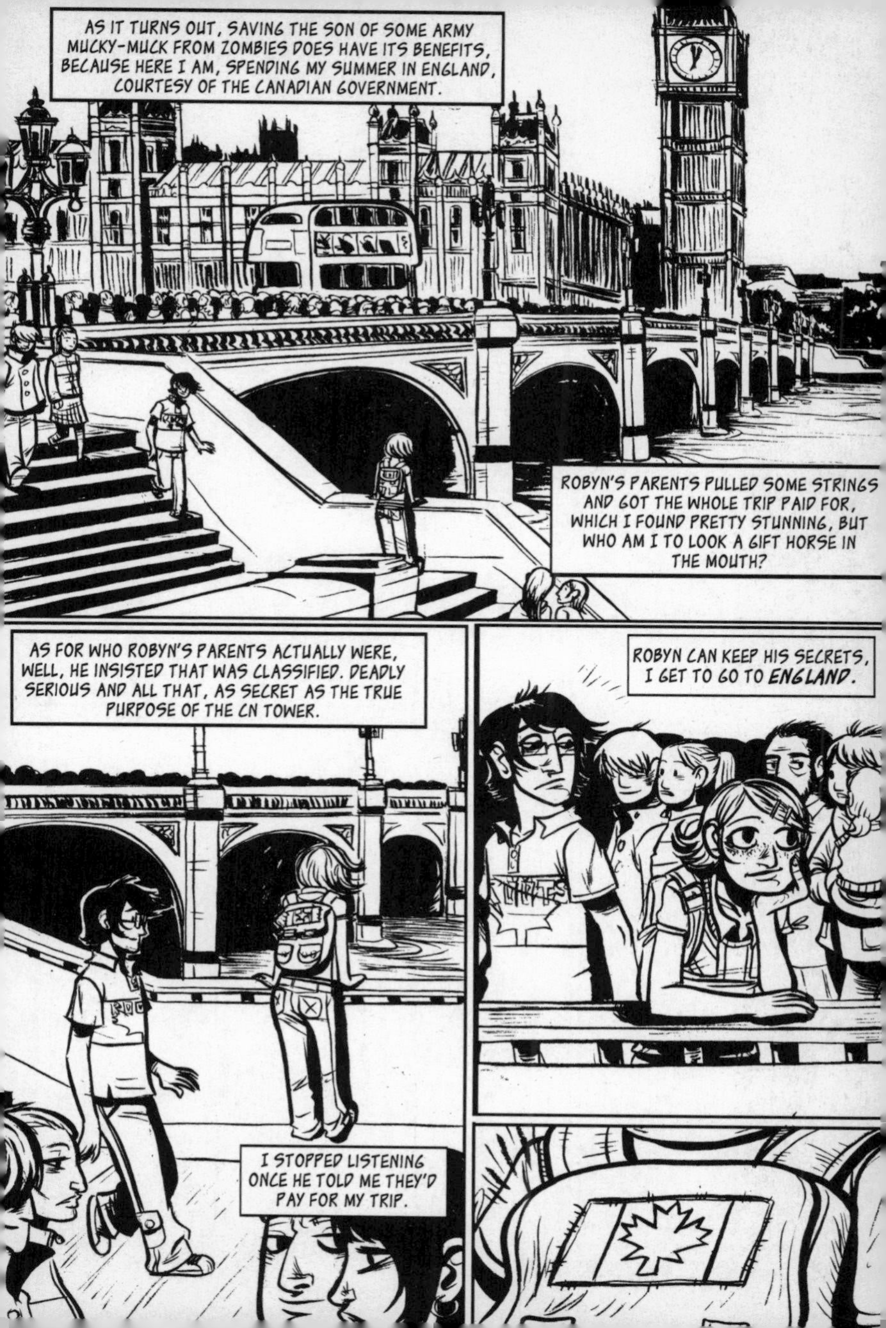
AS IT TURNS OUT, SAVING THE SON OF SOME ARMY MUCKY-MUCK FROM ZOMBIES DOES HAVE ITS BENEFITS, BECAUSE HERE I AM, SPENDING MY SUMMER IN ENGLAND, COURTESY OF THE CANADIAN GOVERNMENT.
ROBYN'S PARENTS PULLED SOME STRINGS AND GOT THE WHOLE TRIP PAID FOR, WHICH I FOUND PRETTY STUNNING, BUT WHO AM I TO LOOK A GIFT HORSE IN THE MOUTH?
AS FOR WHO ROBYN'S PARENTS ACTUALLY WERE, WELL, HE INSISTED THAT WAS CLASSIFIED. DEADLY SERIOUS AND ALL THAT, AS SECRET AS THE TRUE PURPOSE OF THE CN TOWER.
I STOPPED LISTENING ONCE HE TOLD ME THEY'D PAY FOR MY TRIP.
ROBYN CAN KEEP HIS SECRETS, I GET TO GO TO *ENGLAND*.

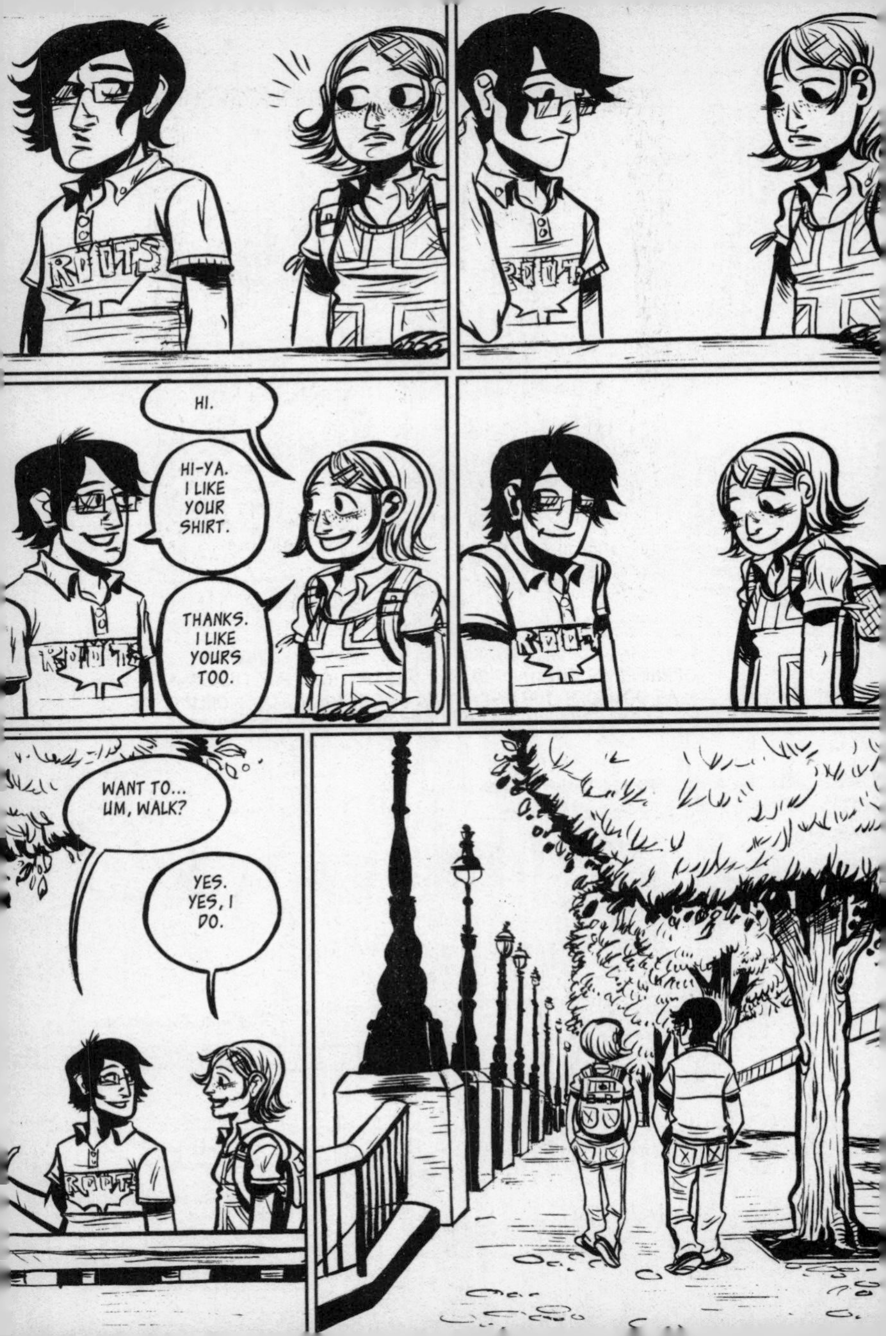
ROOTS
HI.
HI-YA. I LIKE YOUR SHIRT.
THANKS. I LIKE YOURS TOO.
WANT TO... UM, WALK?
YES. YES, I DO.

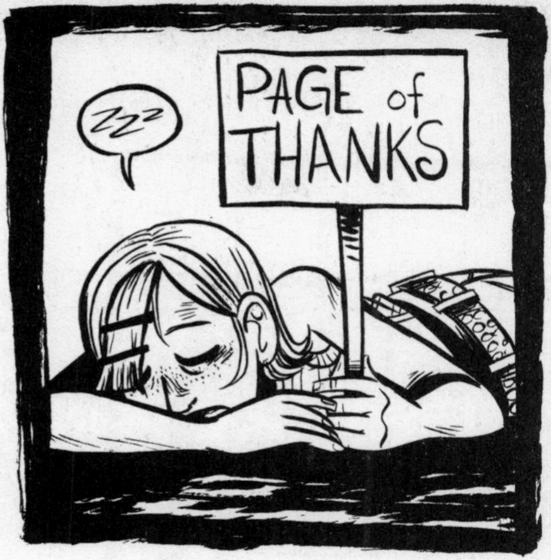

ZZZ
PAGE of THANKS

FIRST OF ALL, THANKS TO SLG, AND ESPECIALLY TO JENNIFER DE GUZMAN FOR HER SUGGESTIONS FOR THE COMIC. AS SOMEONE JUST STARTING OUT IN THE WACKY WORLD OF COMIC PUBLISHING YOUR SUPPORT HAS MEANT A LOT

THANKS TO MY PARENTS AND BROTHERS FOR ENCOURAGING MY STRANGE DESIRE TO DRAW COMICS. I FEEL LUCKY I ENDED UP IN A FAMILY THAT DOESN'T THINK I'M CRAZY FOR WANTING TO DRAW FOR A LIVING.

THANK YOU TO MY FRIENDS AND CO-WORKERS AT COPERNICUS. YOU HAVE ALL BEEN SHOCKINGLY UNDERSTANDING. 'NUFF SAID.

THANK YOU TO MY ONLINE READERS, WHO READ THE FIRST INCARNATION OF ZOMBIES CALLING AND HELPFULLY SUGGESTED I TRY AND GET SOME POOR SUCKER TO PUBLISH IT. HURRAH FOR THE INTERNETS!

FINALLY, THANK YOU TO THE TEACHERS WHO DID NOT TURN ME INTO A ZOMBIE. ESPECIALLY MRS FRANK, MR KEENE, ANDREW BODOR, KRIS PEARN, PROFESSOR COOK, BETTY SPACKMAN AND PROFESSOR LONEY.

CHEERS, AND THANKS FOR READING.

-FAITH
WWW.FAITHERINHICKS.COM

I ABSOLUTLELY LOVE "MAKING OF" BOOKS, WHERE ARTISTS SHOW THEIR THOUGHT PROCESS FOR WHATEVER PROJECT THEY'VE WORKED ON, BE IT A MOVIE, COMIC OR BIGFOOT INVESTIGATION. I'VE NO IDEA HOW MANY PEOPLE SHARE MY NERDY LOVE OF BEHIND-THE-SCENES MINUTIA, BUT FOR YOUR ENJOYMENT, THE FOLLOWING PAGES CONTAIN OLD SKETCHES AND NOTES ABOUT THE EVOLUTION OF ZOMBIES CALLING.

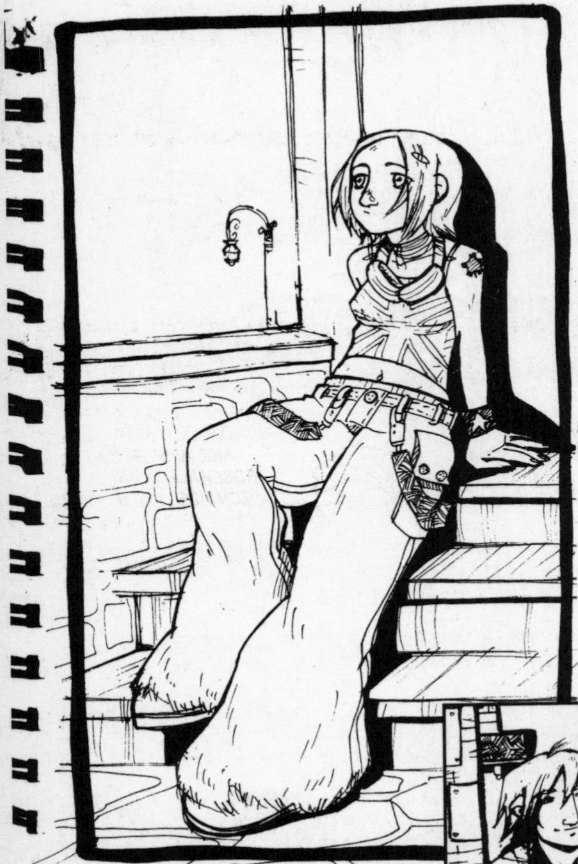

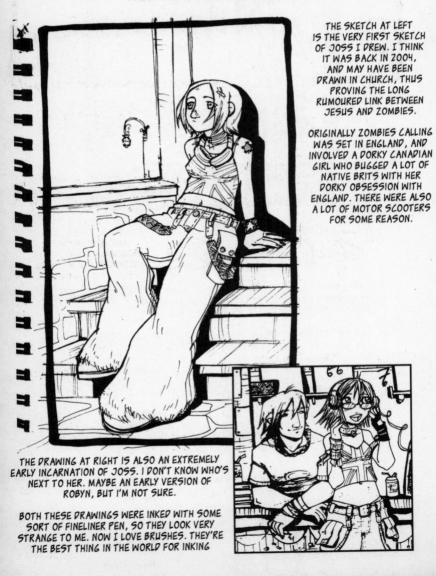

THE SKETCH AT LEFT IS THE VERY FIRST SKETCH OF JOSS I DREW. I THINK IT WAS BACK IN 2004, AND MAY HAVE BEEN DRAWN IN CHURCH, THUS PROVING THE LONG RUMOURED LINK BETWEEN JESUS AND ZOMBIES.

ORIGINALLY ZOMBIES CALLING WAS SET IN ENGLAND, AND INVOLVED A DORKY CANADIAN GIRL WHO BUGGED A LOT OF NATIVE BRITS WITH HER DORKY OBSESSION WITH ENGLAND. THERE WERE ALSO A LOT OF MOTOR SCOOTERS FOR SOME REASON.

THE DRAWING AT RIGHT IS ALSO AN EXTREMELY EARLY INCARNATION OF JOSS. I DON'T KNOW WHO'S NEXT TO HER. MAYBE AN EARLY VERSION OF ROBYN, BUT I'M NOT SURE.

BOTH THESE DRAWINGS WERE INKED WITH SOME SORT OF FINELINER PEN, SO THEY LOOK VERY STRANGE TO ME. NOW I LOVE BRUSHES. THEY'RE THE BEST THING IN THE WORLD FOR INKING

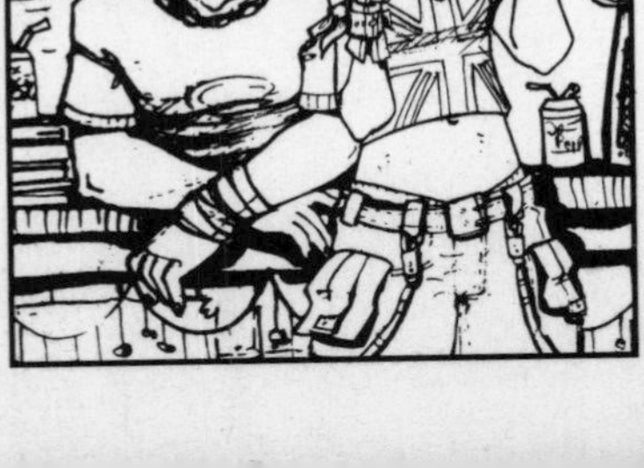

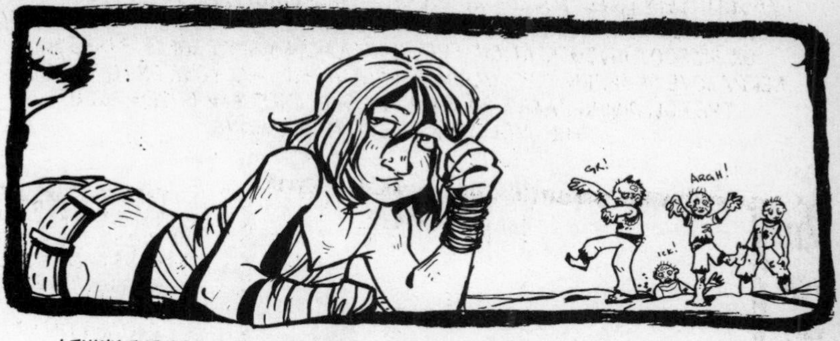
GK!
ICK!
ARGH!

I THINK THE ABOVE SKETCH WAS THE FIRST ONE WHERE I BEGAN TO THINK ABOUT DOING ZC AS A 'FUNNY' ZOMBIE COMIC. I THOUGHT THE ZOMBIES IN THE BACKGROUND WERE HILARIOUS. IT TOOK ME A WHILE TO FIGURE OUT THAT THE 'L' JOSS IS HOLDING UP TO HER FOREHEAD WAS BACKWARDS.

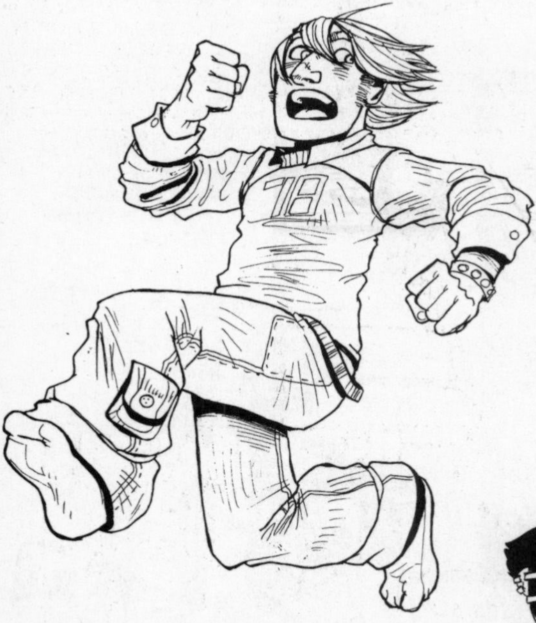
78

ROBYN DIDN'T GO THROUGH MANY CHANGES WHEN THE COMIC STARTED EVOLVING INTO ITS PRESENT FORM. HE WAS ALWAYS A LITTLE BIT OF A LOVABLE PERVERT AND MYSTERIOUSLY NONCHALANT ABOUT THE ZOMBIES. THE DRAWING AT LEFT WAS DONE FOR THE ORIGINAL PITCH I SENT TO SLG BACK IN 2005.

JOSS AND SONNET AS BOBBLEHEAD DOLLS.

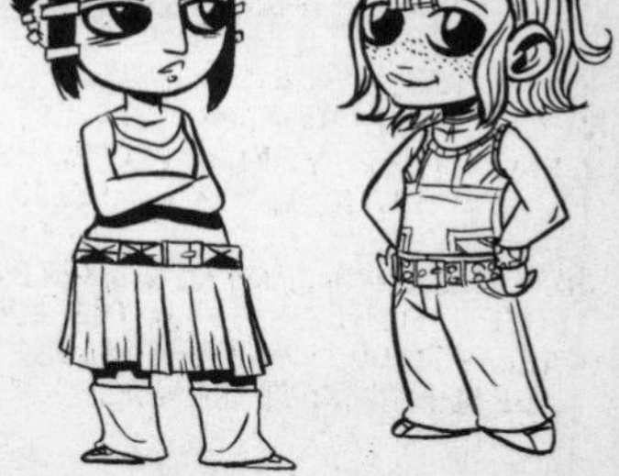

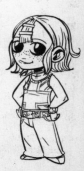

I TOYED BRIEFLY WITH THE IDEA OF TURNING SONNET INTO A ZOMBIE AT ONE POINT IN THE COMIC, WHICH IS WHERE THIS DOODLE CAME FROM. I THINK SHE MAKES A CUTE ZOMBIE, BUT I COULDN'T FIGURE OUT A WAY TO TURN HER BACK TO HUMAN.

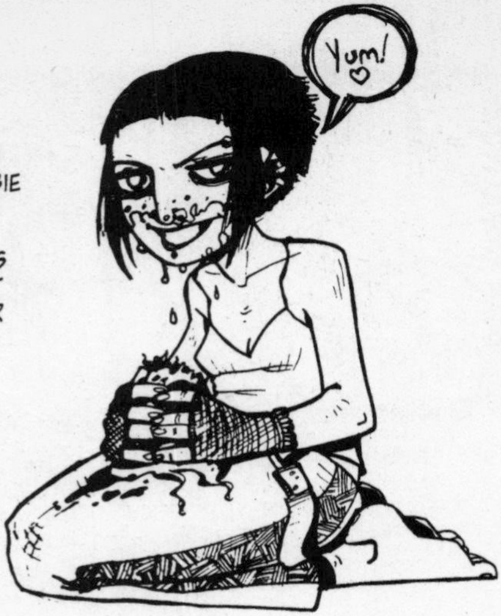
Yum!

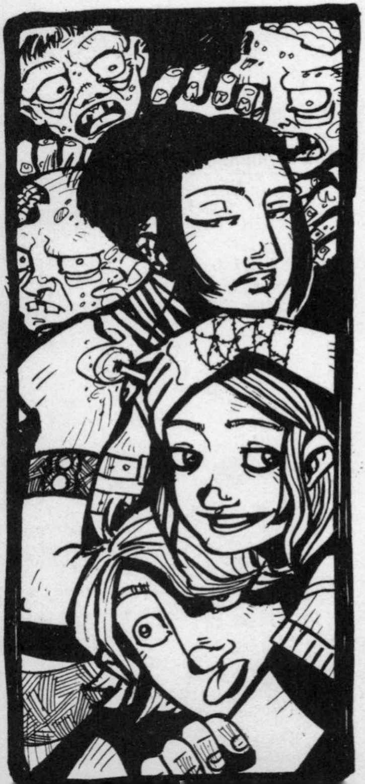

THE DRAWING ON THE LEFT WAS DONE FOR THE ORIGINAL, 15 PAGE, ONE-JOKE ZC COMIC, WHICH YOU CAN SEE ONLINE IN ALL ITS DORKY GLORY AT WWW.FAITHERINHICKS.COM/ZOMBIES. APPARENTLY SONNET WAS ORIGINALLY A SMOKER. I'M GLAD SHE QUIT FOR THE PUBLISHED VERSION OF ZOMBIES CALLING. IT'S A HORRIBLE HABIT.

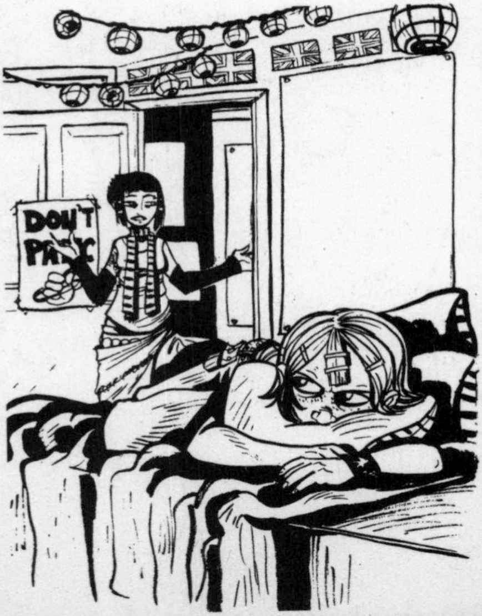
DON'T

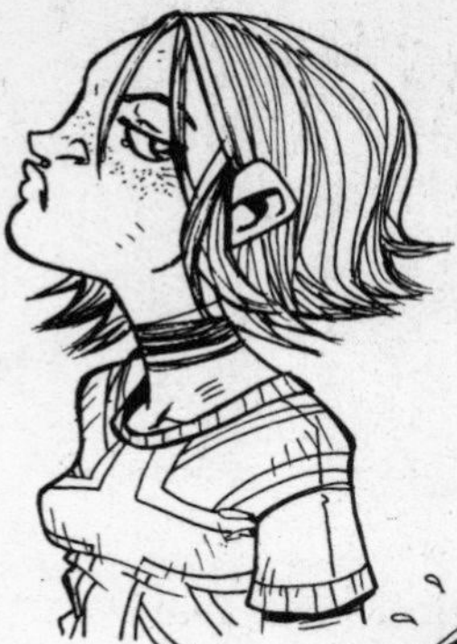

JOSS HAD DIFFERENT HAIR FOR A WHILE. I DECIDED IT WAS TOO TRENDY LOOKING. SHE'S A GEEK WHO WEARS THE SAME SHIRT EVERY DAY. SHE SHOULD LOOK LIKE SHE DOESN'T OWN A MIRROR.

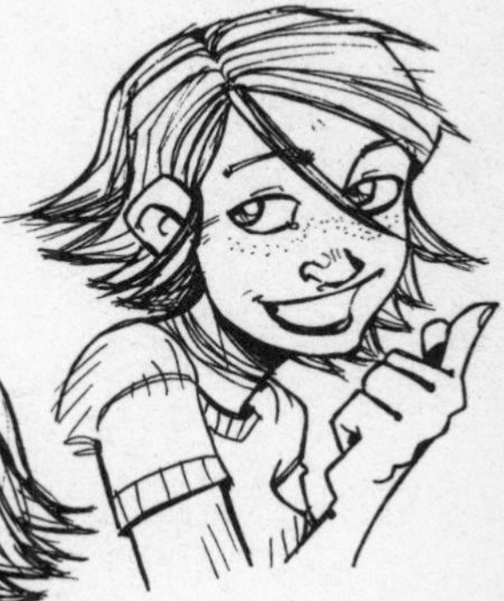

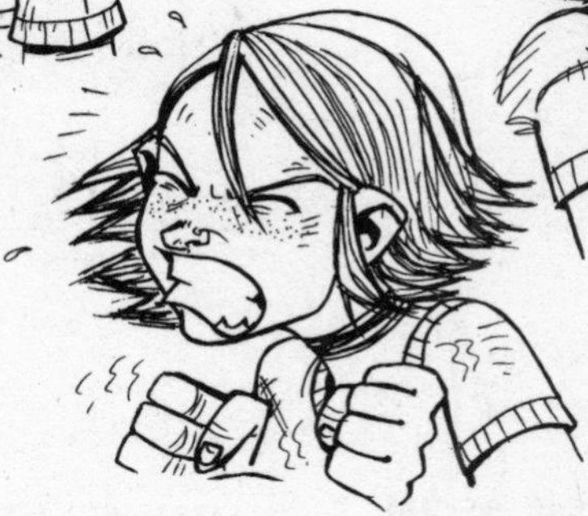

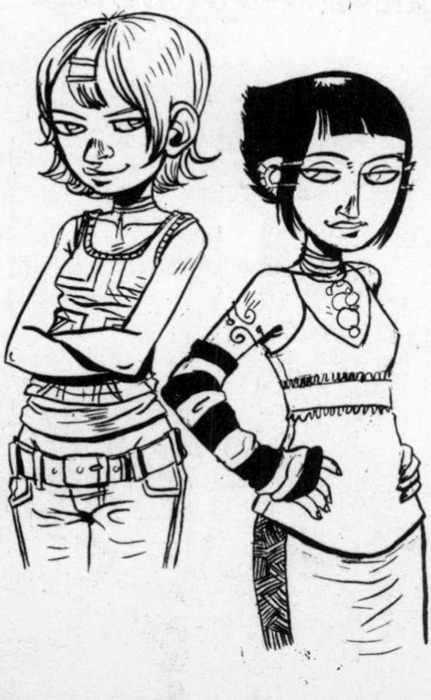

THE DRAWING AT RIGHT WAS THE FIRST ONE I DID OF OF JOSS IN HER FINALISED DESIGN (THE ONE YOU SEE IN THIS COMIC), ALTHOUGH LATER I DECIDED SHE SHOULD ONLY HAVE ON ONE SHIRT.

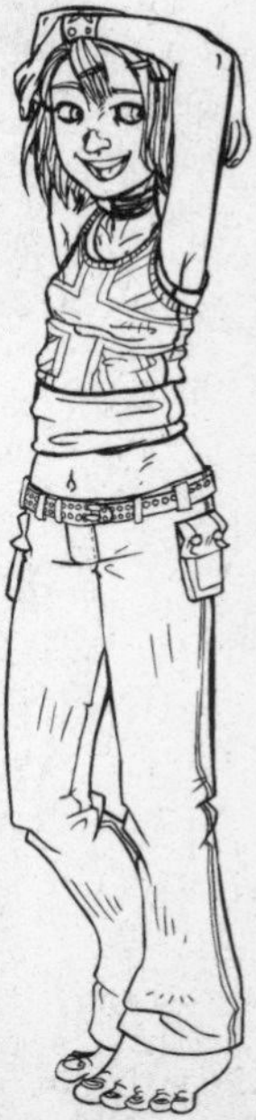

I HAD FUN DRAWING DIFFERENT OUTFITS FOR SONNET. IT'S LIKE PLAYING DRESS UP, OR SOMETHING.

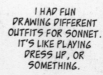

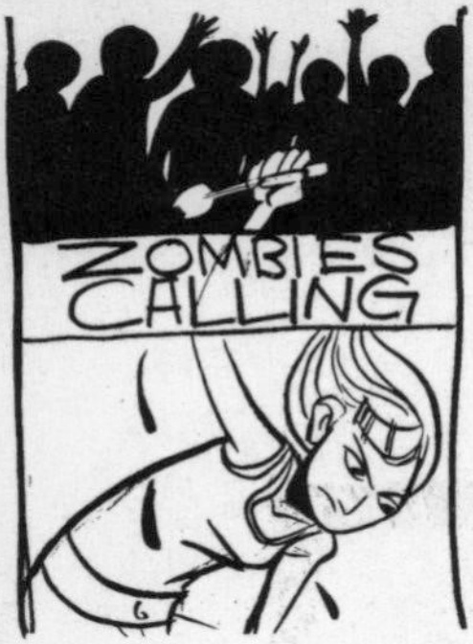
ZOMBIES CALLING

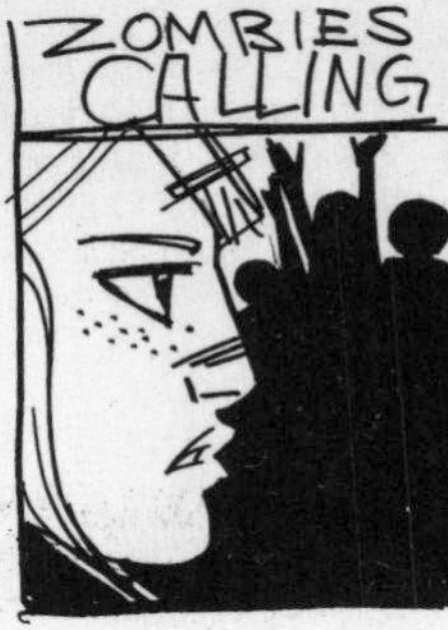
ZOMBIES CALLING

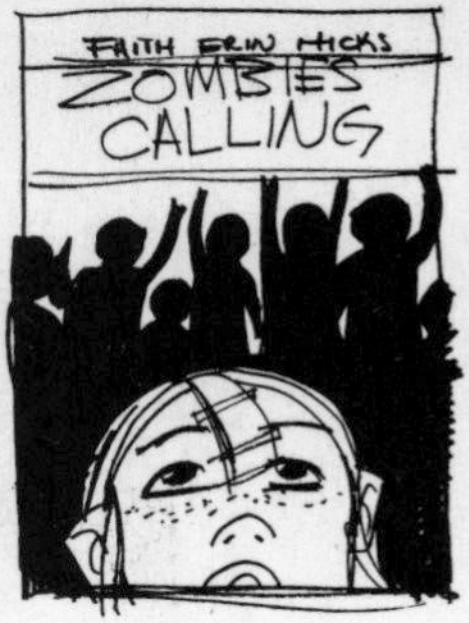
FAITH ERIN HICKS
ZOMBIES CALLING

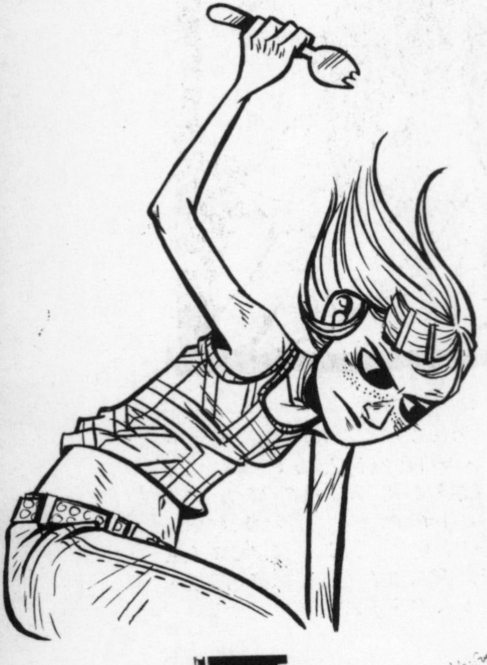

I DID A LOT OF THUMBNAILS FOR THE COVER, THEN PASSED THEM AROUND TO FRIENDS TO SEE WHICH ONE CAME OUT THE FAVOURITE. I WAS KEEN ON THE THUMBNAIL ON THE FAR RIGHT, UNTIL SOMEONE POINTED OUT THAT IT LOOKED A LOT LIKE THE BLAIR WITCH PROJECT MOVIE POSTER.

I WAS SURPRISED MOST PEOPLE SEEMED TO REALLY LIKE THE FAR LEFT THUMBNAIL. I WASN'T THAT INTERESTED IN IT BECAUSE I THOUGHT IT MIGHT BE TOO VIOLENT, BUT THE SPORK SEEMED TO MAKE IT MORE COMICAL THAN ANYTHING. SPORKS ARE INHERENTLY HILARIOUS. I DREW THE FINAL COVER IMAGE DURING MY LUNCH BREAK AT WORK.

SOMETIMES THINGS THAT I DRAW QUICKLY END UP BEING A LOT BETTER THAN SOMETHING I SLAVE OVER.

... WHICH IS ***REALLY*** ANNOYING.

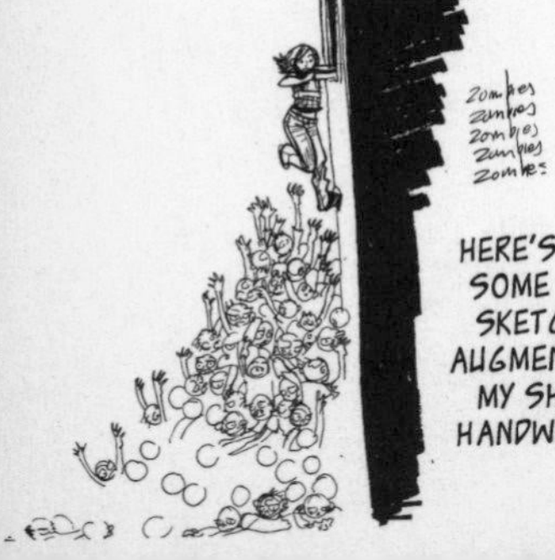
zombies
zombies
zombies
zombies
zombies

HERE'S JUST SOME MORE SKETCHES, AUGMENTED BY MY SHODDY HANDWRITING.

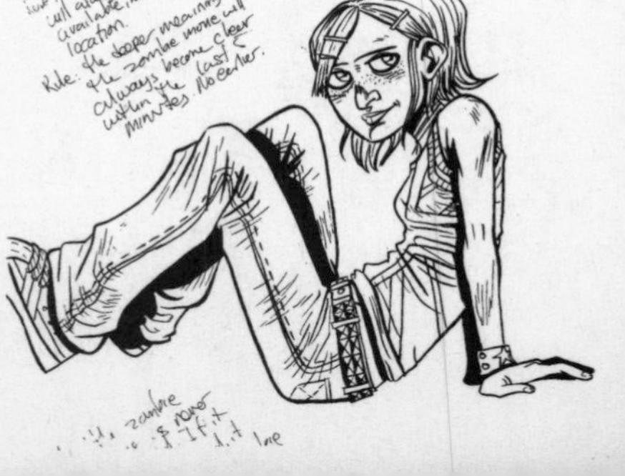
will always be available, no matter location.
Rule: the deeper meanings of the zombie movie will always become clear within the last 5 minutes. No earlier.

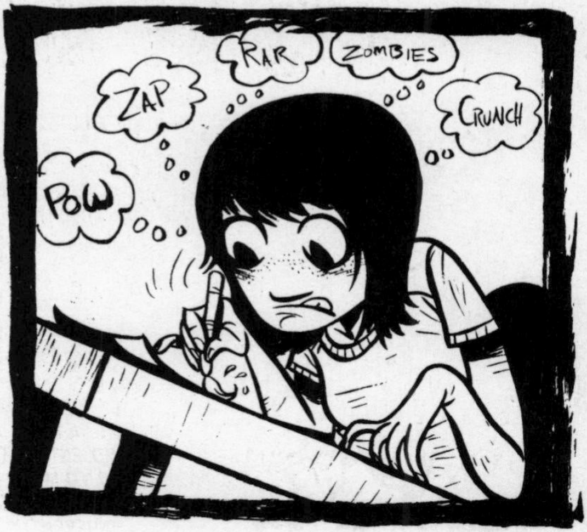
POW
ZAP
RAR
ZOMBIES
CRUNCH

FAITH ERIN HICKS LIVES IN HALIFAX, NOVA SCOTIA. SHE HAS BEEN A SUPPORT WORKER FOR DEVELOPMENTALLY DELAYED CHILDREN, A TURF CARE WORKER AT A GOLF COURSE, A CHURCH CUSTODIAN, A UNIVERSITY LIBRARIAN, A TACK SHOP RETAIL EMPLOYEE, AND A GROOM FOR HORSES, BUT SHE LIKES DRAWING COMICS BEST. SHE WOULD LIKE TO GO TO ENGLAND SOMEDAY.

Also From SLG Publishing

Agnes Quill: Anthology of Mystery

Agnes Quill is the story of a teenage detective, the haunted city she lives in, the strange cases she solves, and the ghosts who help, hinder, or just plain annoy her. Set in Legerdemain—a congested, fog-filled, cobblestone-paved Victorian city built around a cemetery the size of Central Park—Agnes' adventures include confrontations with trapped spirits, cursed souls, possessed relatives, disappearing pets, decapitated scientists, ambitious zombies, and a mess of other supernatural oddities. Written by Dave Roman, and featuring stories illustrated by Jason Ho, Jen Wang, Jeff Zornow, and Eisner nominee, Raina Telgemeier.   ISBN 978-1-59362-052-3 $10.95

Emo Boy
by Steve Emond

Emo Boy's unpopular. Unloved. He has no family. Not only does he need to deal with things like pondering suicide and questioning his sexual identity, but on top of that he's got these emo super powers that only seem to bring destruction and disaster, causing everyone to hate him more than they already do. Volume One ISBN 1-59362-053-5
Volume 2 978-1-59362-075-2 $13.95 each

Outlook: Grim
by Black Olive

Ghosts have taken over Wren's underwear drawer, they're encroaching on the rest of her apartment, and she's not going to take it! Join our saucy heroine Wren and her best friend Chloe as they team up to toss out their unwelcome houseguests from The Other Side. With Ouijah Boards, Voo Doo Dolls, zombies, psychic gypsies and deviant neighbors - it's a paranormal smorgasbord of quick wit, sarcasm and silly humor. ISBN 1-59362-006-3 $12.95

Street Angel
by Jim Rugg and Brian Maruca

Jess Sanchez is homeless and hungry, but she sure as hell isn't beaten down! With her martial arts expertise, trusty skateboard and street smarts, Jesse can take down evil geniuses, ninjas, conquistadors and even the devil himself. ISBN 1-59362-012-8 $14.95

Visit slgcomic.com to order
or call 1-877-754-7877 for a free catalog!